THE MAKING OF THE TWENTIETH-CENTURY NOVEL

THE MAKING OF THE TWENTIETH-CENTURY NOVEL

Lawrence, Joyce, Faulkner and Beyond

John Orr

St. Martin's Press
New York

823.09
O75m

First published in the United States of America in 1987

Printed in Hong Kong

ISBN 0–312–00220–3

Library of Congress Cataloging-in-Publication Data
Orr, John, 1943–
The making of the twentieth-century novel.
Bibliography: p.
Includes index.
1. American fiction – 20th century – History and
criticism.   2. English fiction – 20th century –
History and criticism.   I. Title.
PS379.O77   1986   823'.91'09   86–20353
ISBN 0–312–00220–3

He had a word, too. Love, he called it. But I had been used to words for a long time. I knew that that word was like the others: just a shape to fill a lack; that when the right time came, you wouldn't need a word for that any more than for pride or fear.

Faulkner, *As I Lay Dying*

Contents

Acknowledgements

The author and publishers thank the following for permission to reprint copyright material: Laurence Pollinger Ltd and the estate of Mrs Frieda Lawrence Ravagli, for the quotations from D. H. Lawrence's *The Rainbow* and *Women in Love*; Faber and Faber Ltd and Harper and Row Publishers Inc., for the quotations from Sylvia Plath's *Ariel*, copyright Ted Hughes 1965; Jonathan Cape Ltd, Charles Scribner's Sons and the executors of the Ernest Hemingway estate, for the quotations from Ernest Hemingway's *A Farewell to Arms*, copyright 1929, copyright renewed © 1957 Ernest Hemingway; Chatto and Windus, Random House Inc. and the estate of William Faulkner, for the quotations from William Faulkner's *The Sound and the Fury*, *As I Lay Dying*, *Sanctuary*, *Light in August*, *Absalom, Absalom!* and *The Wild Palms*; the Bodley Head Ltd and Random House Inc., for the quotations from James Joyce's *Ulysses*; the Society of Authors as the literary representative of the trustees of the estate of James Joyce, for the quotations from James Joyce's letter to Stanislaus of 13 November 1906; Anthony Sheil Associates Ltd, for the quotations from John Fowles' *The French Lieutenant's Woman*; Jonathan Cape Ltd, Harper and Row Publishers Inc. and the executors of the Malcolm Lowry estate, for the quotations from Malcolm Lowry's *Under the Volcano*; and A. D. Peters and Co. Ltd and Literistic Ltd, for the quotations from *Selected Letters of Malcolm Lowry*, © 1965 by the estate of Malcolm Lowry; Jonathan Cape Ltd and Tessa Sayle Literary and Dramatic Agency, for the quotations from *Sophie's Choice*, and Tessa Sayle Literary and Dramatic Agency and Random House Inc., for the quotations from *Lie Down in Darkness*, both by William Styron; Faber and Faber Ltd and New Directions Publishing Corp., for the quotations from Djuna Barnes' *Nightwood*.

1 Passion and Compassion; Absence and Desire

Many see the nineteenth century as the high point of the realist novel. Its litany of names includes Dickens and Eliot, Balzac and Flaubert, Conrad and James, Tolstoy and Dostoevsky. Because its aesthetic identity is more secure, its fiction stakes a truer claim to mimesis than its eighteenth-century predecessors. It no longer needs to parade its fidelity to life, nor is it fable which confuses the exposures of existence with the teaching of moral obligation. The author stands back from the text, but fictional characters are not, on that account, puppets to be manipulated. They have their own existence, their own reasons for living. They cannot be construed as the direct embodiment of authorial sentiment or as adjuncts to ingenious plot. The conflict between individual feeling and social obligation, between the tensions of the public and private spheres of middle-class life, are explored more fully than ever before. Above all there is a sense of the fictive world as a social totality. After the French and industrial revolutions, the novel opens out onto reality and history.

It is able to do so because, as Ermath has pointed out,[1] the function of the realistic narrator is to homogenise the medium, like the gaze of the implied spectator in Renaissance painting. The author's narrator is neither omniscient nor personally identifiable with the author. The narrator stands outside the frame of events but within the same continuum. In nineteenth-century realism, the multiple perspective of narrative invokes the moral experience of fictional character as a thing apart from its author. At the same time, realist narrative, through its multiple perspectives of observation, crystallises the fictional character's complex dilemmas of moral choice. Character itself, as a fictional construct of personality in social context, evolves through the process of response to experience, acting upon action, being in the world yet being out of step with it, searching for the elusive rhythms and relationships

1

of a wider social harmony. Such relationships are not always found but the quest itself is fundamental. It becomes all the more poignant, luring the reader's sympathy, by the closeness to hand, socially observed, of injustice and misfortune. Moral experience involves judging others as well as oneself, finding them likeable or loathsome, sensitive or tyrannical. For the reader, narrative perspective mediates that moral experience. The use of past-tense narrative here, with its evocation of time through memory, is vital. For the narrative movement is historical, change over time the movement through social experience, the yardstick of constant and recurrent tension between the personal world of the character and the public world of experience. As specific setting and linear time, the evocation of the social milieu goes beyond the achievements of the previous century, beyond the salutary warnings against temptation and the comic twists and turns of the picaresque.

But, while narrative evolves into something approaching a unified form, its does so, historically speaking, during a century in which the social contradictions of modernising capitalist societies become more manifest. European realism, from Austin and Stendhal to Hardy and Zola, testifies to the perplexing circumstances of a new form of society whose social and economic changes become more pronounced as the century progresses. The novel responds to that complex momentum, but usually in a mediated form. Its response has a double dialectic – response to change and, simultaneously, response to the analysis of change, the quest of philosophy and sociology to theorise change as a dimension of the social whole. There is often an anguished and incentuous alacrity in the novel's response to the new bourgeois ideologies of progress, the diverse, often contradictory, forms of optimism about capitalism which collide with established traditions and conventional moralities. In England, Dickens agonised about Malthusianism and Bentham's calculus, Eliot charted the survival and resignation of the morally capable in a Spencerian world preaching opportunity yet practising restraint, and Hardy tried to subvert Darwinism by elevating the principle of natural selection to the status of human tragedy.[2] Such varied response to the ideological forms of progress show us precisely how the social themes of the novel present a constant challenge to its literary form. The major protagonist of the English novel often experiences the contradiction between a false spirit of optimism in the world at large and a localised reality that is forbidding and brutal.

We might then want to ask, what sustains him or her in such extremes of adversity? There is no single quality but rather a group of complex qualities, structures of feeling which we may term compassion. They involve friendship, affection, reverence, kindness, charity, love and, last but not least, marriage. Compassion is the life-giving antidote to injustice, the face-saving form of mutual esteem which resists and triumphs over adversity. Through it the ego can endure the effects of abusive tyranny, unmerited dislocation from the *civitas*, the dangers of a diminished and embittered self. In the Victorian novel, it has its place within a more specific form, the *Bildungsroman*, where the young hero or heroine often confronts an adult world that is at once vivid and oppressive, attractive in its vitality but brutal in its *modus operandi*. Pip, Becky Sharp and Dorothea Brooke are all innocents abroad in a world of experience which often does not even recognise its oppressiveness or susceptibility to corruption. The Victorian orphan approximates, both socially and figuratively, the general predicament of the outsider subject to ostracism but seeking integration on terms which will lead to personal happiness. As both Miller and Hochman have pointed out,[3] the link between the vivid and the inflexible lies in the individual abuse of authority by eccentric tyrants which excuses the novel from adopting a more critical posture towards authority *per se*. Neither Bulstrode and Casaubon in *Middlemarch*, nor the patriarchs of *Bleak House*, draw the reader's attention much beyond their immediate behaviour to the actual forms of authority they embody. This gives rise to a predictable form of closure. Compassion becomes the consolation of the lone youthful hero or heroine, either through friendship with fellow sufferers, courtship and marriage, or through the Dickensian miracle of charity, which operates like a principle of divine intervention in the narrative. The routes are varied but, in terms of the hero's place within a problematic world, the outcome is clear. Through compassion lies reconciliation.

This closure in the Victorian novel consummates the classic realist form by matching perspective to compassion, feeling to epistemology, ways of seeing to ways of feeling. It recovers the clarity of meaning through the affirmation of a shared structure of feeling. Narrative, as an impersonal force, mediates between character and character and, at the same time, between author, character and reader. In that respect its operation is reflexive but also unifying and consensual. But that affirmative closure only works historically as a response to perceived contradictions between life and value, existence and ideal. The paradox is this. The perceived accentuation of contradiction within society, mediated by analytic interpretation, is a necessary condition of that artistic unity achieved through affirmation.

Where realism is tragic in its conception such closure, however, is impossible, and this raises more disturbing questions about the status of compassion. Compassion, in its literary etymology, is closely linked to that adjacent structure of feeling which De Rougemont in his historical study of Western literature has called passion.[4] Passion haunts compassion in the novel because in the epic poem and the tragic drama it has already preceded it. The rise of the novel was a departure from a passionate structure of feeling intrinsically connected to the forms of nobility and chivalry in feudal society. Henceforth, its most common form of adulteration was the bourgeois romance. But passion still remained as something both peripheral and dangerous to the consensual traditions of the Western European novel. Its intensity and refusal to compromise could destroy lives just as much as compassion could heal them. In the English novel up to Hardy and including James, but with the exception of Emily Brontë, it is the forbidden structure of feeling, that which is manifestly repressed. In the Russian novel of tragic realism, however, passion and compassion co-exist only for passion as the more intense force to destroy compassion's affirmative powers.[5]

In Tolstoy's *Anna Karenina* we bear witness to the courtship of Kitty and Levin side by side with the stormy marriage of the Oblonskys and the doomed affair of Anna and Vronsky. But it is the catastrophe of the last couple, culminating in Anna's suicide, which comes to dominate the book. In *The Idiot*, Nastasyia Filippovna is confronted by a choice between the brutal passion of Rogozhin and the compassionate passion of Myshkin. Her vacillation leads to the breaking of Myshkin's spirit and her own destruction. In both novels passion is the key to a tragic renaissance in the novel which makes Tolstoy and Dostoevsky the historical heirs of Shakespeare and Racine. Yet compassion is a necessary foundation of this renaissance, part of the legacy of Western Europe transformed out of all recognition in the context of pre-bourgeois, absolutist society. Within Western Europe the function of compassion remains central. It resists ideological acceptance of an illusory 'progress', but through compassionate affirmation retains the *promesse de bonheur* by which progress conventionally ingratiates itself. While the tragic marks a break with society's universal laws, compassion is the nineteenth-century reward for the durability of the ego, that measured consistency of response under duress which reaps its eventual reward. It is, in effect, the novel's imaginary resolution of the most deeply felt contradictions of bourgeois society.

In a pre-bourgeois, aristocratic world, tragic realism gives to passion a rather different structure of feeling. The 'nobility' of passion cannot compromise, even fleetingly, with the ideological forms which progress or success take in bourgeois society. At the extreme where passion thrives but compassion scarcely exists, as in the unique case of *Wuthering Heights*, passion emerges out of a peripheral, pre-civilised wilderness of cruelty. In *The Idiot*, where compassion spasmodically flowers, the compassionate presence is vanquished by cruelty and passion in order that passion, the dominant structure of feeling, can finally destroy its victims. Nobility here is a residual class feeling which defies the domesticating forms of bourgeois civility, even if, as in the case of Nastasyia Filippovna, its expressive mode is the cruelty which devours itself. But it is also more. The doomed heroism of Julien Sorel of Nicholas Stavrogin fuses the elevated coldness of nobility with the *passio* of Christ's suffering, which as a religious ecstasy was originally undertaken in the cause of universal human redemption. Thus, irrespective of class background, Heathcliff, Rogozhin, Myshkin, Sorel, Stavrogin and Nostromo are both heroes and nonentities, outcasts mimicking the noble. In their transgressions against the moral code, the passion of loving or rebelling is transmuted into the passion of suffering, a passion which, so merged, often confuses, in the eyes of its protagonists, conquest and redemption, the will-to-power and Christian mercy. Yet the moral codes of bourgeois society or the absolutist state never yield place. They ultimately punish the transgressors and transfer to them the stigma of those who are socially beneath them, the oppressed.

Passion in the nineteenth-century novel is a measure of tragic alienation which points to a deeper sense of social disturbance. As such it remains inimical to the affirmative tradition of the middle-class novel. But the latter, it should be noted, derives its own portrayal of compassion from a specific and necessary social distance from the central forms of the diffusion of capital, and in particular, of industrial capital. The world of Austen and Eliot is the localised world of the provincial gentry and the professions, Dickens's that of the professional patriarch and the small-scale entrepreneur, Trollope's, more often than not, that of the provincial clergy. Though their work deeply informs our whole understanding of Victorian society, it cannot be read – any more than Balzac can – as co-extensive with the Marxian critique of capital. Marx's vision of the dynamic and global diffusion of capital, which takes no prisoners, has its literary correlative, where at all, in the later work of Conrad and James. The earlier Victorian fiction evokes compassion out of the civilising and respectable forms of middle-class culture, where it finds, albeit with difficulty, its necessary social space. By the turn of the century, the major works of Conrad and James – in particular, *Nostromo* and *The Golden Bowl* – cast in doubt the viability of evoking through fiction the structure of feeling we have called compassion. The crisis in compassion here is inextricable from the crisis in narrative seeing, from a major undermining of confidence in the ability of the multiple perspective of realist narrative to produce a unified field of meaning.

Set in an imaginary South American republic, *Nostromo* gives an extraordinary sense of the different levels of connection and diffusion in the global world of capital. These different levels, and the intricate politics of the American hemisphere, create a complex set of events whose significance cannot be clearly seen in a purely local context. Conrad's narrative irony always questions the immediate meaning which can be attributed to events by referring them back to a more opaque set of motives and circumstances. Nostromo acts unwittingly in the context of the misplaced idealism of the Goulds, who in turn are merely acting locally within the global perspective of Holroyd, the rich American industrialist. Multiple perspective reveals contradictory, rather than complementary, meanings, and the regression of motive finds its stylistic expression in the regression of narrative, in the constant chronological looping and the backward movement through time. In Conrad, abrogation of linear narrative indicates a crisis in literary form, the failure of the unilinear progression towards unified meaning at the level of social totality. Narrative of that kind simply cannot encompass the social whole which is unified in such a complex way by capital but equally divided by national power politics and by class. In *Nostromo* the narrative shifts are more abrupt and more dissonant because the focus of the local perspective, the mining of San Tomé silver, would be narrowed in context and meaning by conventional nineteenth-century style. The added focus of imperial power or capital, which is omnipresent in Conrad, calls perspective into question by emphasising its divisive rather than its consensual attributes, and raising the question as to how the reader, given differing perspectives, is to attribute priority.

The focus of *The Golden Bowl* is more directly on the intersection of cultural and economic capital. The novel is probably the author's deepest penetration into an upper-class world where culture, civility, manners and marriage are conducted according to rules of stringent etiquette but actually moulded by more fundamental considerations of wealth and power. Holroyd's economic patronage of the Goulds is more than matched here in the cultural patronage of the Assinghams by the Ververs. Both are instruments of a higher design, compliant and yet thriving on an exaggerated sense of their own autonomy. The outcomes of course are different. The failure of the Goulds scarcely bothers Holroyd, but the mediation of Fanny Assingham is vital in Maggie's eventual success in freezing out Charlotte Stant and saving her marriage. In James, the nature of cultural capital is as perplexing and intricate as the diffusion of economic capital in Conrad's world of political intrigue. Indeed, the Jamesian patterns of intrigue which are conducted socially within a clear and rigid code of order are narratively very far from clear. Narrative perspective and its use of multiple viewpoint, which had previously made meaning absolute in the realist novel, are caught here in the grip of a truly vertiginous relativity.

For one thing, James gives the individual point of view a greater cutting edge than his predecessors. It is the focal point for sustained exploration of the half-formed impression in the character's mind, a technique which is often pedantic and layered in euphemism. Yet the tortuous nature of the narrative is linked to a sensibility of evasion. It is almost as if consciousness were a process of evading things which needed to be thought, and conversation veiled the necessity of saying what needed to be said. Both speech and consciousness act as smokescreen and surface, putting a needed gloss on things which may have a more unpleasant reality. Innocence at times can be a purely upper-class privilege, its fanciful rationalisations testifying to the leisure and luxury of its protagonists. The magnanimity and seeming beneficence of the Ververs comes from their sense of owning a very large portion of the civilised world.

As one of the great, later works, *The Golden Bowl* consummates the Jamesian sense of ambiguity. At one point our sympathies are with the Prince and Charlotte, at another with Maggie and her father. Critics still remain deeply divided over the moral status of the plutocratic magnate and his affectionate daughter. But multiple perspective has here come a long way from George Eliot. The question as to whether the Ververs are angels or monsters can never be clearly resolved. In the course of his narrative, James can shift our angle of perception through 180 degrees and, if Maggie insistently claims not to know where she stands, then neither emphatically do we. The struggle for knowledge and power, centrally engaged in the text, becomes a fundamental part of actually reading it. Maggie strives to separate the Prince from Charlotte without disturbing the delicate balance of power preserved by his pretended ignorance of the affair. Her tenacity puts her in a long line of heroines from Austen onwards who struggle to establish in a patriarchal world what they see to be morally right. Yet Maggie's relationship with her father suggests a higher amorality, a deeper and forbidding conspiratorial power, a nestling within the bosom of ultimate patriarchy.

The Golden Bowl simultaneously calls into question the consensual narrative perspective and the compassionate structure of feeling. Because we do not know what is truly happening, we cannot tell whether the beneficence of the Ververs towards the world and towards each other is truly genuine. The motives behind a magnanimity which is apparently without limit remain dense and inscrutable. The compassion which appears in middle-class life as the ultimate resistence to an ideology which fails appears at the centre of upper-class life to be manipulated as a tool of ideology itself. The realist narrative can no longer effectively provide through consensual perspective an imaginary resolution of cultural contradictions.

This is not to argue for a failure on the part of Conrad or James but rather to suggest that the artistic achievement of raising the novel to a new peak created fundamental problems for any future realist form. Their renewal of the realist form, as with Mann and Proust, also testifies to its decomposition. Compassion becomes problematic because, in evoking through mediate forms the global power of capital upon the lives of individuals, they erode the credible powers of fictional resolution and undermine the certainties of compassion. Passion, on the other hand, remains suppressed as part of the legacy of Victorian morality, assumed but never evoked, recognised as more powerful and subterranean than by the Victorians, but still treated largely as something unspoken. When the renaissance of the realist form occurs in Lawrence, passion is introduced into the English novel in a startling and revolutionary manner, but only because it abrogates the tragic and renews through contiguity the compassionate structure of feeling. Compassion here, though it still manifests itself as friendship, esteem and marriage, shows no closure. Central to Lawrence's transformation is the sense of a life which continues beyond the ending of his fiction, 'the wave which cannot halt', bearing a provisional autonomy from the text which its author cannot fully encapsulate.

Prior to Lawrence, however, there was a totally different resolution for the reading public of the crisis in realist form. The rise of popular fiction among middle-class and lower-middle class readers which came about through the new technologies of printing and the reorganisation of publishing produced its own diluted and vulgarised expurgation of the classic structures of feeling. One of the most powerful of its many forms was the romance. Romance has traditionally been the popular dilution of both passion and compassion, which remained rare as fully articulated structures of feeling. And romance has its own formulae. Infatuation, idealised yearning, gratuitous misfortune, convenient love: all are familiar through their constant repetition. The solidity of compassion is sentimentalised out of existence. The intense mutuality and destructiveness of passion remain out of reach. Instead it is usual for the beloved simply to become a sublimated compensation for what the world of the social, a world 'without love', cannot offer. Even in its most powerful form, say in the work of Charlotte Brontë, romance lacks both the destructive passion of *Wuthering Heights* but also the durability of moral experience to be found in the female protagonists of Austen, Eliot and Gaskell. Yet the way forward for the English-language novel was prefigured by the great French work which came to serve as a model of imitation for much popular romance. The novel which in the nineteenth century most fully dissects romance yet errs in spite of itself on the side of passion is *Madame Bovary*.

Flaubert achieves this by transcending the romantic stereotypes he uses and parodies, by transforming romance into the love of love, distancing himself from Emma's folly but fusing her feeling and action into an almost abstract intensity which is then consecrated as literary form. That historical moment, the decisive departure from Stendhal, whom Flaubert consciously rejected but whose impact he could not escape, links social mobility to the triumph of style. In veering from the aristocratic, in eclipse after 1848, to the provincial bourgeois, Flaubert turns passion from a relationship into an obsession which veers between romance and desire. He repeats the centripetal movement of Stendhal from country to city, but, unlike Julian Sorel, Emma never gets to the Paris of which she dreams, captures no aristocratic lover, no bitter-sweet flavour of her adored capital. The odds are always against the novel evoking the passionate structure of feeling, and in all the later imitations of Flaubert the possibility does not even arise. Why, then, is it here that passion is sustained?

The clue lies in Flaubert's modernity. During the daily round of his heroine, the narrator is always on the outside looking in, cold and distant, never passing judgement, yet at the same time still evoking the world through her eyes. It is precisely this focus which enables him to tread the razor's edge between passion and desire. Emma's love of love emerges out of the conventions of romance and chivalry, which in a calculated way he reduces to daydream and fantasy. But real adultery projects Emma beyond mere sublimation, and itself becomes a consuming passion as her affairs run the gamut from sublimation to sensuality, from romance to a clear but understated sensual desire. This uneven, discontinuous journey of Emma's passion, in which the ideal becomes material and then expires, parallels the phase of her marriage during which domestic profligacy spirals into hopeless irretrievable debt and drives her to poison herself.

Through Flaubert's parody of romance, passion actually strengthens its social referent. The tragic climax rests on the homology between the transformation of credit into bankruptcy and the transformation of passion into desire. The narrative traces a transformation within the text which is later to mark a transformation within the twentieth-century novel. With its evocation of the immediacy of the sense world and its consistent narrative refusal of motive and value, *Madame Bovary* points to the absence of the social as a cushioning force and, despite the blind and doting Charles, to the absence of a moderating compassion. Emma cuts herself off more and more from the world outside adultery as the love of love transforms itself into desire. In one sense Flaubert and Lawrence are poles apart. Lawrence wrests passion from tragic realism by assimilating it to the English tradition of compassion and makes it a durable structure of feeling even within the context of marriage. It is an achievement which in retrospect seems to make Flaubert incredibly brittle. Yet Flaubert in turn looks forward to the great transformation Lawrence inaugurated. He looks beyond *Women in Love* to the point at which the pain and exile of passion lead to the abyss of desire which destroys Gerald Crich and which Birkin consciously and ideologically repudiated. In a sense Emma Bovary, too, is already there.

This transformation of structures of feeling marks a stylistic reworking of the literary sense of the real. The new form is characterised by a textural heightening of the immediacy of the sense world, and this significantly alters narrative perspective. For Lawrence it entails the vividness of nature called forth by allotropic states of feeling, elemental states akin to carbon which dissolve the stable ego of the bourgeois personality and its literary representation in the nineteenth-century novel. For Joyce, narrative sustains its focus on 'the ineluctable whatness of a thing'. Prior to *Ulysses* he had already set forth the epiphanies of sense experience, in which the equivalent of religious or mystical revelation is at hand in the intense, often unexpected, experiences of daily life. Through the intensification of the unexpected in the midst of the humdrum, epiphany links memory and emotion, past and present, hope and desire. It is Bloom's hallucinations in Nighttown, Ursula Brangwen confronted by the horses in the storm. It is Proust's narrator's sensation of the madeleine or the flagstone, Joe Christmas riding through the black cabins *en route* to murdering his white middle-aged mistress. These instances of epiphany all dissolve the duality of nineteenth-century narrative, the connectedness through separation of author and character, the public and the private, the inner world of the hero and the outer world of experience. All dissolve the relationships of connection crystallised by the perspective of multiple narrative.

Before the turn of the century, Flaubert and Zola had already prefigured Freud in addressing the forms of sexuality in European culture which were generally censored out of public discourse. While pointing out the disasters of repression in the 'civilised' sexual morality of his period, Freud also recognised some of the difficulties of sexuality without constraint. In *Beyond the Pleasure Principle* he points out that the self's attempt to pursue pleasure through the lessening of tension can at times lead to a denial of pleasure itself. *On Narcissism* reveals through its analysis of the asymmetries of loving, of the disadvantages of loving rather than being loved, the important dimension of power in sexual relations. In the twentieth century the epiphanous writing of Joyce, Faulkner and Lowry matches and parallels these insights but does so by concentrating on the love object, the other, as the lost object of desire, the love object desired because of and in spite of the impossibility of love's consummation. Into the facticity of desire as material presence, desire desublimated in the union of self and other, is introjected the lostness of absence. The absence is literal when the beloved is in à place apart, a place inaccessible, or when, because desire has no object, he or she cannot be constituted at all. Absence is metaphorical where wounding memory of the other negates the pleasurable presence of the other, or, conversely, when pleasurable memory of the other supersedes, in its sensuous immediacy, the other's actual and oppressive presence. Geoffrey Firmin's response to Yvonne's unexpected return in *Under the Volcano* makes it all too clear how absence can penetrate into the very presence of the other as beloved.

There are, however, significant departures from Freud. In psychoanalysis, absence is tyranny of the past bounded by the unconscious. What has existed in the recesses of childhood is the prime mover of human action, even though it is not usually present to the conscious mind which it governs.[6] Each love object of adult life is a displacement of the love objects of childhood, the Oedipal love of the mother and the father. The novel gives us a different version of displacement, more social in nature. The object of desire is not an object because it displaces the mother and father of childhood. It is the love object which the present rules impossible through law or circumstance, and it is the love object for *that very reason*. The love object is socially lost to the subject within the adult world of desire. Though absence here can be seen as a metaphorical resolution of Freudian displacement, it is something much more. The epiphanous novel defies Freud's evolutionary mythology of libidinal development, the myth of adulthood healing the wounds of childhood. In challenging Freud's adaptation of social evolution to a linear model of selfhood, its relationship is similar to the earlier relationship between the nineteenth-century novel and the ideologies of progress.

The novel defies Freud essentially by reinstating the social as the ubiquitous condition of absence in the contemporaneous world of the fictional character. The conflict between conscious and unconscious, adult and child, is transposed into the self's conflict with a social world which cannot integrate it, which does not so much alienate the fictional self as rob it of identity within the very integument of its being. The absence of the other can then be seen as a mirror of the absence of the subject within his or her own world. And the self finds in the absent other a mirror of its own predicament. It is the very displacing of the love object which acts as a stimulus to desire so that desire is excited in proportion to the impossibility of its ever being consummated. Desire invokes itself by losing the objects it possesses or by choosing others which it cannot have. Though childhood and family, kinship and memory, are central to the epiphanous novel, the dialectic of absence and desire is usually existential and immediate, located within the world-as-such. It does not refer back in the Freudian sense of the unconscious to an absence outwith itself. It refers to an object which in mirroring the subject has been lost rather than repressed.

Epiphany is the stylistic rendering of absence in the realist form, usually an incandescent flattening of perspective, often a blurring of figural dimension. It mirrors the intense experience of absence of self in the lost other, the lost community, the lost society. But though it has links with the demonic nature of the Gothic novel, this intensification of loss is not, primarily, a new romantic convention. It shares with Freud and Heidegger the rejection of nineteenth-century romanticism. The lost other or community is experienced as lost within the immediate world of the present and is part of the texture of lived experience. Absence has no hiding-place. The historical source of this development can again be found in Flaubert. As Genette has pointed out,[7] the daydream in Flaubert has as great a sensuous reality as the character's experience of the immediate world. Ontologically, both are equally real for the subject. Flaubert's protagonists live simultaneously in this world and in a world apart, a world of hope and dream and memory. That balanced but disruptive duality is clearly shown in the second section of *The Sound and the Fury*. On his last day alive, Quentin

Compson is confronted by the same accusation in New England as the one he has made against Dalton Ames, the seducer of his sister, Caddy, in Mississippi. An Italian immigrant falsely accuses Quentin of having kidnapped his little sister. Facing the accusation in the world of the present, Quentin daydreams of his previous role as accuser and faces once more the crucifying absence of Caddy, whom he is never to see again. In the immediate world of encounter are mirrored the absent historical terms of his own damnation. In *Under the Volcano*, Geoffrey Firmin similarly endures a world which he is ceasing to recognise through the haze of alcohol, while vainly attempting to resurrect an absent world he can no longer alter, yearning, with no fixed identity of self, for what is lost and impossible to attain.

Epiphanous narrative subverts perspective because loss of the other at times entails the strategic evasion of intersubjectivity. But loss of the other also points unambiguously to the impossibility of passion. Imaginary incest predominates in Faulkner and Styron because incest is universally taboo and therefore the most dangerous form which passion could take. The yearning for the absent beloved is a passionate longing which, because it cannot hope to recover its displaced object, falls back upon itself and converts itself into a hopeless desire. Desire, it is true, contains a trace of the illusion of passion – historically grounded in previous fiction – and this goes far beyond the idealisation of romance. Immersed in the solipsism of desire, the hero falls prey to this central and tragic illusion. As if to prove that incest is not its only form, in *Sanctuary* Faulkner creates a desire based on the mutual hatred of strangers, the class hatred of Popeye and Temple Drake, and in *Absalom, Absalom!* he converts desire into miscegenation. Desire, in its various forms of hopelessness, becomes the destructive mode of transgressing the social which passion once was, but, in place of the shared alienation from the social world of the transgressing lovers, it reveals the anguish of absence at the heart of the social world. Here all dyadic union is chimerical, and desire is unrequited.

There is a further sense, however, in which the modern novel is closely linked to the Freudian concept of repression, and it lies largely in the forms of repression associated with language. In Freud this originates in the way in which the sound of words can impose direction upon the meaning of dreams, but also in the way in which language, with its capacity for double meaning, can become a prisonhouse of feeling, channelling and curtailing emotional expression and generating neuroses. In Lawrence, Joyce and Faulkner, repressed language has a social as well as a psychological significance. What is repressed, and what the author must liberate, is the inarticulate voice of those in the represented society of the fiction who exist beneath the level of public discourse, a discourse which cannot through its own conventions accord to them the words or thoughts for what they mean, the voice for what they feel. Here the novel gives a substantial presence to what is conventionally absent from the analytic discourse of the society, language as the fullness of expressive voice, of the hidden voice which is normally never heard. The Brangwens and the Morels in Lawrence, the Blooms in Joyce and the Bundrens in Faulkners are all literary landmarks in the new form. Faulkner's Joe Christmas, Wright's Bigger Thomas and the unnamed hero of Ellison's *Invisible Man* extend that fullness explosively into the arena of race.

In its reconstitution of the social world, it would be wrong to see this form as what Williams has termed 'the language of community'.[8] That more conventionally has been created within a tradition of revolutionary romanticism which adheres more closely to the narrative of nineteenth century realism. The danger, which is already implicit in Zola, of eulogising the proletarian community as a collective voice is also be found, in more euphemistic and sentimental ways, in London, Malraux, Steinbeck, and many of the Soviet writers of socialist realism. This tradition, which can be more didactically subversive, has also proved to be more aesthetically conventional. The epiphanous novel, on the other hand, in changing realist narrative, forges the language of absence-within-community, so that, rather than acting as an analogue to class consciousness, it is a testament to its lack of crystallisation. Instead of identifying the collective sentiments of the homogenous community, the reader must uncover, from within a divided community which is lost to bourgeois civility, the contours of the character's lost and hopeless desires.

The voice of absence and desire can be seen not merely in terms of the class hierachy of bourgeois societies, but also, geographically speaking, in terms of the dialectic between centre and periphery. The epiphanous novel invokes the cultural and spatial distance of the fictive community from the metropolitan centres of bourgeois civilisation. It is, above all, a novel of periphery and exile. Joyce's Dublin is to London and Paris what Faulkner's Jefferson, Missis-

sippi, is to New York and Chicago and what Lowry's Quauhnahuac is to the whole of North America. This gives to absence its
social and historical perspective. Absence is both the absence of
the distanced community, and more important, the absence of
the hero *within* the distanced community. The latter operates,
fictionally speaking, within the social context of the former.
Historical 'backwardness' as immediate context signifies the
absence of the 'civilised', the most modern and, by implication, the
most advanced metropolis. Backwardness, though its immediate
presence is most palpable, coalesces with figural absence in the
text as an absence within the social – an absence, in its full nineteenth-century connotation, of compassion.

The classic pattern of alienation as the narrative movement of
the hero away from convention, from a nexus of values which
appears to contradict the pattern of his own life, is replaced here
by a primal absence, an absence which is existentially given and
which narrative perspective cannot readily contain. Absence-
within defies the narrative balance of estrangement-from. The
intensity of its experience approximates at times to visceral
sensation, evoked in narrative through the use of the first person
and the present tense, the interior monologue and the language
of extensive feeling. Narrative operates at opposite extremes of
subjectivity and objectivity, and ranges, very suddenly and
abruptly, between them. In order to reconstitute totality, perspective is fragmented and subjected to internal rupture, stylistic
patterns which have conferred upon the great realist novels of the
twentieth century the honorific and sometimes misleading title of
'modernism'.

The absence of the fictional subject, which, as we have seen, is
mirrored internally through desire in the absence of the other, is
mirrored here *externally* in the 'absence' of society – mirrored, that
is to say, through periphery. This links the levels of individual
and social dislocation in a way which goes beyond Freud and
which subverts in turn his own psychologised subversion of evolutionary narrative. In reconstituting the social totality of the realist
text through periphery it also undercuts the rational powers of
recovery imputed to the methods of psychotherapy. The thrust of
the novel is not psychoanalytic, not to search out motive in the
deep structure of the unconscious, but to search out the repressed
voice of the disprivileged in the deep structure of society. But it
usually is the structure of a 'backward' society at one remove

from the ambience of bourgeois civilisation in which Freud and psychoanalysis have always been at home. Through its varied uses of style, the new realist form uncovers the double contradiction which is thematic and social. A rooted sense of place becomes, paradoxically, the essential condition of absence by juxtaposing the lost hero to his lost community and his lost community to what by implication is, between the lines, the true standard of civilisation. Absence becomes possible through the very rootedness which contradicts it, through the inner space within the peripheral habitus where the hero lives out his implosive isolation. That special sense of absence is the socio-literary correlate of periphery, of a transient, provisional backwardness at the dynamic and ever-changing margin of the modern capitalist world.

The distance of periphery operates obliquely through the world of value to mediate the perceived contradiction between life and ideal. But the greater the distance the more impossible the process of mediation becomes. In Lawrence, where the country operates as an imaginary and topographical border adjacent to the city, the sense of distance is already there, but usually minimal. In Joyce and Faulkner, it is enhanced by greater national and cultural differences originating, respectively, in imperial rule and in slavery. At times the contradictions are so great that they threaten to hive apart, to shatter the form which tries to encompass them. But at the same time there is in all three writers an electrical charge to the epiphanious form which comes from their refusal of literalism – that is to say, of conscious didactic intent. Their artistic strength comes from the fact that during an era of increasing social and political awareness they have refused to graft onto fiction a hypostatised knowledge of power and society.

Instead one finds, reading between the lines, in the interstices of narrative, the intimation of something unspoken and, for the novelist, almost but never quite unspeakable. In *Women in Love* it is the destructiveness of war. In *Ulysses* it is the dead weight of imperial rule. In *Sanctuary* and *Absalom, Absalom!*, it is the horror of racial tyranny. In *Invisible Man*, it is the unspeakable injustice of being falsely named. These themes, at times understated and at other times unstated, can be construed as absences of political statement, absences of ideological intent and also, perhaps, refusals of absolute truth. Such absences and refusals can be referred back to the perceived contradictions which act as a stimulus to the writing, which arise almost out of a sense of wonder and stupefaction, an astonishment which appears at times almost too paralysed to express itself. In Joyce and Faulkner, Lowry and Ellison, this arises when the metropolitan centres serve as an implicit yardstick for the realities of the peripheral culture. Out of that contrast comes an implosive sense of absurdity which pervades the whole text – largely comic in Joyce, comic and tragic in Ellison, profoundly tragic in Faulkner and Lowry. Yet that sense of the absurd is ontologically rather than philosophically grounded, differing for that reason in its expressive form from the fabulism of Kafka or Borges, and later from the magic realism of Marquez. For the rupture with progress which characterises the greatest works in English-language fiction is never complete, never total. The idea of progress is rooted in the living history of Western societies. In many Third World countries, it is often seen as an artificial transplant, volatile and meaningless and ultimately absurd. The tragic fiction of Faulkner and Lowry should be seen in this historical context as treading the razor's edge between acceptance and rejection, absorption and repudiation, operating at a level in which the contradiction between life and value is strained to its highest pitch.

That definitive strain, that dramatic polarisation, is contiguous with the movement from passion to desire. In a sense Lawrence straddles the two traditions, breathing into the English novel a passion it never had, yet dissolving in the next breath the very structure of feeling he himself created. The role of the heroine, and of female character generally, is crucial in this respect. It is through the hopes and ambitions of the Brangwen sisters, and previously their mother, that the nature of passion is forged and challenged, triumphs and fails. In subsequent fiction, the language of feeling is diminished, and there is a stringent artistic purity in the progressive elimination of motive from the realist novel – motive, that is, conceived of as a connecting link between the personal and the social, and as a vital prop in the multiple perspective of narrative form.

This stems, paradoxically, from an affirmation of the role of sexuality in human discourse, an affirmation which naturally confronted a number of novelists with the pitfalls of censorship and hostility. While Freud celebrates motive, the novel finds it obtrusive, creating in the purity of its absence the structure of feeling and the expressive human voice which official culture had previously suppressed. In the epiphanous novel there are two stages of development. Like Freud, Lawrence recognised sexuality as a fundamental and ubiquitous feature of all human striving, but his relationship to classic realism is maintained by virtue of the fact that its very expression is achieved through existential discourse with the other, the active engagement with the other through encounter, in the passing moment of time where feeling explodes off the page and unlike its literary precursors, almost forgets its own history and genesis. The Brangwen sisters are quite unlike any Victorian heroine, but, for any reader of Victorian fiction, the shift in Lawrence, though startling, can be readily understood.

It is a rather different story with the later heroines of the epiphanous novel. With Molly Bloom, Candace Compson and Temple Drake, Robin Vote in *Nightwood* and Peyton Loftis in *Lie Down in Darkness*, mutuality of feeling is absorbed by a primal desire, a desire which both precedes and supersedes its love object, which latches destructively onto the other to crystallise the selfish wishes of the ego, and then abandons the object which cannot gratify its longing, or, conversely, chooses in advance that very object which it knows cannot do so. The departure from the cultural and fictional conventions of romantic love at this stage in the development of the novel are by any standard remarkable. For it is largely in the popular fiction and cinema of the same period that the convention of romantic love has been sustained. The novel undercuts that not by celebrating the discovery of desire but by pointing to its deeper and disconcerting realities, as Jane Bowles does in her extraordinary novel *Two Strange Ladies*, where female desire is an uncanny presence without recognition or name. Desire then brings no formula for liberation but still affects us all, doubling as a hidden means of emancipation and possible form of imprisonment – an imprisonment, that is, which occurs in the context of the very freedom which it brings. For in the absence of a compassionate world, which is the defining absence of the epiphanous form, the pursuit of desire ultimately bears no fruit. In the twentieth-century novel after Lawrence it thrives under impossible circumstances which eventually bring about its own destruction.

2 Lawrence: Passion and its Dissolution

I

The work of Lawrence was a turning-point for the fiction of the twentieth century. He took the crisis in the English novel at its deepest point and tried to forge a new kind of writing after the end of the Victorian era, a quest he saw as being diametrically opposed to the worst forms of Edwardian complacency. For him that complacency was at its clearest in the work of Wells, Bennett, Shaw and Galsworthy.[1] He considered that, by using literature for didactic purposes, the Edwardian 'Uncles' ignored fundamental questions not only of artistic form but also of human feeling. Without doubt theirs was a social and political response to the uncertainties of Edwardian Britain, but for Lawrence it was not enough. For a changing and developing structure of feeling in industrial civilisation, the novel had to find a new form.

He sensed in the Edwardians an incapacity to break the impasse previously created in Victorian fiction by the omission of sexuality and its associated language of feeling, by what Bersani has called realism's 'terror of desire'.[2] The challenge they had ducked demanded a complete recasting of the relationship between body and psyche. Thus Lawrence was prompted to say about Galsworthy that he had put 'a soft sentimental poultice' on the modern soul instead of wielding the surgical knife it needed so badly. The Edwardians had failed to sense that the crisis of industrial civilisation had undermined the stability of the bourgeois ego. The promise–threat of progress which had fuelled the fire of the Victorians had deepened into greater crisis. Problematic evolution had been harnessed to the bandwagon of reform at the very time when, in the eyes of Lawrence, the industrial and technical developments of the age had created deeper differences between social classes and deeper schisms within the individual ego.

Like Hardy, Lawrence saw evolution as a process of human struggle, but his initial optimism about the consequences rested on a close relationship between nature and culture, in the organic relationship of landscape to community which is the vital starting-point of *Sons and Lovers*. Consequently he not only repudiated reformism as an artefact, but also reacted strongly to the dark pessimism of Conrad, noting in a letter to Edward Garnett that he could not forgive the other novelist for his melancholy and surrender. Yet Lawrence must have been disturbed by Conrad's vision of the world, which constituted a formidable challenge to the pastoral elements of his own organicism. Conrad, in taking up the theme of the human cost of imperialism at the periphery of its operations, had portrayed a world where all organic values seemed redundant or in disarray. It was not fatalism but a deep sceptical irony which informed his vision of the globe – a vision which, to say the least, dispelled the myth of the national society as an independent and self-sufficient entity, and where those seemingly harmless terms 'home' and 'abroad' signified that the left hand need not know what the right hand was doing.

It is the experience of the imperial periphery – European and American, not just the British Empire – which creates in Conrad's characters the increasing vertigo of self, the 'horror' of Kurtz and its 'strange commingling of desire and hate', the self-destructive scepticism of the talented Decoud who cannot believe in his own success since he beholds 'the universe as a succession of incomprehensible images'. Imperial rapacity, stillborn revolution and the volatile demands of capital turn the world literally upside down. In *Victory*, finance capital defies the laws of nature: 'a mysterious world in which, incredible as the fact may appear, evaporation precedes liquidation'.[3] But the human consequences are not shirked or forgotten. The liquidation of the Tropical Belt Company prompts Axel Heyst into a series of urgent yet aimless pilgrimages through the Malay Archipelago, since 'Going home to Europe was nearly as final as going to Heaven. It removed a man from the world of hazard and adventure.'[4]

How, then, to recentre the lost world of community? The most obvious resource had been Hardy's view of nature as the source of organic life for the community, and prior to this the pantheistic tradition which Lawrence inherited from Wordsworth and Emerson. Certainly he aimed in his early fiction to fuse that tradition with the Spencerian notion of progressive differentiation.[5] In *The White Peacock, Sons and Lovers* and *The Rainbow* Lawrence tries to link the scheme of individuation within unity to the growth of humanity within nature. This ironically optimistic view of evolution allowed him at first to overlook the worst nightmares which had assailed George Eliot and Hardy. For, as Lester has pointed out,[6] Hardy seized on the most relativistic aspect of Darwinian theory, the concept of 'chance' mutation, and injected into evolutionary narrative those random variations of human misfortune out of which he tried to create tragic fiction.[7]

Hardy's horror at the injustices of chance can be seen in the rise and fall of his individual heroes, of Michael Henchard, Tess Durbeyfield and Jude Fawley. But chance in Hardy can be both poignant and contrived. Time and again it invokes the dreaded spectre of coincidence, the same kind of machinery of plotting which haunts the early plays of Ibsen. For that is how we are forced to read the circumstances leading to Tess's seduction, the fate of the letter to Angel she pushes under the door but also under the doormat, and the constant failure of Jude to meet the right person at the right time, failing to find the woman he wants as often as he bumps into the one he wishes to avoid. Thus chance in Hardy becomes as deterministic as environment – indeed, it becomes *the* determinism of environment, evoking, as it does so, an enduring but misplaced sense of the powerlessness of the human will.

Clearly, Hardy had sensed the growing individualism of modern English society as well as the new pressures of uniformity which lay behind it and at times appeared to contradict it. But his fiction falters because he matches the two in an arbitrary way. It was this arbitrariness which Lawrence sensed that he had to avoid. The note of tragic pathos which his predecessor sought but only very occasionally found struck him as a risk that was too great to take. With the achievements of the Russian realists in mind, he duly noted in Hardy the pardox of a contradictory attempt to create tragegy. Hardy had a clear *'predilection d'artiste* for the aristocrat' and yet the aristocrat was precisely the figure to whom Hardy exhibited an open moral antagonism. In his hands, Lawrence noted, the tragic form had degenerated into the revenge of the bourgeois community upon the aristocratic hero, in which its author vicariously participated.[8] The wider sociological impasse for Hardy is of course the effective dovetailing of the material interests of the two dominant classes in Britain by the end of the century. In terms of the resilience of the British aristocracy, fictive evocations of a 'lost' nobility seem historically artificial. And Hardy's non-aristocratic heroes seem shackled by their inability willingly to transgress, by the closeness of their sensibility to existing mores, by their hypersensitivity to a coercive public opinion.

Lawrence concluded that in his own period neither the tragic nor the 'social', meaning a coagulated public opinion, could reproduce the classic antagonism of the law and love which resonates through Aesychlus. His own literary response worked in two stages. First, in *Sons and Lovers* he tried to establish a naturalistic plateau for the 'social' in the working-class community which produces its own internal antagonisms, where a shallow public opinion is replaced by a deeper compact of community. Secondly, he absorbed the classic tradition of passion into the English tradition of compassion by portraying the endurance of relationships, not their tragic demise. In *The Rainbow* he based his creative remodelling of society on the passionate structure of feeling, which he rescued from the uneasy realm of Hardyesque nobility and placed within courtship or marriage as a form of permanent ambivalence. It seems no coincidence that Lawrence was writing *Women in Love* at the time when Freud published his famous paper *Instincts and their Vicissitudes*. For through successive generations of the Brangwens Lawrence explores the vicissitudes of passion. One finds, without reference to infantile sexuality, an astonishing vision, during a changing culture, of successive co-existences of love and hate.

First, however, Lawrence powerfully added to the pastoral brilliance of *The White Peacock* the working-class community of *Sons and Lovers*. The latter stemmed from the Victorian novel of initiation, but instead of the uprooted orphan we have solidity of class and family solidarity, a sense of community which was inseparable, as Lawrence noted, from the sense of a special affinity to nature among Nottinghamshire miners.[9] In the family life of the Morels, compassion is something which endures suffering and conflict, the myriad antagonisms between wife and husband, parents and children. But, though the novel deals with the pain of separation from family which must eventually come for Paul Morel, there is a further resonance. The compassionate structure of feeling lodged in family life outweighs the attachments which Morel later strives for at the beginning of his adult life. His relationships to Miriam and Clara do not have the same primal power as his attachment to family, and particularly to his mother. Though no longer Victorian in its sensibility, Lawrentian compassion at this stage still predominates over passion.

In *The Rainbow*, where the emphasis is equally on men and women of successive generations, Lawrence makes the decisive breakthrough. The novel is not an accurate naturalistic account of the life of English rural society. The Brangwens are less typical of their class than the Morels are of theirs. But, for Lawrence and for the novel, this becomes a significant advantage. The world of *The Rainbow* is a naturalistic but idealised social space where work, property, nature and the intimacies of family life are all closely fused. The Marsh Farm and Cossenwaite cottage are close to nature yet also within distance of 'the rind of the world: houses, factories, trams, the discarded rind; people scurrying about, work going on, all on the discarded surface'.[10] This dialectic has a specific force. The greater and closer the growth of town and city, the more the Brangwens profit from the sale of their produce, and the more secure they are, consequently, from the fragmentary and dislocating effects of that very same urbanism. Prosperity and the geographic margin – properly speaking, *they* are on the rind – grant the necessary social space for the passionate marriage. Tom and Lydia, Will and Anna are free from the fluctuating tides of fortune which afflict the traders and tenant farmers of Hardy's Wessex, and which are rendered as vicissitudes of Darwinian chance. Through an isolation which is both lived and metaphorical, Lawrence narrows the panoramic spectrum to this self-contained nucleus within a changing world, a nucleus which remains intact until it is split open by the ambitions of Ursula Brangwen.

Passion in *The Rainbow* is made possible by two things. The close relationship of nature and culture is joined to the intensity of religious feeling which is cast adrift from the world of theology and introjected back into the intimacies of relationship. Two processes of the period in which Lawrence had started writing are linked: the embryonic secularisation of Christian belief with the growing interdependence of country and city. The absorption of Protestant faith into the passion of Will and then later Ursula occurs only through a painful sundering of the deep ties with doctrine and worship.

The way is clear for Lawrence to wrest passion from the tragic, unequal conflict of law and love and integrate it into the Victorian novel's resolving form of compassion – marriage. But unlike its fictional predecessors the Lawrentian marriage can never fully reconcile the different levels of the personal and the social. In its new technological phase, industrial society hinders the quest of passion to dictate its own terms of reference. In Lawrence, passion's always vulnerable success implies an enduring loss. For it is only achieved, finally, through the loss of community. As sequential texts, *The Rainbow* and *Women in Love* chart passion's genesis and its dissolution. In the later novel, Rupert and Ursula are forced to accept one another in the shadow of isolation and exile, where they strive against all odds for 'the perfect consummation' of marriage. That there is no margin for error is revealed clearly when Gerald and Gudrun, traversing the same route, see their abortive passion turn to ice. The dilemma of exile as necessary flight is implacable. Industrial civilisation reluctantly sanctions the implosive, monogamous relationship as a haven from its own heartlessness. In giving to the enlightened bourgeois the freedom to create a new form of intimacy, it takes away with the other hand the conditions for enduring intimacy.

In retrospect we can see in *The Rainbow* the importance of an unpolluted nature, three generations back. It has a special insularity from the tyranny of provincial public opinion which had haunted Eliot and Hardy. The tie to nature produces an unreflexive form of interior exile so that in the initial relationship of Tom and Lydia the voice of passion stumbles haltingly into life. This is no mystical rootedness to the soil, no anglicised *Blut und Boden*, but the freedom for new forms of emotion, which the narrative expresses beyond speech in a new language of feeling. Tom's naturalised and inarticulate passion for Lydia is partly the lack of an expressive voice but also a failure to meet the challenge of marrying a woman from another country and a higher social class, a woman who, with her own independence and pride, presents a challenge to the conventions of Victorian patriarchy. On his marriage night, Tom discovers that his passion cannot absorb the resistant foreignness of his new wife. In remaining beyond his understanding, she also remains beyond his power.

Tom tries to compensate for his failure through the affection he showers on Anna, his daughter, who becomes the other centre of his love, illustrating amidst his confusion his power of retaining compassion. She in turn is fascinated by her parents' unspoken and unarticulated passion, seeing in it a greater mystery and freedom than is to be found in adult life away from the farm:

> There was over the house a kind of dark silence and intensity in which passion worked its inevitable conclusions. There was in the house a sort of richness, a deep, inarticulate exchange which made other places seem thin and unsatisfying. . . . The whole intercourse was wordless, intense and close.[11]

At times Anna wishes to escape, but the outside world offers no alternative comparable to that intense relationship which both sustains and stifles her. The emotions of religions are explosive, but 'the *language* meant nothing to her: it seemed false. She hated to hear things expressed, put into words.'[12] It is initially with nature that she has to seek communion. In her relationship with Will, the gathering of the sheaves is more than just a metaphor of sexual awakening. In it the rhythms of nature fuse with the rhythms of the human embrace, leaving no discernible pause between the act of gathering and the act of passion. Embedded in nature the rapture of the kiss is beneath the threshhold of a self-conscious knowledge.

Uncomprehending, Will's response is the socially conventional one of marriage, but marriage is more than just the completion of courtship. It provokes further antagonisms of passion, in which the continuing tie to nature is matched by epiphanies of religious experience. In the second generation, greater contact with the outside world creates conflicts which are introjected back into the germinating passion of marriage. Through the fusion of nature and religion, Lawrence evokes the co-existence of love and hate which Freud formulated analytically as a central feature of sexual intimacy. Passion no longer means the social transgression of lovers, or their tragic alienation, but love and hate co-existing with a primal intensity which allows them to endure within society and points to passion's durability, not its disintegration.

The conflict is never fully articulated in words. Anaïs Nin has suggested that much of Lawrence's writing can be called inter-linear because there is a constant effort to articulate the silent and subconscious dimension of human communication.[13] Certainly the new language of epiphanous narrative must accord greater force to the perceptions of all five senses, to what Birkin in *Women in Love* called 'the phosphorescent ecstacy of acute sensation'. In

Lawrence contact with the other is often wordless, trembling with inarticulate presence. But the love–hate relation of Lawrentian passion makes that presence an authentic bond. At the same time it only gains its full meaning through wider social relationships. Anna rejects the limited life her local community offers her in order that she may summon all her energies to deepen her own intimacy. At the same time Will's diffuse religious mysticism acts as a catalyst, arousing her nascent antagonism towards him. She refuses to see his striving for belief as an attempt to articulate feeling at the level of speech, but instead interprets it as an attempt on his part to raise his voicelessness to a new and more dangerous level of mystification. She senses here a danger for both of them, the danger that passion will become submerged beneath 'nameless emotion'. In Will she sees the coherence of religion disintegrating, a detachment of feeling from meaning which destroys its transcendent unities. But, when she fights against his impossible desire for a religion of feeling, she paradoxically assures herself of her own identity. Through the very fury her beloved provokes in her she can define her relationship to the world and celebrate her stable, emergent self.

The struggle is intensified during their visit to Lincoln Cathedral, whose mystery for Will is a world above the material world. But, though the architecture arouses her, Anna resists Will's ecstasy. She wants to 'get out of this fixed, leaping, forward-travelling movement',[14] and starts to ridicule the faces carved in stone. The love–hate of passion revolves around the division between the material and the ideal, between Will's impulse to transform feeling into mystery and Anna's wish to expropriate it from its religious source. Eventually Anna wins. Will exchanges ardent worship for the practical tasks of maintaining and repairing the local church. But this sequence of events has already shown us the importance which religious fervour has for the world of passion. By charting the secularisation of that fervour, Lawrence strengthens the affirmative element of passion in his narrative, which then becomes permeated by the evangelising zeal of Protestantism without a God. Later, in *Women in Love*, that zeal is conspicuous by its absence and Rupert Birkin has to confront a world whose discourse is more secular and abstract, and where a declining Christianity has little effect on his cerebral ideology of 'love'. Meanwhile, in defying the male mystifications of God in a previous generation, Anna Brangwen manages to give a new and active meaning to female identity. She has not only defined but also expropriated passion.

Anna's subsequent pregnancy cannot therefore be interpreted as a female refuge, a lapse into passivity. The scene where naked she dances 'his nullification' illustrates the feeling of sensuousness her condition gives her, 'the violent trance of motherhood' whose rapture he is denied. Equally Will's fleeting encounter with a girl in Nottingham refuses all romantic conceptions of reconciliation. It precipitates instead an emotion which goes beyond all conventional love and tenderness: 'This was what their love had become, a sensuality violent and extreme as death. They had no conscious intimacy, no tenderness of love. It was all the lust and the infinite, maddening intoxification of the senses, a passion of death.'[15]

Desire, hitherto repressed and subterranean, lying deep beneath the social encounters of most Victorian fiction, surfaces here as an exhilarating triumph of passion. It is assimilated into the passionate relationship as a shared impulse, male and female, devoid of all connotation of sinfulness. In Flaubert it had issued in the love of love, but in Lawrence it issues in the triumphant love–hate of the other, of mutual love–hate, where antagonism deepens in proportion to desire. Taking *The Rainbow* and *Women in Love* as a whole, the passion of Will and Anna is a mid-point, equidistant from the polar extremes of the concrete and the abstract, community and exile, silence and speech. It emerges as a renaissance of the passionate structure of feeling at the crossroads between country and city, nature and civilisation, instinct and self-knowledge. Above all, it represents a movement of language in Lawrence behind convention to renew a structure of feeling which cannot be delineated naturalistically, or translated into the lucid categorisations of the everyday event.

With each generation of the Brangwens, the forms of turbulence into which passion dissolves the conventional ordering of experience increase. They do so through the shattering of the real and metaphorical insularity of the farm, the widening circle of experience. Ursual engages her father's affection in the same way as Anna had engaged that of her stepfather. But Ursula differs from her mother by desiring to burst the narrow boundaries of Cossethay and break away from its limited people. She possesses both her mother's quest for autonomy and her father's religiosity. Her religious upbringing determines both the freedom and constraint of her awakening to passion. Vexed and uncertain about the monotony of weekday life, she seeks solace at first in the visionary world of the Sabbath, finding on that day alone signs of Christ's passion, which the everyday world so disappointingly lacks.

As she grows up, her swollen ego indulges in a fantasy which is a prefiguration of her adult passions, the fantasy that Christ died for her alone and that the sons of God will come to the daughters of men. But, as adolescence alters her, religion changes its meaning. She craves a sense of Christ's passion in weekday terms and becomes ashamed of religious ecstasy. Yet she persists with her search for the sons of God, finding their first emanation in the figure of Anton Skrebensky, the army officer whom she sees as a secular divine, a self-possessed aristocrat making no attempt to prove himself because of his 'nature-like fate'. Anton is a diminutive Stavrogin, proudly alone in society because his true home is the army which acts as a cushion for his archaic sense of honour. For Ursula, the enchantment of their relationship rests on the illusion of its exclusiveness. On the carousel ride at the fairground, moving at a great height, she feels them both to be elevated above the common mass. As a fantasy of the 'noble', that precious sense of elevation replaces the Christian *passio* and its redemptive emotions. The transmutation of passion has its own weakness and its own price.

In the relationship of the two lovers, Lawrence astonishingly reverses novelistic convention. What starts as the romantic female adoration of male 'nobility' is stood on its head as the affair develops into a passion which attacks male dominance and ends up destroying itself. While Anton is still captive to mechanical notions of honour, Ursula strives to subordinate 'nobility' to the expression of open and equal passion. Passion is no longer a socially superior structure of feeling but a relationship whose provisionally equal status is such a fragile entity that its very existence is constantly under threat. The first indications of conflict come at the Brangwens' dance, a conscious reversal by Lawrence of Anna's adoration for Vronsky in *Anna Karenina*. Here it is through the dance that Anton fails to sustain Ursula's infatuation. Instead she fights her way through transient captivation to a 'fierce, white, cold passion' which emerges out of communion with nature and links back to the conflictual intensity of the earlier Brangwens. When she and Skrebensky walk into the stackyard, the passion of Will and Anna is doomed not to repeat itself. For

Skrebensky, as modern mechanical man, views the stacks with 'something like terror', while Ursula 'like glimmering gossamer seemed to burn among them, as they rose like cold fires to the silvery-bluish air'.[16] Her feeling for nature is deeper than her feeling for her lover, whom nature threatens to devour. Only through resistance, conflict, the transformation of love into hate, could Skrebensky compensate for his terror of nature. But for Lawrence the noble passion which mingles infatuation with social superiority is the relic of a bygone world.

Anton's capitulation is the second disenchantment of passion after Ursula's disillusion with the Christian *passio*. But his departure for the Boer War puts it in abeyance. In his absence, Ursula develops an independent identity through her affair with Winifred Inger and her struggle to establish herself first as a student, then as a schoolteacher, in a male world. The resulting autonomy of self more than matches her mother's because it overcomes greater public obstacles, and from that position of strength she is able to confront Skrebensky when he returns from the war. This is the crucial test of whether he can satisfy her demand for intensity, which still lacks its full articulation. But passion's post-Darwinian struggle for survival through the delicate and dangerous equilibrium of love and hate is also post-aristocratic, an intensity which the previous Brangwens could sustain in a subterranean way through proximity to nature, but which now cannot be sustained by nature alone.

The implicit and at times repressed absence of hate from passion is why Ursula disassociates love and passion, seeing the latter as fierce yet transient, 'only part of love' and not all of it, to be played out with a score of Skrebenskys. The dividing-line between love and passion in that sense is spelled out later by Birkin as a matter of equilibrium, an equilibrium of opposites created by autonomy and the equal intensity of feeling. The end of *The Rainbow* shows the demise of a passion which lacks not only this elusive equilibrium but also the even more elusive ambivalence underlying it, which even Birkin could not fully acknowledge. It is a revolutionary moment in the English novel. We witness for the first time in a text subject to immediate censorship the triumph of the erotic within the passionate structure of feeling, which had formerly been repressed, denied, unspoken. It is here that Lawrence most fully extends and deepens his attempt to forge a new narrative language for the complex relationship of feeling and

desire. The attempt has been wrongly seen at times as an attenu-
ation of the romantic when it is in fact a subversion of romantic
love. One anticipates in the flow of narrative a romantic consummation of Anton and Ursula's love. But it proves instead to be on
the verge of self-destruction.

The climactic scene on the beach, in which the reader might
anticipate through the very setting the consummation of love,
actually charts the swift and turbulent passage from joy to disillusion, from desire to nullity. Moreover, that transformation is
achieved, quite brilliantly, through the act of love-making itself.
Conventionally speaking, the absence or actuality of love-making
would be alternate signs of failure or success. Lawrence makes
the conventional sign for triumph an instance of destruction. The
most powerful eroticisation of passion in the English novel up to
that point emerges at the very moment of passion's destruction.
Because he cannot respond to either the irreducible difference of
male and female passion or the promise–threat of nature, the male
beloved becomes a dilution, a weakness, finally a nothingness.
For Ursula, Skrebensky fails by comparison with 'the salt, bitter,
passion of the sea' and the 'great whiteness' of the incandescent
moon, feeling himself 'fusing down to nothingness, like a bead
that rapidly disappears in an incandescent flame'.[17]

The subsequent act of love is like a fight to the death in which
Skrebensky cannot come to terms with the element of hatred
within love:

> She held him pinned down at the chest, awful. The fight, the
> struggle for consummation was terrible. It lasted till it was agony
> for his soul, till he succumbed, till he gave way as if dead, and
> lay with his head buried, partly in her hair, partly in the sand,
> motionless, as if he would now be motionless for ever, hidden
> away in the dark, buried, only buried, he only wanted to be
> buried in the godly darkness, only that, and no more.[18]

As he watches the tear which rolls afterward from her 'wide, open,
rigid eyes', he feels 'as if the knife were pushed into his already
dead body'. Lawrence avoids the Wagnerian *Liebestod* because
passion's failure is a human failure, above all a *male* failure. Anton
fails to recognise the hatred which can be born of love. Because
their passion is more open and independent of marriage, it is more
than the culmination of life in three generations of Brangwens. In

a world which is more mechanical and militaristic, it is more difficult and more dangerous. And it is even more dangerous because it can provoke the anger and resistance of a woman who has risked all in a man's world.

The two epiphanies at the end of the novel, the scene on the shore and the horses in the storm, express in sequence the presence and then the absence of the beloved. In the first instance Anton fails to maintain his presence as the palpable and immediate other. Thereafter Ursula tries to eliminate all traces of his presence. She cannot condone Anton's decision to leave for India to lead the sterile life of a colonial officer, but neither can his absence arouse her desire. Unlike the tragic figures of Faulkner, Lawrence's heroine erases the pain of memory instead of repeating it, the past being a bondage, a heaviness she struggles to cast aside. In the thunderstorm, the heaviness is felt in the oppressive threat of the horses' flanks as they swivel and panic. Yet, even though they threaten her, their frantic search for release is also hers. She wishes to annihilate Anton's memory just as she wishes to annihilate the foetus in her womb which is his physical legacy. With Ursula, passion is presence or it is nothing. When she aborts the child amidst fever and delirium, the involuntary act is almost consciously willed. And in the future passion must change its nature. It must 'come from the Infinite'. She awaits the other who is totally other, who will emerge out of the charged metaphors of God, the Infinite, Eternity.

II

In *Women in Love*, Lawrence's metaphor of 'a new germination' is not sustained. Instead there is a radical departure. The urban–industrial world of the future seemed so bleak in Lawrence's eyes that no metaphor of unified nature could sustain it. Beyond that, the trauma of the Great War, which affected Lawrence daily as he wrote, destroyed his residual attachment to any idea of progress. For that reason war, in the new novel, becomes the hidden signified, the unidentified happening whose horror cannot be accommodated retrospectively into Edwardian life by so portentous a device as prophetic warning. By omitting any reference to it as the source of their urgency, Lawrence actually gives to the plight of Ursula and Birkin a tauter and more immediate desperation, and one to which his reader, confronted by the evidence of mass murder during the war, could more willingly respond. Rupert and Ursula sense the destiny which awaits their civilisation without that evidence which Lawrence's readers will come to possess. The elimination of the wider circumstance of motive aligns itself with the general historical momentum of the epiphanous form, so that, while personal motivation is still to the fore of Lawrentian narrative, there is the vital omission of a wider context. In Thomas Mann's *The Magic Mountain* the retrospective judgement is more measured and more calculated. Hans Castorp's paralysis of will is shown as a response to the incessant and unresolved struggle of conflicting ideologies. But the Lawrentian hero cannot afford to be so passive. Ideology has to be forcibly expropriated from the corrupt public sphere and made the basis for a new relationship between personal destiny and the wider society. The way is then clear for the entry of the active, ideologising Rupert Birkin.

The vital difference from *The Rainbow* here lies in the severing of the link between nature and passion. In the face of the new forms of mechanised warfare the fusion of Spencer's progressive differentiation with pantheism seemed an archaic utopia. The vital connections between nature as metaphor and passion as a viable structure of feeling could no longer be maintained. Passion had to be able to exist independently of nature in order to survive, and could only do so by changing its meaning. The unacknowledged war becomes the main catalyst to Birkin's urgent quest to seek out 'a really pure single activity', which he defines to Gerald as 'the finality of love'. The focus is more than a cerebral updating of romantic convention. It is an ideological quest for an alternative world to the militaristic one which has made a nonsense of human progress. It combines the intensity of the passionate relationship which thrives on the co-existence of love and hate with the search that is abstractly conceived for impersonal equilibrium. But it is a combination which is so frail and vulnerable that it constantly threatens to fall apart.

The crisis in liberalism provoked by the widespread disenchantment with progress after 1914 created new political choices as the war finally collapsed in successive spasms of mutual exhaustion – revolution and counter-revolution, communism and fascism. In a country which remained strikingly immune from these wider convulsions, Lawrence's response was strikingly different.

Regarding the public politics of ideology as eternally damned, he tried to recast it through fiction whose form allows him to cast a sceptical and distanced eye on his own didacticism, to place it as an imaginary hypothesis in the context of an imaginary discourse which operates at the most intimate *and* most public levels of society. Here it is the figure of Birkin who tries to appropriate passion with a new abstract language as passion in turn flees from the devastations of an expropriated nature. Because of the systematic expropriation of nature for industry and war technology, nature can no longer provide the language of fiction with a metaphorical foundation.

The quest for impersonal equilibrium arises out of the breakdown of passion in *The Rainbow*, where Ursula failed to find a lover of equal intensity. Here, in place of the conflicts over nature and religion, there is a different reflexive factor constituting passion. Rupert and Ursula fight furiously over the actual definition which Birkin seeks to give to their relationship, so that passion in its full sense of love–hate intimacy is engendered by the process of giving it a name, and by Ursula's refusal to accept his willed and abstract definition. The context of that struggle is created by juxtaposing Birkin's ideological scenario to the alternative scenarios of Hermione Roddice and Gerald Crich. For Birkin engages not only with Ursula but also with them. His rejection of Hermione mirrors Lawrence's own rejection of the most precious elements of English bohemianism. He condemns her adoration of the animal instincts as the worst form of a self-conscious spirituality which founders on its own dualism. Just as Hermione could never go back to living like the early Brangwens, so all bohemian imitations of a 'natural' rural life end up as unintentional parody. His sense of Hermione's weakness also leads him to an appreciation of the dangers facing Gerald, who acts out the malaise about which Hermione can only talk incessantly. For Gerald uses passion as a mask for the exercise of pure will and the lust for power.

The danger is crystallised in a typical scene where Birkin himself is the subject of mockery. Gerald and Gudrun sit in the back of the car castigating Rupert, who cannot hear them over the roar of the engine. Their smugness suggests something which becomes increasingly clearer as their relationship develops. They deliberately and consciously reject the need to articulate a language of passion, preferring instead the danger of a self-conscious abandonment to sensation, the decadent cultivation of an illusion that passion in a technicised world speaks for itself. In exposing the contradictions of Hermione and Gerald, Birkin merely supplants them with his own. To offset the dangers of a self-conscious animal spirituality, he seeks the monism of 'physical consciousness', an imaginary equivalent to the unconscious in which the bodily self renders spirituality superfluous. It is a desire for mental oblivion, later embodied in his physical attraction to Gerald Crich. But here he has to use such a hopelessly abstract language to communicate it that he is impaled on his own contradictions. In trying to persuade Ursula with supposedly rational proposals about a psychic state beyond reason, he provokes instead a deep and hostile resistance to his sublime absurdity. Yet, for all that, resistance is the start of intimacy.

The nocturnal meeting at Willey Water is one of the central epiphanies of an intimacy which each seeks to define by struggling against the other, the crystallising of a passion which neither has recognised and which neither can name. The central image is that of Birkin throwing stones at the reflection of the moon in the pond. The act is a calculated attempt to break with pantheism, foreshadowing the later explication of love as impersonal equilibrium and of nature as unromantic, beyond humanity, a thing unknown. The destructive act fails: 'But at the centre, the heart of all, was still a vivid, incandescent quivering of a white moon not quite destroyed, a white body of fire writhing and not even now broken open, not yet violated.'[19] The tie with nature cannot be completely broken. Their intimacy has to take place both against the shattering of the moon's image and its reforming on the surface of the water. More generally, the intense conflict between life and ideal is embodied in Ursula's furious resistance to the excesses of Birkin's abstraction.

Earlier, in 'Mino', where they witness Mino's attack on the female stray and interpret it differently, the antagonism has already crystallised. Birkin has set forth his idea of 'impersonal equilibrium' and used the example of the cat fight to support his belief that the male must initiate the move to 'a pure stable equilibrium':

'What I want is a strange conjunction with you –' he said quietly; '– not meeting and mingling; – you are quite right: – but an equilibrium, a pure balance of two single beings: – as the stars balance each other.'

She looked at him. He was very earnest and earnestness was always rather ridiculous, commonplace, to her. It made her feel unfree and uncomfortable. Yet she liked him so much. But why drag in the stars.[20]

After the incident with Mino, whom Ursula regards as a bully, he pursues the analogy. Ursula resists with fury and derision:

'Oh yes. Adam kept Eve in the indestructible paradise, when he kept him single with himself, like a star in its orbit.'
'Yes – yes – ' cried Ursula, pointing her finger at him. 'There you are – a star in its orbit! A satellite – a satellite of Mars – that's what she is to be! There – there – you've given yourself away! You want a satellite, Mars and his satellite! You've said it – you've said it – you've dished yourself!'[21]

The argument ends in stalemate, emotionally as well as intellectually inconclusive. But it sets the pattern of the future encounters where he will exhort and she resist until both reach the verge of exhaustion. Its cyclical and epiphanous nature, in which Lawrence moves the point of view interchangeably between them to shadow Birkin's idea of equilibrium, leads the reader both to the absurdity of their predicament, though feeling with them as well as against them, and to share in their emotional purgation.

Here the source of mutual attraction verges on the romantic but involves a deeper ambivalence, attraction and resistance which come from the failure to make love a thing that can be known and named. Birkin is attracted by the contradiction in Ursula between a 'luminousness of supreme repudiation, nothing but repudiation' and a desire for 'love, only pure love'. Ursula is attracted to Birkin in spite of his egocentric solemnity and his cryptic wish to attain, through Hermione, a desire that is devoid of passion, because his quest is authentic in an inauthentic world, because he wishes to turn his back on the corruptions of technological efficiency and the conventions of domestic marriage. In manner, movement, gesture and speech their resistance to each other has a luminous presence, and their hatred becomes a source of love. In 'Excurse' the consequence is dramatic. Each finally capitulates to the other's refusal to yield. That mutual capitulation, as sudden as it is unexpected, coming as it does where their relationship seems to have broken down beyond repair, is experienced as a sensual release, bordering in exhaustion on delirium. At a stroke Birkin's ideal is both substantiated and destroyed. They both reveal their independence and integrity, their equality of emotional strength. But that revelation has only come about through Ursula's very resistance to the ideal which he tries and fails to impose upon her. In bouncing back from abstraction they find passion beyond nature and religiosity, they rediscover passion as love-and-hate in an alien mechanical world.

This explains in the same chapter the alacrity with which they turn their backs on England and choose exile. It is passion *against* with an urgency which would be inexplicable without the unstated factor which dominates the book, the carnage of mechanised war. It would be wrong to see Lawrence here as giving the reader what he sometimes imagined, an exemplary monogamous relationship, the blueprint for 'irrevocable marriage'. There is no sense in Lawrence as there is in Freud that sexual pathology can be stripped away through analysis and self-knowledge to reveal the bedrock of the normal; no sense either, as sometimes expressed by the Victorians, that normality is self-evident. The marriage of Birkin and Ursula is forged through flight, created against all odds and in circumstances of high danger. Society in no sense provides for it at all. If a literary model has to be taken for the free and autonomous relationship in our own society, it would surely be that of Jude Fawley and Sue Brideshead, who exhibit a cloying and excessive dependency, dependency of the kind which precipitates them into orgies of mutual guilt and blame. Modern marriage as the vehicle of a need for dependency which it usually cannot satisfy was alien to the structure of feeling which Lawrence attempted to create and which he credibly consigned to exile.

The structure of feeling also has its historical and cultural boundaries. Lawrentian passion in its abstract phase is prescient of destruction, nihilism and the egocentricity of desire. What Birkin sees in Gerald and what Ursula sees in the 'dirt' of Birkin's 'spiritual brides' is a premonition of desire as pure sensation and the worship of self. The intimacy of Gerald and Gudrun, while not possessing the clarity of focus which Lawrence achieves in its portrayal of the dominant passion, slides through this danger to its nemesis. The contrast is never exact. Lawrence conceived of passion with a purity which never shows in his evocation of desire, largely because elements of that desire, the craving for cruelty and visceral sensation, are at times melodramatically exaggerated to fix the contrast in the reader's eyes. At the same time they are the probable outcome of the mechanistic civilisation Lawrence despises, the most likely scenario, the most credible option. In creating to him what was largely exemplary, the passion of Rupert and Ursula, he had to create it in a void. With Gerald and Gudrun the emergent structure of feeling is often by contrast opaque, because it is overburdened by naturalistic circumstance. Ursula and Rupert reveal the social more clearly by fleeing it than Gerald and Gudrun do by failing to escape its shadow.

Lawrentian passion, then, is a cultural and personal reponse to a historical moment. That it can be seen, even with its incorporation of open antagonism, as an ideal for consecutive generations of readers is a testament not to its viability but to the changing idealisation of intimacy in our own culture. It is an idealism which works within the texture of the realism of relationships, quasi-Freudian in the wider recognition of ambivalence towards the love object and in the co-existence of love and hate. But it remains idealised because of the uneasy relationship of its intense and finely balanced intimacy to wider networks of association and the wider institutions of society. What is more likely for Lawrence in *Women in Love* is also for his readers less desirable, an intimacy which dies its inevitable if hypersymbolic death on a glacier in the climactic extremes of snow and ice.

Gerald Crich is the key to the prophetic tone of the book. In the first instance he can be seen as an Aryan prototype of inter-war fascism, blond hair and blue eyes, his naked will-to-power marked by acts of cruelty – the vicious handling of the Arab mare, the gloating over the rabbit, the attack on Loerke. But fascism in that sense was not merely violence and the desire for domination personified. His corrupt version of Nietzsche's will-to-power is fused with the new, dehumanising demands of the industrial world. As an industrial magnate, Gerald has abandoned the paternalistic approach of his father towards running the coal mines. In a new era of mechanisation and managerial efficiency – as Zapf has pointed out, his opinions here are strongly informed by Lawrence's understanding of Taylorism[22] – all economic calculation becomes, in his eyes, highly depersonalised. Yet the continuity is not forgotten. The unrepentant Taylorist was also the small boy who watched with glee as soldiers fired at the miners striking in his father's collieries.

The planned mechanical rationalisation of his enterprise, which consumes his life and empties it of meaning, has two different consequences. It leads Gerald to rely on women, drugs and his strange friendship with Birkin as extreme forms of sensation, instant sources of gratification which alone can assuage his boredom. But at another level the power to rationalise becomes symptomatic of the will-to-power in the world of efficiency. Thus Gerald is both cruel and rational, hedonistic and incapable of feeling. He prefigures the articulate fascist mentality of the coming decade, the resolution of intellectuals such as Marinetti and Jünger to solve the perceived contradiction between the mechanical and the organic world by worshipping technology as a new form of domination linking extreme forms of efficiency to extreme forms of cruelty. And his self-destruction in the Alps, though flawed in the writing by over-elaboration and excessive symbolism, echoes fascism's own destruction later in the century.

The figure of Gerald defies in many ways the Weberian critique of rationalisation, pointing both to the fascistic embrace of the unlimited will-to-power and to the later forms of decadence which have become central to Western culture – the reaction against rationalisation in liberal–capitalist societies which has led to extreme cults of visceral sensation in violence, hard drugs and pornography. But Lawrence evokes both largely within the microcosm of intimacy where Gerald and Gudrun, fuelled by the illusion of sheer abandon, discover themselves void of feeling. For the impulse towards abandonment is egocentric and the abandonment itself hollow. The feeling which can be stimulated only through extreme sensation soon exhausts itself as each form of sensation comes to have a diminishing marginal return. The feeling which consequently devours itself in this way is a form of desire which founders on its own perversions.

The perversion is partly willed for the exile; the escape to Switzerland is the same 'movement away' which Birkin had earlier rejected on his return from France. The intimacy is, then, neither the primal absence we later find in Joyce or Faulkner nor capable of sustaining the passion of Rupert and Ursula. Gerald's fate is not tragic, because it represents the wilful perversion of life by the socially privileged. What is more disconcerting is Birkin's continuing attachment to him in spite of the degeneration in Gerald, which he recognises only too well. It is at this point that the novel's weakness reveals itself, showing the failure of Lawrence to achieve a necessary distance. Birkin capitulates too easily to dangers he has already denounced excessively in Hermione, and that capitulation is not redeemed by the nature of his attraction to Gerald, which ultimately lacks conviction.

The homoerotic idea here cannot be dismissed as the transparent rationalisation of a more carnal desire which Lawrence omitted through fear of censorship. Ross has shown through a close reading of previous versions of the text that Lawrence progressively cut out the idyllic forms of hyperbole and allusion associated at the time with with the literary portrayal of closet homosexuality.[23] Instead he was striving to create a homoerotic structure of feeling which would rival and complement the Ursula–Birkin intimacy. As much as anything, the failure is not primarily at the level of eroticism, but at the level of a social credibility. Ursula can respond to Birkin because of the kind of person she is, whereas Gerald for the very same reason cannot. Birkin does not realise this, and neither, one suspects, did Lawrence. Birkin's desire for Gerald entails a kind of social oblivion, the physical touch of the male conceived utopically as a blissful annihilation. It then becomes a specific kind of release, the release from abstraction.

This explains the place of the wrestling-scene in the general sequence of events. Gladiatorial combat is a release from the epiphany of the scene by moonlight and the consequent domestic farce of the marriage proposal. It is, in Birkin, a weakness by his own standards. The emotional tension of expressing his idea of impersonal equilibrium, then reacting to Ursula's equally intense response, is not self-contained. It demands distraction, the presence of an adjacent intimacy to act as a cushion for the terror and hatred which passion directs towards him. And the intimacy is unquestioning in the sense that Gerald, also sceptical, is also unquestioning and cannot rival Ursula's relentless capacity for resistance. Thus the intensity of Birkin's own idea eventually destroys its credibility more in *him* than in the woman who resists it, but can match its demands more easily than he.

The predicament of exile marks an impasse not only in this novel, but in the novel form itself, in the longstanding English tradition of evolutionary narrative. The crisis in the structure of feeling is also a crisis in form. It was a crisis which in his later work Lawrence was unable to resolve. His response was to take exile as a metaphor of the exotic, a quest beyond established civilisation for the exoticism of alien culture and landscape. Here the doomed Gerald rather than the stubbornly enduring Birkin has a greater progeny. The didactic voice of Somers in *Kangaroo* is clearly meant to match the earlier voice of Birkin, but the authorial lack of distance and the fascistic blood mystique suggest instead a further extension of Gerald Crich. And the mystique of blood spreads itself not only across the Australia of *Kangaroo* but also across the Mexico of *The Plumed Serpent* and the Italy of *Aaron's Rod*. In *The Plumed Serpent*, instead of the Rupert–Ursula pure single relationship *against*, we find the marriage of Kate Leslie and Cipriano, the Indian general, sanctified by the mystic religion of Quetzalcoatl and already compromised by ritual murders and the slaughter of innocents. While the adoring Kate is still glad of her white skin, Cipriano behaves like a brutal Latin American *caudillo*, with little sense of human justice. This is Gerald and Gudrun exotically transposed, given a new lease of life through a mysticism which can be exotically misrendered by the Anglo-Saxon imagination in search of primitive vitality.

Lawrence's return home in *Lady's Chatterley's Lover* does not, however, signify a return to the earlier masterpieces. There is, to be sure, an almost puritanical stripping-back of the exotic in the sparse narrative. Yet that is because the style is so urgent that it seems at times to be racing to get to the sex which comes later. In a period of transition for both himself and the novel, Lawrence attempts to match two incompatible structures of feeling. He gropes his way in vain towards a fusion of compassion and desire. True, the language of explicit sexual congress is morally serious. But in the affair of Mellors and Connie Chatterley Lawrence ignores the passionate structure of feeling he had created in the earlier novels, that complex and vulnerable love–hate which strives unsteadily for its own equilibrium. Instead Mellors is the instigator and source of carnal knowledge administering compassion in the instruction of desire. Such magnanimity may smooth the passage to sexual pleasure and rescue Connie from her husband's impotence and the sterility of the post-war upper class. But the tone is false, mixing sentimentality and pornography, placing upon Mellor's heavy dialect the additional burden of the carnal didactic.

The dubious sexual politics does not even possess the compensating value of Strindberg's *Miss Julie*, which it partly resembles, and where by contrast the act of seduction belongs boldly to the mistress and not the servant. At a time when Freud had poured scorn on the idea of active and passive sexuality as functions of gender, Lawrence insists on repetitive images of the earthy male ministering unto the grateful female. The comic cliché which has haunted the history of the novel is never far away: the virile gamekeeper giving the genteel lady of the manor what she secretly 'wants', a stereotype which, doubling as fantasy, offers little compensation for the lack of class power.

The fractured liaison of compassion and desire renders desire at times unintentionally pornographic, compassion at times unintentionally sentimental. This is matched by Lawrence's failure to renew the epiphanous form he created. The language is stripped down, puritanically, of all power of sensuous evocation that is not directly carnal. The narrative has a tone of crude impatience in the earlier sections which suggests the author's infantile anticipation of his later language of desire. By the end and in spite of the inclusion of what could not be published, the return to England has become a settling for a lesser form and a lesser world.

The further disappointment surrounding Lawrence was his failure to bequeath a literary legacy. Of his contemporaries, one finds in Forster a tone of genteel humanism which extends the earlier Victorian language of compassion but which also considerably weakens its impact, and only in Woolf is there an equivalent attempt to develop the epiphanous form. Here though, with Woolf's aversion to the lower class and the demotic, the effects are limited. Certainly she radically alters the balance of sexual politics by evoking significance in the inconsequential events of daily life often designated as 'trivial' and 'female', but the cultural rigidities of class which showed themselves in Bloomsbury's lifestyle are also partially present in her writing, an aura of respectable bohemianism in which she largely explores the unarticulated world of the dominant. The other extension of the form is to be found in Lewis Grassic Gibbon, where the story and voice of Chris Guthrie rivals that of Ursula Brangwen in its remarkable scope and intensity. But, if Gibbon reproduced Lawrence's concern with the demotic voice, he shared with Woolf the disinclination to go further in the portrayal of intimacy. There are similiar comparisons to be made between Lawrence, Gibbon and Woolf and Djuna Barnes, though the chronologies are reversed. For Barnes explored more deeply and explosively than Woolf or indeed any other woman novelist of her time the troubled conjunction of passion and desire. But the achievement of *Nightwood* would not have been possible without the prior accomplishment of work that was most more widely known. For it is Joyce in *Ulysses* who achieved in the epiphanous form the first, unparalleled synthesis of absence and desire.

3 Joyce: The Lineaments of Desire

I

Joyce's role in the making of the twentieth-century novel can no longer be denied. But the exact nature of his role is still open to controversy. As an Irish writer using the English language in the idiom of his native Dubliners, there were many preoccupations he did not share with British writers. Like his literary *alter ego*, Stephen Dedalus, he was brought up in a colonial city as the servant of two masters, the British imperial state and the Holy Apostolic Church of Rome. Rebellion against that dual authority became the focus of his hero's, and his own, initiation into adulthood. But, while the values of the imperial British were so alien to him that he satirically named them 'the seven beastly beatitudes', the moral code and rituals of Irish Catholicism had been firmly implanted in his young conscience. To fight against them, when many other Irish merely fought against the British, entailed artistic as well as doctrinal struggle. *A Portrait of the Artist as a Young Man* is centrally about that struggle, an Irish novel of initiation in which the demands of faith and remorse of conscience are finally displaced by the worship of art. The supremely self-confident Dedalus, poised for exile, casts aside the Aquinas of religious rapture for the Aquinas of aesthetic beauty. Yet his version of that beauty remains hopelessly scholastic just as Dedalus remains in spirit a callow undergraduate.

Nonetheless his first novel shows that Joyce, immersed in Catholicism and its unitary vision of the social organism, seemed very distant from the intellectual controversies of Protestant England. His work was never consumed by the imagined horrors and seductions of progress to the same degree as that of T. S. Eliot, Hardy or Lawrence was. In its retotalising of a fragmented universe, Dante and Aquinas were more apt models for *Ulysses* than Darwin and Spencer. So equally were Flaubert and Ibsen, and so equally was Freud, who provides the greatest analytical clue to the author's middle-aged hero, Leopold Bloom. Joyce's Europeanism marks him off from the other writers of the Irish Renaissance, from Yeats and his resort to Gaelic myth, and from Synge with his exploration of the Connacht peasantry. Ibsen, Flaubert and the Russian realists led him to the life of the living present, the world of the city in which he had been born and raised and whose elusive forms he wished to capture in the imagistic rhythms of his prose.

His fiction of the city attempted to create a new materiality in the novel by breaking with the moral code which had earlier guaranteed his deep opposition to British culture and British rule. By rejecting the parochial grip of Catholicism, which other Irish Catholic writers could not or would not do, he was able to confront the general crisis of value in European civilisation on a scale equal to Lawrence, Proust and Mann. In *Portrait* he demonstrates, self-consciously, that he has absorbed Aquinas. In *Ulysses* he successfully challenges Freud. Psychoanalysis, after all, was beginning to open up the hidden world of desire that religious morality still continued to suppress, and to lay bare the workings of the unconscious mind. But Joyce's interest ranged beyond the fetishism of motive and the predicaments of the individual personality. He was interested in the more complex social world of the city and the place of the individual within it. In *Ulysses* this world becomes the foreground of desire.

The extended definition of epiphany by Stephen in *Portrait* can be seen as exemplary of a new literary form that Joyce helped to shape, a form which Lawrence, Joyce and Faulkner inherited from the modernist legacy of Vorticism and Imagism and appropriated to the realist form in the novel.[1] To Lynch Stephen claimed that 'the instant wherein that supreme quality of beauty is apprehended luminously by the mind which has been arrested by its wholeness and fascinated by its harmony is the luminous silent stasis of esthetic pleasure'.[2] The word 'epiphany' of course has a religious root. Joyce's development of epiphany as literary form is therefore religious in origin and context. The major epiphanies of *Portrait* concern youthful transgression of the religious code. They are material revelations of sin, guilt and remorse dictated by and inseparable from Catholicism as a moral code but situated as secular revelations in the context of daily life, creating their luminosity from what lies beneath the surface of the moral code which triggers them.

The focus here is on the carnal sin of the young male, in thought and deed. As Martin has pointed out, the intense crisis of conscience which Stephen undergoes can be better understood as a phenomenon of its time through the extraordinary reverence for the Blessed Virgin which permeated Irish Catholic education.[3] The cult of the Virgin intensified the veneration of women as sacred untouchable objects, and so precipitated traumas of intense guilt when these same women became, for young Catholic men, secret objects of intense desire. *Portrait* pinpoints the conflict between conscience and desire, which can only be resolved either through abstinence or alternately, through the cycle of sin, confession to sin, and repentance. The metaphor of Stephen's anticipatory constraint bears an uncanny likeness to the hydraulic metaphors of Freud in visualising the dynamics of repression, the dam to the flood, the breakwater to the tide: 'He had tried to build up a breakwater of order and elegance against the sordid tide of life without him and to dam up completely, by rules of conduct and filial relations, the powerful recurrence of the tides within him.'[4] The veneration of the Virgin runs deep but cannot stop his undoing:

> The glories of Mary held his soul captive: spikenard and myrrh and frankincense, symbolising the preciousness of God's gifts to her soul, rich garments symbolising her royal lineage, her emblems, the late flowering plant and late blossoming tree, symbolising the agelong gradual growth of her cultus among men.[5]

In *Portrait* the encounter with the prostitute signifies the crumbling of the breakwater, the breach in the dam. Though transgression occurs where it is expected to occur, in the bowels of the city, it is still internalised by the young transgressor as guilt. It is transformed, after the sermon on hellfire, into the extremities of remorse. In *Ulysses* the structure of feeling is significantly altered. As Joyce moves to a consideration of adult sexuality, the Catholic yoke is broken. For the central protagonists, the Church cannot rightfully define the sinfulness of desire. Its religion is a presence among presences, a burden among burdens, a fact among facts.

Neither for the Blooms nor for Stephen is it life's most pressing issue.

The movement from *Portrait* to *Ulysses* is a passage out of the religious universal, a shattering of the sacred canopy. The movement crystallises most clearly in the realm of desire, since desire is no longer the sinful transgression of religious conscience but human need and human wanting, part real and part ideal, never entirely removed from the realm of conscience but with its own bodily autonomy. Desire and its thwarting provoke a secular desperation. In 'Nausikaa', 'Circe' and 'Penelope', the emergent structure of Joycean desire has its origins in Flaubertian passion. Yet the finished structure of feeling is markedly different. If love is an idyll which romanticises its object to suit its abstract principle, then desire craves materially for that which it cannot name. Its secret wanting is beyond cathexis, or that is how the reader is led to witness it. The copulation of Molly and Blazes Boylan takes place beyond the reader's gaze. Within focus, what does take place is the unlikely encounter of Bloom and Gerty Macdowall, fantasy at first sight, where desire is always in view but always beyond touch – the touch, that is, of others, though not of oneself, as Bloom soon finds out. If Emma Bovary's love of love ends in the passions and betrayals of actual lovers, Bloom's desire hovers at the threshhold of masturbation and hallucination. In its physiological rhythms, its progress from dawn to dusk and day to night, it continually reminds us of the absence of others, the absence of touch and the absence of consummation. Stephen too, with no immediate desire to be thwarted, reminds us in his discourse on Shakespeare's sexuality of the vicarious wishes of the artist-not-yet-formed for the artist formed only too well by experiences he wished he never had.

Like Flaubert before him, Joyce's personal letters bear a crucial relationship to his fiction. In his letters to Nora Barnacle we find an autobiographical source of Bloom's desire. There too desire is secret and subterranean, its intimacy consisting of the poetic obscenities Joyce would never have allowed himself to use in public and whose frankness was so remarkable that the full text was not published until 1975. The tendency of some critics to regard them as salacious needs to be challenged. They are above all an act of passion. The beloved is Nora Barnacle and can be no other. Out of that passion thwarted by temporary absence, out of the distance between Dublin and Trieste, Joyce was able to transpose an autobiographical intensity of feeling into Bloom's desire. But it was essentially a transposition. For in the marital bed Bloom is impotent. Desire no longer has any object, only a range of unarticulated possibilities.

But the letters contain something else, too. They contain a violent oscillation between the extremes of body and soul, between a carnality which is at times spiritual and a tendency to idealise which is at times material. Joyce idealises his love for Nora through constant and obscene evocations of desire. His love allows him to burst into tears of pity at some slight word or cadence as it alternates with the delirium of his imagined desires, of the variations of carnal pleasure, which are elaborated with a blunt and candid desperation.[6] But this alternation of body and soul has almost disappeared from the fictional Bloom who emerges in print in 1922. Instead of the passionate dualism of Joyce, the man, we have the radical strategy of absence of Joyce the author. Desire in Bloom is deromanticised, and the passion for the absent love object is replaced by the diffuse longing of the absented subject, the passion of absence by the absence of passion.

The difference between letter and fiction is also manifest in the act of writing itself. Extensive and episodic, the novel perambulates around the perimeter of desire. Masturbation is one thing among many that it observes. But Joyce's obscene letter-writing is inseparable from the onanistic act. Writing and masturbation act and react upon one another as a different letter candidly confesses, ending bluntly in the bitterness of self-recrimination.[7] In *Ulysses*, on the other hand, where passion is absent, fictional desire has a cooler, more detached and more comic air. But that is because the desire of Leopold and the desire of Molly are turned away from each other. Living in the same house and sleeping in the same bed, their formal co-presence precipitates a variety of absences, absences where imaginary love objects are interchangeable and even Boylan cannot satisfy Molly's desire. For both, the breaking-free is not an emancipation but a breakdown. Here Joyce very boldly attempts to do what Freud was trying to do for infantile sexuality – to uncover the deeper structures of adult desire, to discover the origins of the Fall in the lover's first love and show regression in adult life.

Following Flaubert, the convention would be to focus on the adulterous wife. But, for all its poetic audacity, Molly's consciousness in 'Penelope' goes back over the events of the day on the verge of sleep, reliving the actions which have already come to pass. Instead the constant focus is on the cuckold, the impotent husband. Bloom is a moving presence through the narrative and the city, the elusive mover in an elusive city. His elusiveness of movement, which the varieties of Joycean narrative attempt to pin down, comes not only from the urban setting but also from Joyce's recognition that this particular city could in no way be seen as a typical metropolis of the age. In conversation with Arthur Powers he confessed he had seen Dublin as an almost medieval city, certainly not the coming metropolis of modern times.[8] Writing *Ulysses* during the period of the Irish uprising and completing it at the time of the founding of the Free State, the novel had already become an act of historical excavation, of recovering a city of memory which the Easter Rebellion had damaged physically and changed politically. Destruction and change provoked in Joyce the mixed responses of nostalgia and modernism. Dublin was no longer the city he knew, and he sensed that it had passed beyond his gaze into a dubious modernity.

Yet the novel, like *Manhattan Transfer*, was highly prophetic. From the setting of a pre-motorised city, the text seems to capture the physiological rhythms of what was yet to come, of dense, mechanised and electronic forms of energy. Dublin becomes at time as electrifying as it is lackadaisical. Moreover, the episodic and epiphanous nature of Joyce's narrative gives it a distinct advantage over the novel of Dos Passos. Whereas the American tries to convey the sense of simultaneity in city life by moving laterally from one story to another through a series of layered narratives, the movement in Joyce is more imagistic. It gives us people who are simultaneously isolated and connected, discrete atoms of experience all closely interwoven in the same narrative. The strategy is part of the turn away from romanticism, as explicitly stated to Powers. In working against the idealising tend encies of the romantic imagination, the realist form provides the crucial connections between the city and desire. Joyce wished to fuse the materiality of everyday life as moving presence with the deeper structure of desire in the psyche. Dublin was used, in particular, to subvert the new idealisations of the Irish in cultural nationalism, particularly the early Sinn Fein. Reacting to an article by Gogarty purporting to demonstrate the 'venereal excesses' of the occupying English, he wrote, 'I am nauseated by their lying drivel about pure men and pure women and spiritual love and love for ever. . . . The Irish consider England a sink: but if cleanliness be important in this matter, what is Ireland?'[9]

In the first seven episodes of *Ulysses*, the materiality of everyday life is established chiefly through Bloom and Dedalus. Instead of idealising reality, his two heroes try to bind the imagination to the world of the senses. Each has a unique voice which forges languages out of the sense experience of bodily motion. Each tries – and often fails – to extemporise with language in order to encompass meaning. What Joyce gives us here is the interior realism of the half-formed impression, the dexterity of free association which lacks the composure and the public obligations of speech. 'We are always tired in the morning' Stephen tells Haines at the tower, hinting at his later, listless meandering along Sandymount Strand. 'The sacred pint alone can unbind the tongue of Dedalus',[10] remarks Buck Mulligan, prefiguring the afternoon convocation in the National Library, where alcohol has given Stephen the courage to launch his alternative life of Shakespeare.

The turn away from romanticism is paralleled in the narrative by the turning-away of Stephen and Bloom from the dominant values of colonial Ireland, their existential derision for the 'two masters' of Irish life. If Bloom deconstructs the religion of the Church to which he does not belong, it is because Stephen has already deconstructed the Empire for which he has no use. At a deeper level that dual deconstruction of priest and king is a setting-loose, a disintegrating which makes immediate recomposition a near-impossibility. Both dissolve meanings but cannot confer a single definitive meaning upon life in the city or, indeed, Ireland in general. A formless narrative forms the experience of dislocation, the protean nature of wandering.

The movement against value is complemented by the movement away from habitus. Bloom is set adrift by the prospect of his cuckolding, Stephen by the perfidy of his mocking friend. Each feels homeless. In Stephen's case the absence is deepened by a profound bereavement, his mother's death: 'Her glazing eyes, staring out of death, to shake and bend my soul. On me alone. The ghostcandle to light her agony. Ghostly light on the tortured face. Her hoarse loud breath rattling in horror, while all prayed on their knees. Her eyes to strike me down.'[11] His remorse concerns his failure to kneel, his refusal of her last command. That morning the failure has depressed and confused him. It continually repeats itself in his memory, so that his mind, with all its vast compendia of knowledge, can scarcely move beyond the half-formed impression or idea, continually subverting what it starts to think, failing to confer meaning. The stream of his consciousness runs too freely. He cannot answer his own questions on the nature of perception or decide whether to visit his Aunt Sara's, and so he atones for his indecision by visiting her in his imagination, thus wounding two birds with one stone.

Two things more oppress him, fuelling his failure to forge a voice of inner clarity. They are the two companions in the tower: Haines, the English conqueror, and Mulligan, the gay betrayer. The conqueror has two personas, Haines and Deasy, whereas the mocking voice of Malachi Mulligan is clearly unique, if anything a doubling of self. For Mulligan's words do what Stephen wishes his own to. They trip easily off the tongue and confer their facile meaning through sacrilege and gaiety. They have the instant composure which Stephen needs to rehearse at length, a surface elegance below which he knows he needs to penetrate. Mulligan is the desired and hated *alter ego*, attracting like and dislike, envy and repulsion. Momentarily, his attractiveness links language to desire, cryptically, through Wilde's 'love that dare not speak its name'. His lyrical obscenity excites ambivalence. The 'Ballad of Joking Jesus' is something the cautious Dedalus would not dare to sing, but eventually it becomes something he no longer wishes to hear three times a day after meals. The use of language has a veiled erotic attraction, impulsive but evanescent.

The public voice of the mocker is a temptation which in the end Stephen must forgo. Alone, the spellbinding magic of the word cannot atone for the sensation of void. For Mulligan's speech fails to impose any deeper significance upon its own utterance. His words are thrown away in jest or parody and unwittingly become a *reductio ad absurdam* of all discourse. Stephen in turn mocks the mocker just as Joyce shows his contempt for the clichéd love of Irish conversation as spellbinding and unique. Mulligan's words are a false solution, for, though they act as a narcotic, they leave Stephen afterwards with an even greater sense of futility. Thus the walk along the strand is also a leave-taking, a disapproving reaction to Mulligan's flippant mastery in the tower and his toadying to Haines, the Englishman.

Drawn effortlessly, Haines is the archetype of the well-meaning but patronising and insensitive English colonial. 'It seems history was to blame', he concludes without irony after Stephen has admitted to being the servant of two masters. Later, when taking tea with Mulligan in town, he says with forbearance, 'This is real Irish cream I take it . . . . I don't want to be imposed upon'.[12] His oppressiveness, complemented by the schoolmaster Deasy, is then part of Stephen's daily life, manifesting itself in occasional trivia. Haines and Deasy simply take the superiority of their own nation for granted, and by implication its right to rule. Such a presumption is ironically echoed later in 'Circe', when Stephen confronts the drunken Cockney soldiers. They believe in the same right to rule but cannot afford the luxury of the civilising qualities which are meant to accompany it. And, going beyond Ireland, Haines the 'decent' Englishman also prepares us for the impending entrance of Bloom through his anti-semitism.

Alienation from English values operates as a source of humour rather than a source of anguish. Stephen's conversation with Deasy satirises the contrast between the largesse of Empire and the parochialism of the homegrown utilitarian:

– . . . Do you know what is the proudest word you will ever hear from an Englishman's mouth?

The seas' ruler. His seacold eyes looked on the empty bay: history is to blame: on me and my words, unhating.

– That on his empire, Stephen said, the sun never sets.

– Ba! Mr Deasy cried. That's not English. A French celt said that. He tapped his savings box against his thumbnail.

– I will tell you, he said solemnly, what is his proudest boast. *I paid my way.*

Good man, good man.

– *I paid my way. I never borrowed a shilling in my life.* Can you feel that? *I owe nothing.* Can you?

Mulligan, nine pounds, three pairs of socks, one pair brogues, ties. Curran, ten guineas. McCann, one guinea. Fred Ryan, two shillings. Temple, two lunches. Russell, one guinea, Cousins, ten shillings, Bob Reynolds, half a guinea, Kohler, three guineas, Mrs McKernan, five weeks board.[13]

For most of Stephen's waking life, the Irish art of borrowing has been a more pressing affair than the Irish borrowing of art. It is only in the Library when he seeks to abscond with the Saxon bard that the latter trait comes into its own. As with Mulligan, the voice of the double, the voice of the self-righteous Englishman, is comically oppressive. But its unintended comedy can be easily pinpointed, whereas Mulligan's incestuous kinship cannot. In either case the effect is the same, prompting Stephen to bide his time, making his own voice abrupt and elliptical as he hopes to explode into eloquence later in the day. The irony is that, while the opinions of Haines and Deasy are laughable, it is their fellow countryman's voice, not Mulligan's, which Stephen wants to usurp as his own. Or, rather, since he feels that Mulligan has usurped his own voice, he cannot merely replay the ingratitude by borrowing his friend's clothes. He has to perform the same act of usurpation on someone immeasurably greater. In 'Proteus' the stream of consciousness echoes the public suppression of the early-morning voice, the failure to find value either in the forlorn exile of Kevin Egan or in the love of women, an aborted passion which tries largely in vain to focus upon a particular woman. Thus the fuzzy-headed philosophical quest to capture the ineluctable modality of the visible ends in predictable disarray.

Bloom, by contrast, does not gently rage for an order which has eluded him. Plunged into the detritus of city life, he watches it circle around him, repetitive and without semblance of order, either advancing to the margins of meaning or leading his mind into daydream, into the mythic wanderings of the imagination. He shares Stephen's absence but his goes deeper. Jew and cuckold, his confrontation with the city resembles an interior estrangement, a failure to belong to what he cannot fail to cling to. In a way, Joyce is placing his exiled self back into his native city fifteen years on, fictionalising himself as the outsider on the inside just as Stephen, his other fictional persona, portrays him in youth as the insider on the outside. He thus gives to his autobiographical absence an imaginary presence while preserving in the text the quality of that absence. But he is doing more. At first sight, Bloom's senses seem to blend harmoniously with their surroundings, making him a natural inhabitant. But the harmony proves to be deceptive. The close encounter with city life occurs because he lacks anchorage in the two most significant features of Catholic Dublin – the church and the home. And at work, the most significant feature of any society, he makes the briefest of appearances, disapproved of by nearly all, treated as a pariah. True, his job as an ad-collector takes him out and about as a matter of course. But it does not explain his resolve, knowing that Boylan will visit Molly at four, to stay out all day and half the night.

As a Jew twice baptised into the Christian Church, a rarity among rarities in the Hibernian metropolis, his distance from the Catholic conscience gives him the mixed blessing of an estranged freedom. Unleashed from the devotional moorings of his fellow Dubliners – and their hypocrisies – he drifts free with the city's currents, flows and meanders. The Catholic God is something he does not think about – except profanely. His wife's adultery is something he dare not think about. Though at times he presses against it with his nose, he sees the life of the city as without shape or value. Bloom is constantly on its margin, the odd man out at Dignam's funeral, the nonentity in the newspaper office, a fly in the ointment during the Citizen's tirade against all things un-Hibernian. At one with the flux of life, he is frozen out of its frail human ordering, *l'homme moyen passif*.

Bloom is a wandering Jew with a vengeance, a native stranger in the city. In that respect he is the alien vessel of epiphany, the interior datum of his master's Irish art, un-catholicised by Stephen's remorse of conscience, unromanticised by Celtic mythology. His passivity is a set of failures and aversions, a failure to make decisive interventions in the life of the city. The failures are comic, distances, as Joyce himself once remarked, between aspiration and fact. As its hour approaches, the prospect of his cuckolding strangles his consciousness with its stifled horror. In the National Library, taking on the Dublin literati, Stephen feels he must stand or fall by his own voice. Voiceless, Bloom tries to escape from his own thoughts. He escapes into his surroundings, into the imaginary wanderings which will take him far from his domestic predicament.

Bloom thus contrives to exist beneath the symbolic ordering of value in Catholic Dublin. Dignam's funeral proves the point. If 'Hades' consists of the funeral procession to All Hallows, once he gets there Bloom is in little danger of being consumed by hellfire. He has his own sacrilegious thoughts on priesthood and the crucifixion: 'He saw the priest stow the communion cup away . . . . Bald spot behind. Letters on his back I. N. R. I.? No: I. H. S. Molly told me one time I asked her. I have sinned: or no: I have suffered, it is. And the other one? Iron nails rain in.'[14] The heresy is mild but inventive, an effortless making strange of ritual, an easy lack of reverence. The point had already been confirmed a moment earlier when Bloom walked in the back door. Seeing a notice for Father Conmee's talk on the African Mission, he inverted the anthropology, viewing the priest as the Chinese might, as a heretic ripe for conversion to Buddhism. Religion comes easy to Bloom because it is the least of his material worries. He has his nose to the ground, too low perhaps to sniff out incense, but low enough to sniff out death.

In the wanderings of Stephen and Bloom, epiphany, 'the sudden realisation of the whatness a thing', comes to consciousness through the locus and momentum of the body. In 1904, Heidegger had not yet formulated his ontology of *Dasein*, but Bloom had his own kind of answer to Cartesian dualism. Nothing escapes from him and he in turn escapes from nothing. He is the unified being whose feet move south as his mind wanders east. Boland's bread van and the legends of leadpapered tea packets in Westland Row lead him twice to the Orient in the same morning. In between, thoughts of oranges and olives bring him to the melon fields north of Jaffa. But they disappear as a grey cloud covers the sun. The promised land becomes a barren land, 'the grey sunken cunt of the world'. Vision fuses with sensation, the near with the far, the 'dead sea in a dead land, grey and old' with the act of 'hurrying homeward' as 'grey horror seared his flesh'.[15] As he turns into Eccles Street, there, then, here, now are all interwoven. Nightmare visions of cherished myth became as real as walking home. This may well be the average beginning to the average day of an average man, but this particular average man is permanently on the run.

The narrative progression from 'Telemachus' to 'Lestrygonians' provides us with a paradox. The progressive loss of certainty is matched by a progressive uncovering of reality. Only in the absence of certainty is the latter possible: depth of perception without perspective, enumeration without totality. The achievement is made by interweaving the interior point of view with an omniscient narrator, whose disembodied speaking is textured by Bloom's point of view. Whether or not the narrative goes beyond the presence of either of the two heroes, as in 'Aeolus', it becomes a more distanced commentary on the sights and sounds of Dublin. Yet even here the narrative with its newspaper headlines and bewildering succession of cameo scenes is phenomenologically appropriate to Bloom's role as ad-collector – that is, as small time *bricoleur* of exhortatory signs. Through the metaphorical connectedness of the materially fragmented, Joyce produces a language of the sense world which is as visual and oracular as it is verbal.

In this episode, the text is both cinematic and pre-cinematic. It both presages and rivals a form whose development would come to influence the novel profoundly yet also narrow at times its inventive scope. But *Ulysses* also focuses on what the cinema can never do. Film narrative cannot adequately capture the free associations of the interior point of view. It cannot give direct reality, as Joyce does, to the stream of consciousness without simultaneously evoking it as a distortion of exterior reality.

This achievement, to be highly cinematic and yet go beyond cinema, is one of the great accomplishments of the first half of the novel. Consciousness seen in this way delineates for the reader Bloom's perpetual absence. Absence from value propels Bloom into peripatetic *Dasein*, his closeness to the everyday mirrored through estrangement, his kinships with its rhythms mirrored through loss and loneliness. In the second half of the novel the strategy for unveiling absence is altered. Joyce plays with the different forms of distancing which absence entails, and often the forms become too microscopic or too portentous. But the forms themselves indicate that the author himself has taken over the mantle of his characters in the quest for totality. The ploy is ingenious but it is also obvious, since he is their creator. 'Ithaca' proceeds to let us know it with a vengeance. Yet in 'Cyclops' and 'Circe' Joyce penetrates the deeper structures of myth, and in 'Nausikaa', 'Circe' and 'Penelope' he penetrates the deeper structures of desire.

The turning-point comes with 'Scylla and Charybdis,' where Stephen's waking day reaches its anti-climactic peak in a display of ostentatious virtuosity. Prior to that, in 'Sirens', Bloom's thoughts have rummaged through fervent chaos during the imagined moment of cuckolding, and it is left to Stephen to restore a mannered and aesthetic order to the world. His mythologising of Shakespeare is not only an answer to his failure in 'Proteus': it also introduces us to the subterranean connections between art and desire and paves the way for the transformation of style in which Stephen's author will finally take over. The temporal movement then becomes clear. As the day moves towards night, diurnal absence precipitates nocturnal desire.

The mythical figure Stephen reinvents as 'Shakespeare' to suit his own purposes, mixing fact and fiction, is the first real link to Bloom, for the story of the poet joins youth to middle age. Stephen views the bisexuality he imputes to the Bard with a mixture of scorn and vicarious envy. But it later becomes clear that, without the artist's advantage of sublimation, those same sexual proclivities would lead, as they do with Bloom, into furtive androgyny and masochism. In wilfully taking Hamlet as the text of the play-wright's life Joyce also takes issue, as Ellmann has pointed out, with Freud.[16] During the writing of *Ulysses*, Ernest Jones located the tragedy of *Hamlet* in the Oedipal sexuality of its hero. Joyce, by contrast, sees the figure of the author not in the prince but in the ghost of his father coming back to warn him of his murderous uncle and perfidious mother. In Stephen's version the figures from life are Shakespeare's elder brother, Richard and Ann Hathaway, Hamlet himself the hypothetical extension of the son Hamnet, who had died a child. The sexuality of the young prince, attributed by Jones to a repressed desire for his mother, loses centre stage to the cuckolding of the murdered king. Stephen's Hamlet does not discover the prisonhouse of childhood so much as the voice from the dead which warns youth not to repeat its own mistakes.

From that point on, the novel is about the prisonhouse of adult sexuality, the lineaments of adult desire. The episode itself proceeds like a play, so mirroring the original's play within the play. Stephen's discourse is rehearsed and stage-managed and his silent asides are phrased as commands, stage directions to himself. To start with, he must combat Russell's Platonic idealism – 'Form-less spiritual. Father, Word and Holy Breath' – with Aristotelian mimesis. 'Unsheathe your dagger definitions. Horseness is the whatness of allhorse.'[17] But the epiphany which constantly mirrors itself links WS to Joyce's two heroes in two different ways. 'The player Shakespeare, a ghost by absence', is almost a mirror of the ghostly absence of Bloom, who has noticed practically everything on the streets of the city while remaining largely unnoticed himself. The 'stagyrite' Shakespeare, on the other hand, is clearly a mirror image of the tale's youthful teller, obsessed by the sexual fall from grace which in his eyes precipitated the greatest written art, and yearning to experience the trauma himself.

Stephen's expropriating of Shakespeare is a metaphorical kidnapping of genius, the only person or thing English which is worth taking. But the key to genius lies in desire, in what the traumatised artist sublimates to gain immortality. From that dangerous and elusive form of feeling, Stephen tries to keep a guarded distance behind the critical language of judgement. But interpretation has its tell-tale bias, never more than in the subplot of how Will is chosen in order that he can choose:

> He chose badly? He was chosen it seems to me. If others have their will, Ann hath a way. By cock, she was to blame. She put the comether on him, sweet and twentysix. The greyed goddess who bends over the boy Adonis, stooping to conquer, as prologue to the swelling act, is a boldfaced Stratford wench who tumbles in a cornfield a lover younger then herself.
> And my turn? When?
> Come!
> – Ryefield, Mr Best said brightly, gladly, raising his new book, gladly brightly.[18]

The ravishing of the Stratford Adonis brings forth tragedy. But Stephen is not destined to share his fate. For, though she idly dreams of *cherchez l'écrivain*, not even Molly Bloom can bring forth *Ulysses*. The narcissistic aesthete who understands materiality yearns vicariously but in vain. For life cannot imitate the art which has imitated life. And Dedalus knows it would not be the same thing. History may be the nightmare from which he cannot awake but it does not repeat itself in the guise of his rehearsed mythology. He claims the genius makes no mistakes, but in his version of the Bard the genius is clearly the beneficiary of his mistakes in so far as he is their victim. Because genius consists in being chosen, it cannot be kidnapped through conscious emulation. Already ambushed by Ann Hathaway, the Bard's seizure by Stephen is at best metaphorical, an extended form of wishful thinking. All he can do in his discourse is to maintain the pose of the scornful narrator, concealing the fact, but not too deeply, that he too wishes to get laid. With no object for his own desire, Stephen dreams of being chosen and ravished so that he can bring forth great art.

His wish dreams observe a dialectic of active and passive, of being acted upon in order that he can act. But his myth-making also tells of a prisonhouse of desire created by the primal act, of how, in the thrall of repetition which goes beyond the pleasure principle, the act will always come to haunt him:

> Why does he send to one who is a *Buonaroba*, a bay in which all men ride, a maid of honour with a scandalous girlhood, a lordling to woo for him? He was himself a lord of language and

had made himself a coistrel gentleman and had written Romeo
and Juliet. Why? Belief in himself had been untimely killed. He
was overborne in a cornfield (ryefield, I should say) and he will
never be a victor in his own eyes after nor play victoriously in
the game of laugh and lie down. Assumed dongiovannism will
not save him. No later undoing will undo the first undoing.[19]

The prisonhouse of desire is the myth linking Stephen to Bloom.
In mythologising Freudian repetition, Stephen makes its reality
utopian. For the aspiring writer, the desire to be ravished by desire
has the added advantage of being, like Shakespeare's, a spur to a
new and even more wounding desire which is a darker shadow
of the primal act. Desire as wounding unlocks the key to art. But,
if Stephen's Bard shows us the poetics of desire, Bloom later shows
its reality. He too is a ghost, a shadow, an absence haunted by
his own androgyny. And his masochism celebrates other kinds of
failure. If Stephen uses the Bard to mythologise repetition as Fall,
Bloom subverts him. For Bloom's sexuality has no Fall. It emerges,
piece by piece, out of the amorphous textures of absence in a
mundane, fragmented world. Bloom is the other ghost who cannot
correct Stephen's dogma, because he does not yet know him. Later
he is to become the demythologising reminder that first love need
not dictate the wound 'where love lies ableeding'. But, unlike the
story of the Bard, his own story stays plotless. While Stephen
invents the story of an artist, the artist who invented *him* deliberately refrains from inventing a story at all.

At the end of 'Wandering Rocks', the limits of Stephen's
endeavour are cruelly exposed by the Viceregal cavalcade, making
its way after luncheon through the city. With simpler intent and
no pretensions to art, the Viceroy triumphs where Stephen has
failed. He expropriates with ease the salutes and reverential gazes
of passing Dubliners. What Stephen has failed to take from the
English at a deeper level of truth he extracts from the Irish in the
world of appearances. It is a token victory, but its very nature
makes the point. His carriage crosses the paths of all the fellow
wanderers Joyce has already introduced, and who in being Irish
are not the Viceroy's fellows at all. The journey formally connects
the disconnected, the movement of the thread of meaning absent
in the previous episodes with Stephen and Bloom. It is the false
closure of imperial rule made after no other closure is possible.
Despite the obsequious gestures of Simon Dedalus, the final salute

to the cavalcade is the image of Almidano Artifarni's sturdy trousers vanishing behind a closing door. Thus the procession connects nothing and nobody and the city remains fragmented as day passes into night. The previous journeys are ironically paralleled by the emissaries of priest and king. Unlike Bloom, the pious Father Conmee is recognised and respected everywhere he goes. He exudes a false compassion, while Bloom's capacity for compassion remains hidden and stifled. And, by the power invested in his office, William Humble, Earl of Dudley throws into relief the total lack of influence which Stephen has on his fellow countrymen. It is significant that during the cavalcade Stephen and Bloom are the only two characters who do not see him.

II

The second half of the novel, starting with 'Cyclops', marks a significant departure in style, or rather in the juxtaposition of very different episodic styles. It deepens the epiphanous form in some episodes by attempting to etch more clearly the contours of absence and uncover a deeper structure to desire. At the same time the omniscient narrator jumps out of his own skin in an act of extreme disassociation with his characters. The formal parody of styles in 'Oxen of the Sun' and the mathematical catechism of 'Ithaca' are forms of self-conscious playfulness which distance themselves from the sensuous world of human events, and the act of narration takes precedence over what is narrated. The parodic spirit is maintained too in 'Eumaeus', which returns to the realist form as, at best, a satire of provincial journalism. In all three episodes Joyce is more concerned with satirising other modes of writing than with developing his own. The result is a crisis in form, a sense of attenuated exhaustion, redeemed only by Molly Bloom's soliquy in 'Penelope', which restores the dominant tone of the book and at the same time acts as a kind of epilogue, going back over the events of the day. The climactic episode is 'Circe', arguably the *tour de force* of the novel, in which Joyce links the conscious and unconscious levels of the mind, the hallucinatory and the real, the contrasting human rhythms of day and night.

Prior to that, Joyce creates the comic tone in 'Cyclops' and 'Nausikaa' which contributes so much to the novel's artistic success. This works initially through the mannered separation of styles, the vibrant contrasts between the euphemistic and the demotic within the same continuum. At the same time, they are used for a specific purpose, to reveal Bloom's humanity and, at the same time, his failure to realise that humanity, to give it a decisive impact. We are shown in rapid sequence his failure in politics, compassion and desire. His humanity is thwarted by his own incompetence, his retractions, his failures at self-expression. The feebleness of his proclamation of universal love in Barney Kiernan's paves the way for his failure to connect, other than through an obscene and minimal body language, with Gerty Macdowall on Sandymount shore. The failure of his attempts to convince his fellow drinkers of the need for compassion is followed by his dismal failure to be passionate. The humour which Joyce extracts from the gap between aspiration and actuality is almost pitiless.

Among critics there have been two different strategies for claiming Bloom as a quintessential hero.[20] One is to see him in nineteenth-century terms as a man of basic decency and compassion, an Irish Pickwick surrounded by all forms of human folly which he tolerates through thick and thin – Bloom harassed and put-upon, caring and devoted. The other is to centre upon his concealed desires and see those desires as a revolutionary step forward in the sexual politics of the novel – Bloom as the caring, uncared-for citizen or the exemplar of a new androgynous desire. In truth he is neither. For the most part compassion lacks opportunity or expression, while his desires remain furtive, vicarious, unfulfilled. The overall effect, especially with the distancing narrative techniques in the second half of the book, is to suggest failure in middle age. Bloom is a Quixotic figure with the degraded status of Sancho Panza. As Joyce looks down more and more distantly on his hero's failure to be heroic, his authorial gaze is pitiless. One senses that Bloom's situation is already chosen. The determination – that is, the setting of limits to his heroism – is irrevocably social. In that sense, Bloom's day is the daily culmination of all the disadvantages of his disadvantaged life.

'Cyclops', in which the disadvantage really crystallises, has a schizophrenic narrative. It is the deliberate act of an author who knows the Ireland of his own youth has already passed into history and will one day become myth. The nameless first-person narrator, suspected by critics of being Simon Dedalus, narrates with his derisory nose to the ground. The authorial narrator, narrating the same events, self-consciously transports them back into the semantic realm of the ideal. The Citizen, the central focus for both narrators, comes over at times as the ghost of Cuchulain, yet he and Bloom are also Vladimir and Estragon. The split narrative has its place both in the history of Ireland and in the history of modern fiction, suggesting in both cases a gap which cannot be closed.

The conscious manipulation of the gap is what makes the episode so wonderfully comic. As a sharp reminder of the contradictions between formal discourse and demotic speech, it is also a warning to all aspiring proletarian realists. But it is more clearly a direct attack on the pretensions of the Irish Renaissance in mythologising the demotic. Joyce renders the Citizen in both the demotic and the idealist style. He is seen by the nameless narrator as 'up in the corner having a great confab with himself and that bloody mangy mongrel, Garryowen, and he waiting for what the sky would drop in the way of a drink'.[21] The alternate version mythologises him as a Celtic hero:

> The figure seated on a large boulder at the foot of the round tower was that of a broadshouldered deepchested stronglimbed frankeyed redhaired freely freckled shaggybearded wide-mouthed largenosed longheaded deepvoiced barekneed brawnyhanded hairylegged ruddyfaced sinewyarmed hero.[22]

Adjectival hyperbole drives home the arbitrary reworking of history. As a Gaelic nationalist with his own compulsion to mythologise, the Citizen is a fair target and Joyce constantly turns the Citizen's own weapon upon himself. Yet the eulogistic tone of the authorial narrative also works to counter the derision of the nameless narrator, who degrades his fellow Dubliners through the fact of propinquity. One by one, the nameless narrator scorns all his fellow barflies in turn, seeing little of value in any of them. The euphemistic narrative then gives the reader an amusing but deliberately false relief from that oppressive tone of vilification.

One is reminded, by Joyce's juxtaposition, of Pearse in *The Plough and the Stars* orating his patriotic vision of purgation through blood outside a pub full of Dubliners who remain deaf to his call because more intent on berating one another. In both cases the city acts as a microcosm of the contradiction between the actual and the ideal, which paves the way for deeper conflict, in Joyce's case, in the encounter between the Citizen and Bloom. By this time the outcome of the argument no longer matters. They have both been the subject of so much parody (objective) and contempt (subjective) that neither can win on the substance of what is said. All that is left is hollow eloquence, and here the Citizen wins his pyrrhic victory. For Bloom, arguing in favour of compassion, is immediately cast as the alien, the outsider, the betting cheat who stumbles pathetically to find the words to make his point. While he cannot find the words for compassion, the Citizen cannot find words enough to send it packing. Joyce sensed that much of Irish eloquence fed on hatred because the seeds of hatred had already been sown. The Citizen draws on the authentic images within the collective memory of a colonised people: Drogheda, the potato famine, the brutality of the British navy and the arrogance of empire, nostalgia for the prosperous trading Ireland which 'existed' before the English invasion. As the sense of injustice is reduced to rage, history is converted by declamation into myth. The scorn of the nameless narrator for the pub's habitués is inverted in the Citizen's contempt for everything outwith, everything that is *not* Irish. Self-hatred is projected ironically outwards on all those who are not there to be vilified.

To all this Bloom, the despised outsider, has no answer. Compassion is a lost cause. His tentative effort at linking the persecution of the Irish and the Jews is met with an ethnocentric contempt. In trying to answer that contempt, both narrators hold him up to ridicule:

> – Persecution, says he, all the history of the world is full of it. Perpetuating national hatred among nations.
> – But do you know what a nation means? says John Wyse.
> – Yes, says Bloom.
> – What is it? says John Wyse.
> – A nation, says Bloom. A nation is the same people living in the same place.
> – By God, then, says Ned laughing, if that's so I'm nation for I'm living in the same place for the past five years.[23]

As the Citizen spits at Bloom's claim to be Irish, the meaning of hatred becomes clear. When Bloom then proclaims that what is really life is 'love', circumstance has already undermined him. Love, if it had any meaning at all, no longer does, and both narrators deride it, Dedalus through anti-semitism, Joyce through a pointed parody of a word whose currency modern life has utterly devalued. Thus, as Bloom utters the word 'love', the world of absence and desire has already cut the ground from under him.

Dissolution of 'love' provides the continuity between 'Cyclops' and 'Nausikaa'. After failing as compassion, love now fails as passion. Instead we have masturbation as desire's surrogate, the shared excitement of total strangers, a man and a girl who neither touch nor talk to each other. The two narrative styles convey, as in 'Cyclops', the respective failures of the purely ideal and the purely material. Bloom's narrative deflates the romantic pretensions of Gerty MacDowell just as the sudden stride of the lame girl down the strand shatters the perfect fantasy which Bloom has formed of her to aid his self-abuse. Gerty holds out hope by inventing romantic fantasies of a middle-aged lover. Seeing her lame, Bloom can no longer hold out hope at all. The mutual images which excite desire are achieved furtively. Speech or touch, any open gesture would destroy the spell. For Gerty sudden orgasm is cruel compensation for the deformity which makes her unattractive. For Bloom it is cheap compensation for his failed contest in the pub, since, after all, he has just run like a scared rabbit from his belief in universal love. Gerty sentimentalises a love ideal from which her life falls ignominiously short. Bloom, ignominiously, falls short of his own ideal. He remains a 'man of inflexible honour' but only down 'to his fingertips'.[24]

The general process of fragmentation thus continues apace. After Gerty has orchestrated consciousness into the swooning illusion of romance, Bloom dissolves it into separate particles whose parts constitute no whole. The effect is disturbingly forlorn. We have an even deeper sense now of Dublin as the city of desolate day, a city in which all encounter seems to have a pitiless transience. Bloom's consciousness seems to have internalised completely the verbal icon of the advert which dominates his daily life and puts money into his pocket. His mind points out objects to him through garbled associations, acts of describing in shorthand. All discursive connections, on the other hand, are merely there to be ridiculed.

Yet, as author, Joyce still wants to reconstitute totality and give the separate wanderings of Bloom and Stephen a simultaneous meaning. He does this, however, only when reality itself is dissolved in the episode he referred to as hallucinatory, and in which he transforms narrative into an unstageable play with myriad stage directions and a cast of thousands. As French has pointed out, Circe is written in the most objective of literary forms, drama, yet it is the very episode in which the objectively real is most difficult to identify.[25] And it is the one episode in the book where Joyce constantly traverses the epistemological boundaries of the real. Hallucination becomes a sustained metaphor for the intersection of dream and reality, where the different worlds of day and night, waking and sleeping, merge into one another. In an extraordinary *tour de force* Joyce supersedes the Freudian divisions of conscious and unconscious, re-creating all levels of the mind in a metaphorical unity. And, precisely because of the phantasmagorical nature of their meeting, it is the one episode in which Bloom and Stephen truly connect. The real contact of the aesthete son and the mythic father can only take place beneath the level of reality, beneath the reality of absence which governs in different ways their peripatetic lives. At the conventional level of encounter, as in 'Eumaeus', all feeling is buried beneath a shiftless mundanity, and in 'Ithaca' they are already dehumanised and microscopic as Joyce plays at being God.

The brothel scenes do not focus around gratified desires, but circle around imaginary ones which turn to wish dream and nightmare. It is Bloom who occupies the centre of the stage, but largely in his own imagination. The play within the novel concerns that which the erotic setting induces in his own mind, that which even it cannot fulfil – the fears, guilt and desire which go beyond the normal capacity of an establishment which caters for male fantasy. The brothel precipitates what it cannot accommodate, since Bloom is too unconventional for what it has to offer. Yet the hallucinations have no clear-cut proprietorship. Characters from earlier episodes are joined by those newly invented to make their dramatic entrances, so that they appear at times to all the actual persons in the brothel and at other times, like Banquo's ghost, exclusively to the person – Stephen or Bloom – who is haunted by them.

There are, however, discernible sequences amidst the babble of voices with which Joyce bombards the reader. Bloom is put on trial for the weakness evident during the course of the day (guilt) and which shadows his secret androgynous and masochistic desires. He is then given the freedom of Dublin and emerges as the ruler of Ireland (power), a great reformer addressing his subjects and promising them, 'ye shall ere long enter into the golden city which is to be, the new Bloomusalem in the Nova Hibernia of the future'.[26] After being ignominiously discredited and stripped of his power, he indulges in a third hallucination which is the very opposite – a dream of submission (desire). His fetishism, voyeurism and masochism are all orchestrated into a deep and focused yearning to become 'the new man woman'. He swaps gender with Bella Cohen, the brothel madame, who then becomes his male tormentor making him submit, in a parody of *Venus in Furs*, to a chaotic routine of discipline and bondage. In a clear echo of Stephen's myth of 'the allwisest stagyrite', he is triumphantly unmanned by Bella, 'mine in earnest, a thing under the yoke'.[27]

This hallucinatory passage, from guilt to power and then from power to desire, follows the pattern of an initial weakness offset by a wishful strength which gives way to a deeper and more central weakness. Politically, Bloom's abortive vision of power and of himself as Ireland's humane saviour is 'buttocksmothered' by his masochistic desires, which themselves bespeak a paralysis of will. His comic bewilderment as popular leader at the entreaties made to him by all his subjects, and which they expect him to resolve on the spot, gives way after his humiliation to the abject but desired state in which he does not have to choose at all. In pornography sexual masochism is often the ritual abdication of the right to choose, the eroticisation of the loss of will. Bloom's desire is then a secret ritual solution to a public failing of daytime life, repeating at the level of fantasy the actual movement which had preceded it that afternoon, the motion of flight from Barney Kiernan's pub, when he has failed to win a political argument, to the compensations of furtive self-abuse on the strand. The fantasies go deeper than the reality they supersede. But the extraordinary thing here is that Joyce actually eschews any secret answer at the level of desire, which, regressing back into the unconscious, then purports to explain the failures of Bloom's conscious life.

If we take all three moments in the process of hallucination, guilt power and desire, the relationship is actually circular. Bloom's guilt is a cause of his failure to be powerful, but his failure to be powerful is in turn a catalyst to his masochistic desires. The circle completes itself, however, without solving anything, because we know that Bloom's guilt is precipitated in the first place by the socially unacceptable nature of his desire. There is no Freudian regression into infantile sexuality but, as with Faulkner, a focus on the secondary derangement which fictional narrative makes primary. Bloom's derangement is involved in its own infinite regress, conscious of itself but too conscious for its victim to bear, because it is related to the other things of which he is conscious, and which his dream world merely confirms rather than discovers. In Nighttown, Bloom suspects the worst and finds it.

The deeper sense of his public weakness which 'Circe' reveals is also a consequence of it. The failure of desire is grounded in the failure of politics, the failure of politics grounded in the failure of desire. The embryonic challenge to embryonic Freudianism is startling and unique. There can be no regression to an unconscious level to explain a conscious process without, at the same time, an inversion of roles by which the unconscious becomes conscious only to be explained by the conscious which has become unconscious. In explaining each other, guilt, power and desire constantly regress and re-emerge. Because of his public anonymity – cuckolded nonentity in the newspaper office, ineffectual Jew in the world of Sinn Fein – Bloom chooses not to choose at all. That existential choice not to choose finds its instant symbolism in the transvestite rituals of masochistic desire, where Bloom takes on the female role because he identifies it with submission. In choosing his deepest secret he chooses the illusion of oblivion, thinking that secret beyond all conscious knowledge. By putting himself willingly at the mercy of his deepest desire, he puts himself at the mercy of the women who appear to willingly desire him.

For those who see in Bloom a genuine androgyny, an authentic but repressed male desire, the last link must be the weakest in the chain. There are no women who desire Bloom in the way he wants them to, so that his imagination invents them, invents them as female circus freaks who appear to be consumed by will but in reality have no will at all. Bello Cohen, the horsewhipping circus master, is at best an amusing charade, at worst a gross caricature of active female sexuality. In fantasy Bloom invests her not merely with his own gender but also with his own will. That projection is an act of estrangement by which he turns his will against himself, externalising it as the attribute of the dominant other. As drama, in the ritual world of appearances, the will appears to emanate from her. In reality, the deeper reality of the psyche, Bloom's wishful fantasy has given *his* will to *her* so that she can use it to punish him.

Once Bloom's secret has been confirmed to the reader, Joyce

makes the link with Stephen through the mounted, cuckolded Bard. Both share the surreal image of WS with the reflected antlers in the mirror, the phantom who is both of them but also neither of them. But there is a crucial difference. While Stephen will never be a great tragedian because his art does not embody a tragic life, Bloom's life does not have the pattern to make it into any kind of art. In sharing the Bard, neither of them has Anne Hathaway. The wounding spur to art which Stephen has failed to find is also the active, predatory lover whom Bloom has failed to discover. None the less, Stephen and Bloom connect in a way which proves subsequently impossible in the tedious, naturalistic 'Eumaeus'. They have connected at a pre-conscious level by sharing the same hallucination. After they leave the brothel, they are politically connected by sharing the same hanging. As Stephen is confronted by the two English soldiers, the images of willing and unwilling victim coalesce. The Croppy Boy, hung from the gallows by his English executioner, prefigures the colonial assault Stephen is about unwittingly to receive. The violent erection after the rope is jerked echoes the prior discussion of hanging and its physical effects in Barney Kiernan's. But the subsequent scene where the manly matrons of the English upper class rush forward with their handkerchiefs to sop up his gouts of sperm echoes the comic attack on the desexed Bloom by Bella Cohen and her prostitutes.

The scene is a play on the meaning of the word 'victim'. It shows the fatuity of Bloom's attempt at self-victimisation by displaying the political execution of an innocent victim. The Croppy Boy of the song is an Irish patriot hung after a confession to a British soldier posing as a priest. Yet his main sin – forgetting to pray for his mother's rest – is similar to Stephen's refusal to kneel at his mother's deathbed. Stephen himself is now about to be victimised, and in the same way the arbitrary punishment has nothing to do with the original act. One central meaning of colonialism is thus revealed: the power of the masters to choose punishments for their subjects for acts which fit no credible definition of crime. It is the freedom of the dominant to be arbitrary in the choice of their victims. After the condescension of Haines and Deasy, the brutality of the Cockney soldiers is the same posture posed at a more central level, and as 'revelation' becomes analogous to the sado-masochism of Bloom's desire. It confirms in its own way what is already known. The soldiers defend with arbitrary force a power which Stephen is not even challenging, a right to rule the Citizen has already denounced and which Haines and Deasy assume to be a natural element in the human condition. But this arbitrariness is the seed of colonialism's downfall. The blood of innocents will later lead to the outrage of protest and the rage of revolt.

After the shared hallucination of WS, the closest moment of the two comes when Bloom tends to the fallen victim. It is a genuine but fleeting instant of compassion. At the very end of the episode, the mythic father has his last hallucination. The inert victim appears to him as Rudy, his dead son. The symbolic union of Bloom and Stephen is phantasmagorical, evoking the evanescence of the half-remembered dream. Thereafter, on the naturalistic planes of 'Eumaeus' and 'Ithaca', where Bloom and Stephen are exhaustively described together, there is no human connectedness. Despite what many critics have said, these latter episodes shows the episodic form in crisis, Joyce frantically overwriting at the point where he barely needs to speak. Thus 'Penelope', though really an epilogue, is also a last-ditch rescue, a humanisation of what has become pedantically inhuman. The effect comes through the one female voice of interior monologue in the novel which is entirely self-contained. And she is a voice rather than a character, an interior female reworking of the events of a distinctively male world. At one level she comments on events, but at another she inserts a complex expression of female desire into what until then has been an almost unbroken flow of male discourse. In its candid eroticism, Joyce's achievement here goes beyond any other work of its period. We see again the central disparity in the novel, the conflict between the real and the ideal, reproduced from the female point of view.

The romantic element in Molly's thinking is connected to her narcissistic wish to be constantly admired and constantly loved.[28] The material element in her thinking comes from a knowledge that any encounter with men has its disillusion and mundanity. Unlike Gerty, who romanticises her pathetic encounter with Bloom, Molly makes no attempt to romanticise her own adultery, dwelling acidly on all Boylan's faults and weaknesses, barely giving him the benefit of the doubt over anything. Bloom and Boylan are both like the other men she thinks of, admired for their capacity to admire her, but castigated for all their personal foibles, vices and hypocrisies. Her thought exhausts itself on the verge of sleep in the endless self-contradiction of criticising all those by whom she desperately needs to feel loved. In the end it is Bloom who comes across in her thought with a greater impact than any of his rivals, who suffers the worst complaints but receives the most respect. Yet the structure of feeling is never finally broken. It is questioned, perhaps put into abeyance, but her respect is bestowed in the absence of speech, definitive and provisional at the same time. Joyce shows us no direct communication between husband and wife, no recrimination, hatred, forgiveness or passion. Molly restores to Bloom secretly what she cannot openly give him.

As she exhausts all his rivals, real and imagined, she returns through memory to the first love of a man for whom she no longer has desire. After Bloom's ungratified perversions, memory alone restores the validity of love as the cornerstone of marriage. But, since desire is impotent and love a bygone passion, memory transplants love and becomes its unfulfilled *promesse de bonheur*. As in Proust, memory sustains and unites. But it does so in Joyce despite of, rather than because of, the actual presence of the beloved. Both husband and wife are trapped, dissatisfied with the day's sexual encounters, which are no adequate compensation for their failing to love one another. In the final passage of the monologue, the Moorish Gibraltar of Molly's memory provides release from the life of the day and the bleak derelictions of dirty Dublin. Then memories of courtship and first love on Howth Head resurrect the bond between love and marriage which the novel has systematically crucified:

> the sun shines for you he said the day we were lying among the rhodedendrons on Howth Head in the grey tweed suit and his straw hat the day I got him to propose to me yes . . . and I thought well as well him as another and then I asked him with my eyes to ask again yes and then he asked me would I say yes to say yes my mountain flower and first I put my arms around him yes and drew him down to me so he could feel my breasts all perfume yes and his heart was going like mad and yes I said yes I will Yes.[29]

This is the final note of affirmation fending off the void, or rather rebutting an aesthetic nihilism which no considers no life beneath the level of art to be worthy. The paradox of Joyce is that the statement of affirmation can only be achieved finally through absence, through the locked interior consciousness of the wakeful beloved while the impotent lover snores in his sleep. It is the remembered moment where desire is inseparable from passion, the moment of original beauty inverting that other moment, in Stephen's mythology of WS, of original Fall. Memory as trauma here gives way to memory as desire. In the myth of Shakespeare the past undermines the adult life which follows. With the Blooms, the beauty of the past is itself undermined by the adult life which, despite the best of beginnings, takes no prisoners. The present may be circumscribed by the past, but as often as not it helps to put itself in chains.

The influences of Joyce on contemporary literature are legion. Beckett, Miller, Durrell, Styron, Updike and Pynchon are just some of the names which spring immediately to mind. But those who were closest to the epiphanous form and who developed it further with the example of his own work before them were Barnes and Faulkner. While the chequered career of Djuna Barnes echoed the plight of artistic exile, Faulkner deepened the concern with periphery and the alienation from dominant value. In contrasting ways both extended the fundamental legacy of *Ulysses*, its creation of new structures of feeling in the novel which transform the realist form. These structures, both thematic and social, linking fiction as an act of writing to Western capitalism as a developing form of modern civilisation, are the by-now familiar ones of absence and desire.

4 Bitter-Sweet: Hemingway and Barnes

In the post-war novel, the trauma of war is transformed into a portrayal of the unspeakable. Literature provided a new language for the conflict between the idea of progress and mass human suffering, whose unrelieved intensity had reduced many to numbness and silence. Analytically, of course, there were other formulations. Marxism reaffirmed the theory of the necessary imperialist war and the ripeness of the capitalist system for destruction, while Freud discovered the death instinct to be an integral part of industrial civilisation. But fiction directed itself more closely to the pulse of the immediate response, where all explanation seemed to pale beneath the immensity of the carnage, where disenchantment and bitterness came easily from the failures of post-war renewal and the widespread sense of shattered values.

Though America was a late entrant into the war and did not suffer on anything like the same scale as its European allies, the dereliction of value finds charged expression in its writers-in-exile, particularly in Eliot's *The Waste Land* and Hemingway's two novels *The Sun also Rises* and *A Farewell to Arms*. Formal patterns of intelligibility are broken down in the fragmentation of the new literary languages. Just as the war was a catalyst to social change in Europe, in the United States fiction became more consonant with the thought and speech of ordinary people, deriving much of its new vitality from the immigrant masses prepared to suffer economic exploitation in their quest for the American Dream. The novel's opportunity lay in the unique American combination of geographical movement and social ambition, in the constant challenge to custom and tradition. Anderson and Dos Passos, Fitzgerald and Hemingway substituted a direct naturalistic mode of observation in place of Jamesian motive and its narrative circumlocutions, presenting their characters on a landscape which is almost pictorial, eschewing the elaborated code of motive and analysis at

72

the very time when, ironically, Freudian theory was coming into its prime.

The novel took from and contributed to the more general forms of iconoclasm and subversion in the European *avant-garde* of the period, and was not written as an adjunct to or reflection of a stable, settled society. After 1918, European civilisation was seen as being permanently under threat, devoid of purpose and direction. The sustained epiphanies of Joyce, the imagistic fragments of Eliot, the terse, staccato prose of Hemingway were responses to the perceived loss of value, a sense that the language of value could not be recovered through fiction in any ordered or stable form. While the 'lost generation' is a somewhat facile way of describing the writers of the period, there was a sense in which literature was seen as having to convey, in all urgency, an immediate and sensuous reality of which it had no intellectual measure. That urgency born out of the void of value also threatened the ordered progression of multiple narrative, subverting that sense of perspective based on reflection which could be located back, ultimately, to a confident and ordered middle-class life.

In the war Germany capitulated from within, through exhaustion. For the West, it was a hollow victory. Fitzgerald's story 'Mayday' begins,

> There had been a war fought and won and the great city of the conquering people was crossed with triumphal arches and vivid with thrown flowers of white, red and rose. All through the long, spring days the returning soldiers marched up the chief highway behind the strump of drums and the joyous, resonant wind of the brasses, while merchants and clerks left their bickerings and figurings, and crowding to the window, turned their white-bunched faces gravely upon the passing battalions.[1]

The tone, of course, is ironic. The patriotism is shallow and unconnected to the life around the observers. Fitzgerald's soldiers, like Faulkner's Donald Mahon and Hemingway's Harold Krebs, are aimless and uncertain, unable to fit into civilian life yet not really knowing what patriotism is at all. What makes their plight worse, as 'Mayday' cleverly shows, is the ability of society to get on without them, for the conspicuous consumption of the jazz age and the world of Jay Gatsby to flourish as if there had been no war at all. If the war had undermined traditional values, then the selfish acquisitors and hedonists of the post-war period had little to put in their place. The Protestant ethic may have had a sting in its tail, as Prohibition showed, but in the life of the city it was fighting a losing battle against the new entertainments of consumer culture.

The growth of the cities had outflanked the arcadian obsession of nineteenth-century American thought and fiction, and its concerns with the frontier society. For Hawthorne and Melville, the American Dream had in part been that dream of innocence which Leo Marx has called the pastoral garden, the arcadian hero facing both ways at once against the threat of the wilderness and the threat of the machine. In Dreiser and Dos Passos, however, the city became a new kind of threat. The machine had already triumphed and turned people against each other. Others were there to be outwitted if one was not indeed to be their victim.

The Great Depression put into rather galling perspective the blossoming prosperity and new lifestyles of the 1920s. But in that period between the end of the war and the Wall Street Crash, the fermentation of American fiction in exile was crucial to the development of the modern novel. Paris, which remained the cultural capital of the West, numbered among it temporary residents not only Joyce and Pound, but also Hemingway, Faulkner, Fitzgerald, Dos Passos. It also accommodated Gertrude Stein, Djuna Barnes and Anaïs Nin, three of the foremost women writers of the inter-war period, whose writing clearly thrived in their exiled habitat. Paris became in that sense the crucial link between European culture and American fiction, acting as the nerve centre of the artistic innovations which fed back into the mainstream of American realism. It did so not only by putting its pulse on the uncertainties of post-war society, but because it could relate these to experiences of war in Europe which passed America by. War and consumer capitalism were both forms of the secularisation of value, and of its devaluation. But there the similarity ends. One offered the blandishment of hollow pleasures, while the other gave a new meaning to human suffering and to the vanity of warring nations.

The alternation of the two phenomena accelerated the development which had earlier begun in the English-language novel through Lawrence and Joyce. This was the democratisation of narrative – that is, the use of a narrative form more congruent with everyday thought and speech. It is a movement which, as we saw with Lawrence, has to be initially naturalistic, in order to extend realism beyond its naturalistic foundations. For democratisation is not a means for the author to make narrative more 'natural' but one for giving it a new poetics. The inevitable departure from the style of Henry James produced its own forms of aestheticism. In Hemingway the search for the demotic voices of everyday living produced a poetics of lyrical repetition, the recurrent use of the terse and simple phrase, a first-person narrative which rediscovered a deceptive simplicity in the telling of the tale. Hemingway attempted through such techniques to establish himself as a writer before a wider reading public, though he was most successful later on with *For whom the Bell Tolls*, a novel in which he risked least.

But his twenties fiction, including the stories, did mark a break with the past. His tense, descriptive style entailed the removal of motive as a defining characteristic of narrative. Absent from Hemingway's writing is a reflective consciousness, an impersonal narrator through which character can be placed under the microscope of analysis. The narrative focus tends to be on the experience of the immediate event, detailed and sensuous, the focus enhanced by the greater congruency between narrative and ordinary speech. While the rhythms of the colloquial are taken into narrative, the focus tends to make secondary the narrator's task of directly judging others and, if need be, the narrating self. From the very beginning Hemingway had consciously elevated his technique to a theory of 'omission'. A terse, compressed narrative which omits comment and reads at times like speech invites the reader to read between the lines, to draw his or her conclusions from what is never explicitly stated.

Looking at his first collection of stories, *In our Time*, the use of omission has mixed results. In 'Big Two-Hearted River' its operation is too literal. Nick Adams embarks on a fishing-expedition in the northern peninsula of Michigan in order to forget the wounds he suffered in the war, but no explicit reference is made to the war or his wounding. His intense concentration on the solitary tasks at hand – hiking, camping, eating and fishing – while excluding any reference to his past life has been wrongly taken as an exercise in self-conscious male virility. But Hemingway's fanatical refusal of wider forms of signification invites this confusion. His technique is more successful in 'Soldier's Home' because explicit reference is made to the war which Alfred Krebs has fought in. What are omitted are the actual details, which Krebs conceals to his family and friends by telling the apocryphal stories which are somehow expected of him. The reader is thus given the context in which Krebs wants to repress the events of his war experience, his sense of speechlessness at the contrast between war and hometown life, his failure to reintegrate and to feel compassion.

As a narrative device, omission is a form of absence forged through the fusion of the demotic, narrative voice and the tactical elimination of motive. Krebs's selective memory echoes Bloom's suppressed awareness of Boylan's impending visit to Molly. But the technique finds it full fruition in Hemingway's masterpiece of the 1920s where he confronts the war experience itself, *A Farewell to Arms*. Here the author's motive for the absence of motive is not the specific homecoming but the impersonal horror of war as such, a war evoked retrospectively by Hemingway during a period which had seen the rise of fascism and the failure of the peace. He uses the Italian front not merely because he had served there briefly, but because the retreat at Caporetto seemed a decisive metaphor for the war as a whole, and a foreshadowing of the revolution and counter-revolution which convulsed Italy in subsequent years. The work is thus far from autobiographical, a brilliant imaginary reconstruction of events in which he was *not* personally involved.

The writing conveys a quintessential bitterness about the relationship of war and peace, a bitterness whose strength lies in understatement, the incongruity between ideal and reality, between what characters expect and what happens to them. The balance here is maintained by compressing the consciousness of Frederic Henry to focus upon immediate events. As Reynolds has demonstrated, the main deletions from the original draft are instances where Henry reflects philosophically upon the wider meaning of events, or, rather, tries to impose upon them impromptu categories of meaning which read as utterly banal.[2] The sharpness of the narrative form is lost and the deletions are rightly made. The ruthless pursuit of omission, involving a radical narrowing of narrative perspective, seems at times a high price to pay. But the intervention of reflection in the draft acts like a sudden jolt to bring down an elaborate house of cards. Reflection cannot compensate for the total loss of value that is deeply felt, a rueful bitterness whose structure of feeling is conveyed through omission and strengthened by the historical ambience of war.

The dialectic of war and passion here provokes comparison with *Women in Love*. In Lawrence passion, properly conceived, is the only genuine alternative to the unstated horror of modern war. In Hemingway war, observed at close quarters, is the catalyst to the passion it sabotages. Hemingway refuses to see war, as Remarque did, in terms of a unifying force which created comradeship under adversity and then took it away through the physical fact of destruction. The distance of his hero, as a foreign Red Cross lieutenant, is there from the start. Henry confidently tells his reader that he will not be killed in this war since it has nothing to do with him. His friendships with Rinaldi, the priest, and the other ambulance drivers on the front are always fleeting. An early visit to Catherine Barclay, only to find she is ill and unable to see him, reveals to him his empty solitude: 'I went out the door and suddenly I felt lonely and empty. I had treated seeing Catherine very lightly. I had gotten somewhat drunk and had nearly forgotten to come but when I could not see her there I was feeling lonely and hollow.'[3]

That sense of isolation, of absence-within-community, is there from the start, and is owing not just to foreign nationality or lack of combat duties. Experience at the front has suggested to him that all traditional and abstract values associated with war were meaningless: 'I was always embarrassed by the words sacred, glorious and the expression in vain . . . . I had seen nothing sacred, and the things that were glorious had no glory and the sacrifices were like the stockyards at Chicago if nothing was done with the meat except to bury it.'[4] Solitude is the other side of the coin in the devaluation of value. Even the sense of soldierly comradeship is fragile; the rituals of male bonding are excessively brittle. In the retreat at Caporetto such are the confusions of war that Henry is physically isolated from his colleagues, shoots a sergeant who tries to desert, and is then wrongly arrested and nearly shot for desertion himself. Hemingway goes beyond the sense of comradeship to the process of disintegration which affected most of the armies in the war in 1917 and 1918. The falseness of heroism in fact foreshadows it. In a previous campaign Henry is decorated for being blown up while eating cheese. He is scathing about Ettore, the fascistic hero who bores everyone he meets. His dependency on Catherine Barclay, who provides the only escape route from his solitude, is increased by his recurrent experience of the front as void and futility.

Superficially the relationship seems to approximate to what one expects in romantic fiction. After telling the priest at the front that he is incapable of love, Frederic eventually feels that he has fallen in love with Catherine. But the development of the relationship undercuts his spare, provisional feeling of passion. Within intimacy there is always a certain sense of distance from the woman he cherishes and who becomes devoted to him, so that she enters his bed only to remain, metaphorically speaking, at arm's length, cherished as an unusual and exceptional object of desire. Unlike Lawrence, who forges an abstract language of feeling to accommodate the volatile relationship of Ursula and Rupert Birkin, Hemingway strips away the language of feeling in his narrator to a zero point beyond which any further paring-down would involve a total liquidation of the text. At times, speech alone, and increasingly a speech which is Catherine's alone, sustains the burden of intimacy. As the couple's intimacy deepens, as she becomes pregnant and he returns later to Milan as an escaped deserter, the same relationship crystallises in two divergent directions held together by illusion. For her it is romantically, overwhelmingly an affair of passion, but for him it is largely a matter of conquest and desire.

It is not that Henry cannot admire the extent of her devotion. He admires it only too well. Between the lines, in the silent, unstated response to her language of devoted passion, we can read the contours of narcissism and vanity, a vanity which is assuaged by her devotion, a narcissism which gazes back in rapt admiration at the spontaneous admiration his love object has showered on him. But the rhythms of Catherine's speech are taken up at times by what she senses Frederic cannot say, by the omissions which sustain the intimacy. In the intimacy of banter she seeks proof of the uniqueness of their affair, knowing that none can be shown ultimately to satisfy her, accepting the idea of romance along with the idea of proof as a necessary illusion:

> ' . . . Keep on lying to me. That's what I want you to do.
> Were they pretty?'
> 'I never stayed with anyone.'
> 'That's right. Were they very attractive?'
> 'I don't know anything about it.'
> . . . .
> 'You're just mine. That's true and you never belonged to

anyone else. But I don't care if you have. I'm not afraid of them.
But don't tell me about them. When a man stays with a girl
when does she say how much it costs?'
    'I don't know.'
    'Of course not. Does she say she loves him? Tell me that. I
want to know that.'
    'Yes. If he wants her to.'
    'Does he say he loves her? Tell me please. It's important.'
    'He does if he wants to.'
    'But you never did? Really?'
    'No.'
    'Not really. Tell me the truth.'
    'No', I lied.
    'You wouldn't', she said. 'I knew you wouldn't. Oh, I love
you darling.'[5]

His deceit is later echoed when he takes her to a hotel before
catching his train back to the front. Around the room are four
mirrors and she realises it is a venue for prostitutes and their
clients, who can witness there the evidence of their own desire.
At one level the parting is idyllic, the solitude of lovers before he
takes the crowded troop train. At another there is in Henry's
desire for her an undertow of deceit, a readiness to say what she
wants to hear, constantly, despite the fact that reflexively both
share the other's knowledge of the deceit which underpins the
banter. Henry's constant willingness to please through speech is
the only form of constancy he has, but it suffices in the shadow
of her devotion to be the vital, connecting link between her passion
and his desire. What acts as an effective catalyst to her joy, her
radiance, becomes in him a lack of dimension, a confession of
failure, a nullity.

The intimacy which polarises passion and desire is produced by
the circumstance of war. The circumstance of war gives to Frederic's desire the urgent need to conquer the object of its attraction
without transforming that attraction into love. Although his feeling
is uniquely for Catherine, and is enhanced by the circumstance of
his transgression, his desertion, he lacks, like Skrebensky, the true
capacity for feeling which engenders passion. The transgressing
context is clearly there, but ultimately works against him. His
experience of the front, his wounding, his disenchantment, his
escape, his power to survive and see through human folly give

him the very strength which makes the hollowness of his emotions significant. In desiring Catherine because of what the war is doing to him and what the war has made them, his fate echoes the classic plight of alienation. But his failure to sustain feeling independently of war, his inclination to hide instead beneath his reverence for her admiration and the pleasure her devotion brings him suggest a structure of feeling that is clearly in transition. It remains transitional, never fully extended or worked through, because Catherine sustains passion as an illusion, lyrically, elegaically, almost in counterpoint until the very end. But the romantic convention to which that illusion of passion tends is undermined by Frederic Henry's lack of substance, his incapacity to feel and to express feeling at those very moments when it is most needed.

Narratively the novel inverts the mythic structure of conventional romance. It starts off with a romantic cliché, the devoted nurse tending to the brave, wounded hero, and proceeds to invert it. In doing so it makes the vital connections between the personal and the social, the public and the private. Catherine's pregnancy is no more a matter of chance than the mortar shell which nearly kills Frederic. The irony is that, while Henry recovers from the blast of the shell which is meant to bring death, Catherine is killed by the consequence of an act which brings forth life. The power in the novel's climax comes from that very inversion, where Catherine is the tragic heroine looking death stoically in the face, and Henry is the narrating anti-hero watching from the wings, the cryptic voyeur become helpless spectator, and in the last pages almost slipping off the page.

Hemingway's first-person narrative conveys a male structure of feeling which is at once reverential and desiring, but always elliptical so that the nature of the writing suggests in Henry a taut mastery of perfidious experience while suppressing its narrator's motive in acting. The reader then has to read off the various absences of narrative, the egocentric desire of Henry, his voyeurism and narcissism, against a structure of feeling captured openly in Catherine's voice. The paradox is that speech here reveals motive more than narrative, in a reversal of the convention of classic realism. That very reversal gives the narrative its supreme momentum. The dominant tone of Catherine's voice, a tone of misplaced devotion, gains strength through misfortune and suffering, through her refusal to care for anyone, herself included, but the love object who no longer suffers, who watches her suffering yet still cares mainly for himself.

This kind of writing was an achievement which Hemingway, in his novels at least, was never really able to repeat. The deliberately flat narrative trajectory of *The Sun also Rises* fails because its hero lacks that very strength which is undermined by desire. And, in a literal sense, Jake Barnes also lacks desire. His impotence is too unfortunate a wound to be a metaphor for the legacy of war. As a narrative device its biological fixity makes the story static and immobile, a fashionable *roman à clef* certainly, but still a shiftless study of a brittle and rather precious bohemian circle intent on devouring itself. In *For Whom the Bell Tolls* there is a rather different departure. The use of a third-person narrative dominated by Robert Jordan's point of view admits back into Hemingway's fiction the recourse to motive and reflection which he had previously taken pains to omit. The effect is twofold: an aggrandisement of Robert Jordan as the all-American revolutionary hero, and, at the same time, a disconcerting sense of authorial intrusion, an intrusion which is forced, a privileged knowledge and scepticism about the course of the Civil War which is largely an artefact, which is preformed and does not emerge from experience.

The novel's strength lies in its epic qualities, which are largely classic in conception, but the point of view of the character, especially the hero, is too manipulated. Narrative perspective gives the author greater scope in depth, yet the narration is always straining to say too much, to encompass a wider truth which the author manufactures for his own purposes. At times Jordan appears, as Frederic Henry does not, as a euphemistic personification of the author, as a tragic hero who is not a tragic hero at all since he has no blemishes. Yet Hemingway's instinct for narrative perspective was right in terms of his own development. For, if one compares the Civil War novel with *Across the River and into the Trees*, we see in the latter the epiphanous novel coming apart at the seams. Verging on grotesque self-parody, the novel of omission here clearly has nothing to say. Because there is no longer any sense of the unspeakable, nothing is finally said. Hemingway's soldier hero self-destructs in a charade of utter emptiness.

Part of the challenge which Hemingway tried to meet in his later work was the reconstruction of value prompted by the rise of fascism in Europe. But his cosmopolitanism tends to become vapid once it looses contact with its original stimulus in the 1920s, with exile, rootlessness and the perceived devaluation of values. *The Sun also Rises* clearly conveys these qualities. But its limitations become readily apparent when it is placed alongside the greatest American novel of exile during the inter-war years, Djuna Barnes's *Nightwood*.[6] In the exile of Hemingway expatriates there is always the impromptu camaraderie of the group to fall back on, the collective cushion for individual collapse. Personal identity is always fragile but never totally disintegrates. But in Barnes the fact of exile and the impact of war call identity seriously into question, always threatening to dissolve it through dislocations which are not fully understood, ever refusing to Barnes's characters the cultural and psychic landmarks which can tell them who they really are. A difficulty with Barnes, never less than breathtaking, is her consistent refusal to start from the naturalistic plateau which characterises the earlier thrust of the epiphanous novel. The poetics of narrative are post-Joycean, rhythmic in their encrustations, at times elusive, distanced quite radically from naturalist representations of thought and speech. Her style, possessing the imagistic and associative resonances of modern blank verse, is on the epistemological margin of realism. But, like all mimetic fiction, her poetic articulation of the inexpressible gives rise to a deep and penetrating vision of social reality.

The ornate and baroque mannerisms which are clearly evident in the first half of the book are not arbitrary or capricious, but have a clear origin in the historical theme of the novel. The novel is not only a comment on the collapse of empire in Europe but a deeper comment on the link between power and the symbolism of the old order, on the loss of traditional pomp and circumstance and the symbolic certainties of cultural artefact. The writing is initially an ironic attempt to blast a way through the debris of disordered and archaic symbol, attempting through its mockery of the pitiable and nostalgic Felix Volkbein to find a new kind of authentic voice in a spiritually threadbare world. But the weight of creation from first principles is a burden which Barnes's characters cannot finally bear. In the vacuum of post-war Paris, they betray each other and finally do not know themselves.

The male characters show the clear influence of Joyce. Felix Volkbein is, like Bloom, an archetype of the wandering Jew, but less palpable, almost a cipher of historical absurdity, worshipping the 'nobility' of the defunct Hapsburg Empire, and parading his dubious title of 'Baron' while working as a bank clerk in Paris. The Irish-American doctor Matthew O'Connor suggests Malachi Mulligan twenty years on, 'a middle-aged "medical student" with shaggy eyebrows, a terrific widow's peak, over-large dark eyes, and a heavy way of standing that was also apologetic'.[7] He combines the mockery of Mulligan with the hypersensitivity of Dedalus, but he shares with Barnes's other characters the lack of a clearly defined self. He tries and fails to serve the souls of others and destroys himself. His gift for words eventually congeals in horror at the human motives it cannot encompass. But Barnes's story focusses on her female characters, where there is a distinct departure from Joyce, and also from Proust in his fleeting portrayal of lesbian intimacies. In Barnes the male characters circle around the periphery of those intimacies, not as points of conventional normality but as signs of cultural confusion. Felix marries Robin Vote so that as an American with no ties 'she might bear sons who would recognize and honour the past. For without such love, the past as he understood it, would die away from the world.' O'Connor comments on events about which he is helpless with a mendacity he cannot control. 'His fabrications seem to be the framework of a forgotten but imposing plan; some condition of life of which he was the sole surviving retainer.'[8]

Like Hemingway, Barnes explores the intermediate context of passion and desire, the forms of obsession and betrayal which betray their tenuous links. But the predicament is more startling, the exploration more profound. Proust and Hemingway both use the first-person narrative to try and encompass the love object only to find that is ultimately impossible. But there is a sense in both in which narrative rationalises the motive of the fictional narrator. Frederic Henry rationalises his obvious conquest, Proust's narrator his own relentlessly solipsistic obsessions. The narrative strategy of Barnes is rather different. Robin Vote is the love object of three different people, Volkbein, Nora Vote and Jenny Petheridge, whose confused and anxious motives are psychologised through the poetics of third-person narrative and embroidered in the fabrication of O'Connor's monologues. But Robin Vote, as the love object of all three, remains an enigma. Her acceptances and betrayals remain motiveless, analysed to infinity by the doctor precisely because they are in a profound sense unanalysable. Her elusiveness is the book's mystery, just as it is her lovers' suffering.

The treatment of obsession shows, then, a marked development from that of Proust. In the retrospective reflections of Proust's narrator we see an attempt to rationalise the meaning of Albertine's betrayals, largely as a catalyst to the suffering which is the necessary condition of the narrator's art. But this reflexive rationalisation, which generalises betrayal and suffering of a very specific sort as universal human experience, seems very tenuous, almost an escape clause for the fact that Albertine seems to have no reality at all as a person outside the narrator's mind. Obsession reduces her to a phantom. In *Nightwood*, Robin Vote is given a palpable presence in the epiphanous style, a living presence which cannot be pinned down, which escapes as she does from the grasp of her lovers and their garrulous fabricator, the transvestite doctor. Barnes's achievement in portraying female desire here goes beyond the lesbian intimacy which provoked horror and outrage when the book was first published. Her achievement differs from that of Woolf or Joyce by being its very reverse. Instead of introducing, through interior monologue, the subjective voice of female consciousness or female desire, she evokes through epiphany the elusiveness of female desire's escaping object.

When Felix first meets Robin Vote, she presents herself 'to the spectator as a picture forever arranged'. She lies on her bed 'half flung off the support of the cushions from which, in a moment of threatened consciousness she had turned her head'. 'Heavy and dishevelled', her legs 'in white flannel trousers were spread as in a dance, the thick lacquered pumps looking too lively for the arrested step'. In the pose of extreme passivity her hands, 'long and beautiful, lay on either side of her face'.[9] The posture, which suggests a still life, masks the active nature of Robin's perfidy. For, as Nora Flood discovers later to her chagrin, Robin is a somnambulist living in two worlds, that of the child and that of the desperado. Thus Nora will be unable to prevent her elusive beloved from abandoning her for the night.

In Barnes's style the arranged picture soon springs to life, seen no longer as a portrait but within a moving frame. The various forms of describing Robin all evoke a profound sensuous dislocation, the image of a woman whose bodily senses have abandoned normal forms of human perception. Thus Robin's voice ignores the conventional forms of talk and speech:

In the tones of this girl's voice was the pitch of one enchanted with the gift of postponed abandon: the low drawling 'aside' voice of the actor, who, in the soft usury of his speech, withholds a vocabulary until the profitable moment when he shall be facing his audience – in her case a guarded extempore to the body of what would be said at some later period when she would be able to 'see' them.[10]

While her voice constantly suspends its power of communication, her hands appear as the instrument of her sight:

> When she touched a thing, her hands seemed to take the place of her eye. . . . Her fingers would go forward, hesitate, tremble, as if they had found a face in the dark. When her hand finally came to rest, the palm closed, it was as if she had stopped a crying mouth. Her hand lay still and she would turn away. At such moment Felix experienced an unaccountable apprehension. The sensuality in her hands frightened him.[11]

She defies the order of things and defers the present, suggesting a presence which constantly undermines itself, which asks itself to be experienced as a mirror of absences within the admiring spectator. Her singular dislocations of sense mirror theirs of spirit, psychic absences which in the case of Felix, Nora and Jenny are made explicit. While Felix demands that Robin's body bear the son whose 'nobility' will reinstate the past, Jenny is the 'squatter' who covets objects she would not desire if they were not the exclusive possession of others. But the central and most difficult absence is that of Nora. Proprietor of a pauper's salon in America, she meets Robin at a circus, the grotesque mirror of the pomp and circumstance in Felix's forgotten world, and which presents to humans images of their own animality. She possesses a quality which Robin will never have. 'The equilibrium of her nature, savage and refined, gave her bridled skull a look of compassion.'[12] But Nora's compassion for others mirrors an absence in herself, an inability to judge and discriminate, a compassion which in loving everything is 'despised by everything'. Condemning no one for failing, 'one would discover in her eyes, large, protruding and clear, that mirrorless look of polished metals which report not so much the object as the movement of the object'.[13]

The form of Nora's compassion is to lose herself for others, to rob herself for everyone, catching herself ever-diminished through the fixated act of giving. As a potential victim of all those she 'loves' through her compulsion always to overvaluate, she sets herself up to be tormented by Robin Vote. Here the general compassion is transformed into a passionate fixation which excludes all other objects. Her obsession with Robin echoes that of Swann for Odette, the paranoia of feeling betrayed blooming amidst the anxieties of caring. In Proust the suspected acts of betrayal, always just out of focus, act as a catalyst to the desire for possession, and lead to the desperate persistence which ends in Swann's marriage to Odette. In Barnes, it is the other way around. Nora already possesses Robin only finally to lose her.

Nora's obsession is in part a *Liebestod*. But the conception of it transcends romanticism, since it is a consequence of a breakdown in a relationship which is at the same time the transgressing intimacy of exiled women in love. The uncertainties of the affair become a mirror of a post-war society, where all purpose is anxiety, all identity confusion. Amidst such uncertainty love appears as a form of grasping which gradually loses its grasp upon its object:

> Love becomes the deposit of the heart, analogous in all degrees to the findings in a tomb. As in one will be charted the taken place of the body, the raiment, the utensils necessary to the other life, so in the heart of the lover will be traced, as an indelible shadow, that which he loves. In Nora's heart lay the fossil of Robin, intaglio of her identity, and about it for its maintenance ran Nora's blood.[14]

Nora retains the indelible shadow while the figure of Robin runs loose through the night. As she thinks of the dangers confronting her escaping beloved, her anxious imagination embraces a corpse. She knows that, despite Robin's tragic longing to be kept, only in death would Robin belong to her. The night into which Robin escapes is the real and metaphorical predicament linking absence to desire. Robin's nocturnal absences are a physical removal, an amputation. She is the lost other who constantly returns in order that she can flee into the dark streets, the dimly lit bars and the arms of other women. The night is the form of darkness in which everything is permitted and all becomes possible.

The difference between Robin and her three lovers is a simultaneous play on the contrast between day and night, free play and determination. All three lovers are bound to the moral order through their grotesque misreadings of it, while Robin's relationship to it is mediated only by them, since her breaking-free is constant insistence that she has no ties to the moral order at all. As an instance of the general form which desire takes in the epiphanous novel, the intimacy of Nora and Robin is probably the most literal. If, through desire, the absent other becomes a reflection of the absent self, then Robin's desire as a desire for someone of the same sex is a literal rendering. Their intimacy becomes a play upon identity and difference, in which reflection has a purity balancing the divergent personalities of lover and beloved. It balances out the difference between a woman whose response to the world is determined by a considered sense of what the world is and a woman whose actions, both ubiquitous and arbitrary, contain no sense of what the world is at all.

Nora knows Robin only as the type of person she could never be, yet, as she confesses to the doctor, 'A man is another person – a woman is yourself, caught as you turn in panic; on her mouth you kiss your own.'[15] The night is seen by Barnes and by the doctor, her surrogate narrator in direct speech, as the supreme instance of escape into the arbitrary, where evil has indefinite extension, where the physiological rhythms of those who should be sleeping and dreaming undergo their severest dislocation. Yet the doctor is more than a surrogate narrator. He himself suffers from the disease he diagnoses and for which he can provide no cure. This becomes clear in the 'Watchman, What of the Night?' episode, where Nora, on discovering Robin's sudden departure with Jenny, seeks out the doctor's advice in extreme desperation. Above all she seeks out a meaning for what seems to her as irrational, the termination of a relationship whose betrayals always struck a note of constancy. The doctor, who witnessed the savage attack on Robin by Jenny in the carriage, already knows what she has come to find but knows too that he has no answer.

The scene where Nora finds him in bed, made up and wearing a woman's nightdress, clearly expecting someone else, works at one level as a parody of all psychotherapy. The therapist appears as the patient, freakish, absurd, in the very horizontal posture which the Freudian analyst demands of his client. He invokes the night as a form of psychic diaspora and yet that diaspora is his own. His nocturnal flood of words is a dramatic performance, constantly on the verge of capturing sense, yet ending finally in nonsense. What comes out sounds like explanation and so distracts Nora from her suffering. But Nora's constant lament, 'What am I to learn? . . . What can I do?', receives no definitive answer. O'Connor is betrayed by his role of fabricator of surrogate truths for truths which cannot be fully known. Like the arbitrary nature of his subject, the night, he disperses himself into nothingness.

O'Connor's despair at the world and at himself springs from an epoch which claims to have forged a secular and scientific knowledge of the human heart, yet has given to its wandering exiles confusions of identity and permanent anxiety. As the doctor knows, knowledge of it, and his poetic gloss on that knowledge, cannot provide an explanation as to why Robin should have left Nora for the last person on earth for whom she should ever have left her. The 'irrational' here is an absence from discourse which discourse attempts to consume with its own eloquence, only to fail poetically. Taken as a whole, Barnes's text itself reads as a constant surfeit of word over deed, where, stunned by actions it cannot explain, speech then holds all actions in abeyance. Yet underlying the whole text are the constant actions of Robin Vote, actions whose lack of specific detail lends to them a phantasmagorical presence, and against which speech rebounds as a visible counterpoint.

Here action is centred on desire. But Robin Vote's desire is predicated on the arbitrary nature of its own object, so that, by dispersing itself through the unknown, it remains itself unknown. It obeys the mandate of a tragic vicious circle. Its truth is inaccessible to the coherence of reason and its nature defines itself through the inaccessibility of its truth. The consistent logic of its irrationality is to choose what cannot be defined by reason, to desire what can have no name. Robin is then seen as the incarnation of motive which is truly motiveless, giving to motive a purity of absence which Nora's grief, in demanding reasoned explanation, refuses to acknowledge. But desire does have a provisional truth which O'Connor finally pins down before his nemesis:

'And why does Robin feel innocent? Every bed she leaves, without caring, fills her heart with peace and happiness. She has made her "escape" again. That's why she can't "put herself in another's place", she herself is the only "position"; so she resents it when you reproach her with what she had done. She knows she is innocent because she can't do anything in relation to anyone but herself.'[16]

Desire in Barnes is not merely egocentric but the nucleus of a structure of feeling which permeates the intimate relationships of rootless exile. Her post-Jamesian reformulation of innocence, of the American in Europe, exhibits a certain perversity but is also a statement about a form of freedom which issues in transience. It is Robin's freedom, her rootlessness, her androgyny – 'a tall girl with the body of a boy'[17] – which make her attractive to others, so that the transience is a feature not simply of personality but also of the mutually anticipated relationships in which she becomes involved. Nora is the exception, in that she presents her compassionate self as the pinnacle of constancy only to be irrationally deserted, and still fails to realise that idealism has been finally broken by the harsh, intractable world in which both of them live.

That world is of course the world of bohemian exile, the elevation and rootlessness of living in another country, a felt emancipation of speech within the ambience of another language, qualities which Hemingway and Barnes, in their best writing, bring out to the full. That form of exile acts as a lever of privilege. The freedom to cross national frontiers and live out a culture which is cosmopolitan in the fullest and most elusive sense of the term – Paris the magnet which attracts like to like from all corners of the globe – is the privilege of those who dare to abjure convention and seek greater personal freedom. In doing so, exile tests the durability of exile to its fullest, and in post-war Paris, where the disenchantment with idea of progress received its richest artistic expression, one finds a fiction in which the ego's identity is tested to the fullest. In Hemingway and Barnes the narrative of omission gives off a bitter-sweet aroma. It presents us with an indelible scent of the dissolving identity, the decentred self, which is part of the 'loss' of progress. Desire, in the fiction of the period, is the nexus of that dislocation, linking privilege to dispersion, iconoclasm to dissolution.

Yet if we look to Joyce and Faulkner we see that exile and periphery, with its double dialectic, has already accomplished more than exile alone will allow. The movement back to periphery is more than topographical: it is also a descent, a search to capture the repressed voice of the oppressed, the poor, the 'insignificant'. This movement, both topographical and social, fuses theme and style through the development of the epiphanous form. The response to the loss of progress strikes to a deeper vein of absence through its double dialectic. Absence within community is not, as in Barnes, absence within civilisation, but absence *outwith* civilisation. What we see in Faulkner is the lost character or the lost family within a lost community, whose undeniable sense of place the novelist clearly evokes precisely because it has been denied, historically speaking, a wider cultural recognition.

In Faulkner, the peripheral community comes to assume its greatest significance in the development of the epiphanous novel. The absent other who mirrors as object of desire the absences of the desiring self has its external counterpart in the peripheral community. The peripheral community within which the hero cannot satisfy his transgressing desire holds up the mirror for the cosmopolitan reader to an absent civilisation, to the absence of civilising features of life which in the nineteenth-century middle-class novel are conventionally taken for granted. The achievements of Barnes are already foreshadowed by those of Faulkner. The flood of sound in Matthew O'Connor's voice is in part an echo of Benjy Compson's sound and fury. The desires of Robin Vote dispersed among the *quartiers* of Paris have an equally outrageous precedent in the desire of Temple Drake in the bleak flatlands of north Mississippi.

5　Faulkner I: The Family Void

For much of the nineteenth century, the American South had been the home of slavery, political rhetoric and magnolia fiction. For a large part of the twentieth it became the home of segregation, the Ku-Klux Klan and William Faulkner. After defeat in the Civil War the South forged a myth of its honour in battle and passed it down through generations, a myth of the nobility of its 'unvanquished' which is one of the main historical fixations of Faulkner's fiction. Such mythologising presented Southern whites with psychological compensation for their continuing sense of defeat and with a continuing sense of their region's distinctiveness when it became subject from 1914 onwards to more intense processes of social change. The glory of the Old South could be revered while the New South painstakingly tried to overcome the stigma of its economic backwardness through greater participation in the American capitalist process. Thus the self-image of the South as a separate entity which deserved to be a separate nation thrived on nostalgia after a long and painful period during which its history had been marked by extreme discontinuity.[1] Often the disruptions caused by the failure of the Reconstruction and stagnation, by the rise and fall of populism and the introduction of Jim Crow legislation, could be conveniently forgotten. After partial entry into the mainstream of American economic life, segregation could be and often was legitimated as part of an earlier tradition of honour when in reality it was the consequence of a ruthless, revanchist struggle for power.

Faulkner's work subsumes both the myths of honour and glory and the realities of historical dislocation – of racism, poverty, corruption and class conflict. It contains its own nostalgia for the Old South, for the cult of honour, which, as Genovese has shown, could only have been created initially out of the fabric of plantation slavery and its paternalistic, pre-capitalist social relations.[2] Yet it also possesses a vision of slavery as the historical curse from which the South will never escape. Though Faulkner thought at times of the old paternalism as preferable to the brutality of the Klan, his own work shows the enduring legacy of slavery not only in relations between black and white, but also in those between poor tenant farmers and heirs of rich planters, traditional artisans and rootless entrepreneurs. It also demonstrates the failure of a new professional middle class to set an example through their civility. Faulkner was as much part of the Southern renaissance as Allen Tate or John Crowe Ransom, but little in his fiction supports their view of the South as a rural arcadia in a corrupt commercial world. For Faulkner, commercialism was already a force within, and resistance already beginning to collapse.

Like the Irish Renaissance, the writers of its Southern American counterpart tried to create authentic values for a peripheral culture at the very time when the South was beginning to lose its insularity. As the penetration of capital proceeded, they asserted the sense of place against a rootless metropolitan culture. In fiction, Faulkner, Caldwell and Thomas Wolfe all flouted the existing conventions of middle-class realism and the assumptions of bourgeois psychology which went with it. Thematic emphasis on the lower middle classes, poor whites, black servants and labourers, and the socially outcast were misread by critics, as Flannery O'Connor points out, in terms of demented 'Southern gothic' or the 'grotesque'.[3] In underestimating the violent traditions of Southern society, which went far beyond the plantation, critics claimed to find in Southern fiction a distortion of the real which was so outrageous that it broke the bounds of any psychological credibility. In truth that same fiction was a profound comment on the misadventures of the modern self.

The distinctive differences of Southern writing were a response to the distinctive differences of a quasi-peripheral culture. They were also a response, as Rubin has pointed out, to a new sense of perspective on Southern history made possible by the time which had elapsed since the end of the Civil War.[4] This new sense of history, of a world mythically continuous but empirically discontinuous, was at its strongest in Faulkner. This was partly because it had, to start with, a wider frame of reference, beginning with the exilic themes of the lost generation, then working backwards through an important but transient phase of middle-class Freudianism, and culminating in the major novels of Yoknapa-tawpha County. The early war stories set in France and England, then the first novels – *Soldier's Pay*, *Mosquitoes* and *Sartoris* – proved to be more accessible reading in their own time than the later masterpieces. But the themes of disenchantment and post-war bitterness showed Faulkner he could not progress as far in writing of a world war without honour as he could by invoking the Civil War, whose honour had been so thoroughly mythologised by the descendants of the vanquished. *Mosquitoes* and *Sartoris* demonstrated there was no easy road in an increasingly psychologised age to the fictionalisation of desire through the use of surrogate Freud. Far from aping the language of psychoanalysis, the language of fiction had to find its own form and create its own world.

The transformation from *Sartoris* to *The Sound and the Fury* was momentous. Not only was Faulkner reaching back to a sense of place after a period of exile; he was reaching simultaneously *down* to the repressed voices of his own community and *upward* to the voices of honour now in decline. Far from abjuring modernism, Faulkner brought it home, rematching modernist aesthetics to the realist form in a society which had little tradition of serious fiction and little contact with modern art. Part of the intensely pictorial nature of his narratives comes from the absence of a visual-arts tradition in the South, as absence of which he was well aware and for which he tried as a writer of fiction to compensate. But the encounter of modernism and regional 'backwardness' really comes from the response to two very different wars which he fused together, one which had perpetrated the myth of eternal honour for its defeated and the other whose devastation had soured the cultural mood of the ensuing decade, making the devaluation of value an attractive proposition. Thus for Faulkner Southern honour had become a historical anachronism which had outlived a more recent nihilism. But it was still an honour that was deeply flawed. For, though genuine in its resistance to the harsh world of capital, it remained blithely immune to poverty and suffering and accepted as natural a new and brutal system of racial hegemony.

As a residue of plantation paternalism and the lost Confederacy, honour invoked the memories of a pre-capitalistic South worlds apart from the development of global capital, in which historically it had played such a vital part. Other institutions, however, helped to explain its durability. The most important is the family. The forms of extended kinship in the South, including intermarriage between cousins, made the family a solidary and protected institution. But defence of family honour often led to self-defeating violence. The protection of land or property, the defence of female virtue or revenge for its violation, often led with fatal consequences to the lower-class brawl or the upper-class duel, a violence that was legitimated by a claustrophobic fusion of idealism and self-interest. Honourable clannishness resonates through *As I Lay Dying*, through Quentin Compson's quixotic attempt to square up to Dalton Ames, through the altercation between Ruby Lamarr and Temple Drake in *Sanctuary* as they give rival class versions of their families' protection of female honour. In his famous story 'Barn Burning', Faulkner goes further and shows how the law itself connives in the maintenance of family honour by turning a blind eye to crime when that honour is under threat.[5] Abner Snopes takes revenge against his planter landlords by setting their barns on fire, but his son Sarty, who is the only witness and is willing to testify against him, is never given the opportunity by the justice of the peace at his father's trial. Compelling a son to testify against his father would be to break the community's unwritten code of family honour, and, even though Snopes is a ruthless villain, such a recourse was unthinkable.

Unsentimentally Faulkner summons up the resources of the Southern historical tradition to forge a new structure of feeling in his fiction. He links the tradition of honour to the nullity of a modern world of capital whose dynamic ubiquity had begun, at the time of writing, to threaten the traditional Southern family itself. The traditional familial intensity which inures it to the wider society is itself under duress. Mythically speaking, family life can still protect the lost hero from a heartless world. But its power is indubitably on the wane. The Compsons try to put a brave face on solidarity only to reveal family life as an empty shell. In Lawrence the organic life of the family thrives on internal conflict and divided feelings. In Faulkner the conflicts are avoided, the divisions suppressed, because there is no open commitment and little sense of value. Enshrining honour through its eminent genealogy, the Compson family becomes honour's abnegation.

In the first-person narratives of the three brothers, Faulkner evokes the family's familiarities of encounter but the narratives themselves are monstrously egocentric, monuments of intensity which testify to no shared life. Instead the Compson children create a surrogate family of childhood whose pivot is Dilsey and which they share with the black children who are supposed to look after them. This family-within-the-family echoes the white plantation family of the Old South, in which, as Blassingname has shown, the white parents distance themselves from their children and the black mammy comes to have a crucial role in the children's upbringing.[6] Through Benjy's time-warped vision, Faulkner gives to the surrogate family an intense, almost Blakean pathos. For the Compson family is in decline, forced to sell its land to pay for Quentin's schooling at Harvard, and unable to reproduce the aristocratic aura of its ancestors. Instead the extended planter family, which should have become, in its new bourgeois phase, a series of nuclear families, of interlocking nuclei each focused around the three sons and the daughter, remains the empty shell of an extended family with no nucleus at all. It is kept going only through the loyalty and informal authority of Dilsey Gibson. The inept grandmother, the tyrannical uncle, the rebellious niece, the perennial idiot who is neither boy nor man, all circle around an abiding emptiness, their household noise a hollow presence. Amidst the sound and fury of the novel's title, they produce and reproduce the family void.

The impairment of Benjy's senses, which makes him incapable of judging others, becomes in retrospect the key to nothingness. He is both chaos and vortex of the epiphanous voice, raging with grief in infinitely repeated sequences, but experiencing the stillness of serene contentment in Caddy's presence, or later, by the golf course after she has vanished, in the mere utterance of the sound which constitutes her name. His memory is impaired, a series of discontinuous associations which have neither sequence or chronology. The sight of Caddy's daughter, Quentin, with her boyfriend in the swing triggers off the image of Caddy with her beau, years earlier, in the same swing. The mute Benjy hollers, incomprehensibly to those around him, because the intensity of the sensation of loss cannot be expressed in words. Yet eighteen years later he would probably not even recognise the woman for whom he grieves. The stillness at the centre of movement is then complemented by the absence at the core of intense sensation, the not-there of Caddy. And this absence which cannot be communicated by a congenital idiot is none the less a mirror of the void within which the other members of the family, who do have the mental and physical capacity to communicate with one another, abjectly fail to do so.

In the first narrative section Faulkner gives both a palpable rendering of what compassion is and what is its necessary doom. Benjy's desire for compassion is mirrored in his worship of his sister's purity, not as an abstract ideal like that of Quentin's but as a form of pure presence to the senses – 'Caddy smelled like trees'. But the movement out of childhood, where Caddy can only give less as she grows into a woman with her own desires, while Benjy remains a grown child, is also a historical movement for the whole family which Faulkner later sets out in the third and fourth sections on a wider canvas. Among the family only the young Caddy has compassion, compassion echoed in her fleeting reappearance eighteen years later when, banished from the household, she tries to ensure that her money reaches her daughter despite Jason's treachery.

In the first two sections, Caddy's voice echoes and re-echoes as the voice of compassion, but for that reason her figure is its vacated centre. Through the use of the present tense, her brothers' memories constitute her voice as ever-present when her own presence is irretrievable. It is only later – ironically, in Jason's narrative – that she makes her sole and brief appearance in the present. By this point her rebelliousness is being echoed by Quentin, her daughter, totally without compassion but instead through selfishness and contempt. Compassion as the lost structure of feeling highlights the family's eclipse, since such compassion could only resonate through the mythic honour or traditional form it can no longer recapture. Caddy's defiant pursuit of her own desire is not arbitrary but a response to the absence of compassion within the family, which leads her to be selfish too, and flout all the conventions of the Southern belle enshrined as a paragon of sexual virtue. She gets pregnant by a passing soldier, quickly marries someone else, then deserts daughter, husband and family alike to lead her own life. Her reponse to a loveless family is not only to repudiate married love but also to dissolve the fragile boundary between passion and desire, since her love object always seems to take second place to the harshness of erotic encounter itself.

One of the few shortcomings of the novel is that the reader is left to deduce the pattern of her future life largely from the abundant memories of Benjy and Quentin. Escaping from the family void, she also loses, to the novel's detriment, the presence she had gained through the 'I' of Benjy and the 'I' of Quentin. Faulkner in fact left few clues and clearly suffered afterwards from his own omission, since he later tried to fill in the adult Candace's life in 'A Compson Genealogy' for Malcolm Cowley's *The Portable Faulkner*. But the interpolations were unconvincing; the original presence was never truly regained. Instead, perhaps one can see some kind of approximation to Candace in the rather different heroic figure of Charlotte Rittenmeyer.

The glimpses we are given of Caddy show us the paradox of Faulkner's narrative strategy, of revealing her only in sequences of great intensity but, also, only from the outside. She cannot be at the centre of the text like Temple Drake, because her desires are substantial and her relationships sequential. The reader infers that, though flawed and unsatisfactory, they have a completion which none of her brothers could ever attain. While Temple's desire has no stable object, Caddy's does. But, for that very reason, Caddy, unlike Temple, cannot return to the fold. As a personal revolution of the collapse of family, her escape also has to be diametrically opposed to the response of Quentin, who makes no attempt to escape but tries to fill out the family void by unnatural means. Her affection for Quentin comes from a love of life, while Quentin's idealised love for his sister comes from a love of death, forcing him to give himself to one because he is unable to give himself to the other.

In the relationship of Quentin and Caddy, Faulkner further deconstructs family honour. Quentin springs to the defence of his sister's honour as convention demands when it is threatened by Dalton Ames. But he can do so only by imagining the act of incest which is the ultimate horror of family life, which preserves it only through deformation. His Quixotic idealism is predicated on material opposites – the high sex drive of his sister and his own lack of desire. Reality throws sexual double standards into relief by reversing societal expectation. Quentin spurns the unspoken privilege Southern society gives him as the young buck while Caddy throws off the restraints imposed upon her as the young belle. Quentin idealises where Caddy desires, and for that reason ends up idealising desire in its absence, confessing to his father the incest he will never commit. The dividing-line between romantic idealism and the pathology of Quentin's death-wish is fine but distinct. Incest renders the ideal primally corrupt, as unrequited passion is transformed by Faulkner into impossible desire.

Quentin's desire for Caddy is more generally an idealised desire for desire which has its roots in the material predicament of the changing South. At Harvard, Quentin's fixation on the past links the vice-like grip of the family to the vice-like grip of history. He tries to resurrect both as they disappear into a bottomless void. His doomed course follows the pattern of fixation and melancholia to the point of self-destruction, so that the second section provides us with a unique and poetic transcription of Freud, Freudianism paralleled and surpassed with uncanny exactitude by the language of fiction as interior monologue, but done so in a specific social context, the passing of the Southern tradition. The primal tie of incest is both the imaginary reality of desire and the metaphorical reality of the Old South passing away before the mercenary world of capital, a world without honour or paternalism or glory. Failing to uphold any of these three values which his imagination reveres, Quentin reverts to his imagination's only other hope. Incest is the last attempt of the intending suicide to remove integrity out of the corrupt world before death removes the subject himself.

The narrative style of the Quentin section is at once banal and turbulent. The external events of the last day are related with an uncustomary flatness. Cambridge, Massachusetts, unlike Oxford, Mississippi, fails to take shape as a definite place. Yet the naturalistic flatness of this external design has an important function in the uncovering of Quentin's interior world. Faulkner echoes Flaubert in the juxtaposition of reality and daydream, but is more ambitious in making it, in addition, a topographical distinction between North and South. Amidst Quentin's craving for death it is daydream which comes to have an accelerating momentum, which finally drowns out the eventful circumstances of his day, where he finds a lost girl, is arrested and accused of kidnapping her, is subsequently released, then gets involved in a fight in which he is badly beaten. But it is not that daydream drowns out such events. It is more that these events only seem to echo the obsessions of memory, in which life is merely the shadow of an interior world.

Memory here is not only the vivid sensation of recalled incident but also the imaginary dialogue, part actual, which repeats Quentin's encounters with his father, with Caddy and with her lover Dalton Ames. Memory gives reality no clear boundaries. In wishing to annihilate in retrospect the incidents it wished to prevent and at the same time inaugurate those which never came to pass, the distressed mind alters both to mollify its grieving. All three protagonists in Quentin's imaginary discourse alternate between the real and the fantastic, and it is precisely from that oscillation that the clarity of each voice rings through loud and clear. In the passage towards death, Quentin no longer wishes to disentangle fact and fantasy. The essence of his romantic longing for self-destruction is that they should be impossible to separate, that they should become, as the end approaches, more and more closely intertwined.

The corollary is the increasing fusion of past and present, which finally become merged at the point where Quentin picks a fight with Gerald Bland for boasting about all his girls. He does this because he identifies the man beside him with the hated figure of his imagination, Dalton Ames. History then repeats itself as Quentin fails for the second time to assert his physical prowess and is badly beaten. By this time the tragic pathos of the epiphanous narrative differs significantly from that of Benjy's. Benjy can only record facts and his response to them, knowing neither good nor evil. With Quentin memory invents as it records,

> poor Quentin
> she leaned back on her arms her hands locked about her knees
> you've never done that have you
> what done what
> that what I have what I did
> yes yes lots of times with lots of girls
> then I was crying her hand touched me again and I was crying crying against her damp blouse then she lying on her back looking past my head into the sky I could see a rim of white under her irises I opened my knife
> do you remember the day damuddy died when you sat down in the water in your drawers
> yes
> I held the point of the knife at her throat
> it won't take but a second just a second then I can do mine I can do mine then
> all right you can do yours by yourself
> yes the blades long enough Benjys in bed by now

yes
it won't take but a second I'll try not to hurt
all right
will you close your eyes
no like this you'll have to push it harder
touch your hand to it
but she didn't move her eyes were wide open looking past
my head at the sky[7]

The passage has a double ambiguity. We cannot tell whether or
how much of what we read is invented and how much has actually
taken place. The narrative, moreover, is deliberately made to read
as if, in the suggested suicide pact, the act of killing is an act of
carnal union, the knife Caddy will not help him use, the penis
she will not touch in order to aid his penetration of her prostrate
body. The scene can be read as invented by Quentin to match
incest and murder in his own mind and his impotence to achieve
either, or as invented by the author to suggest a parallel of which
his hero is not consciously aware, or as a further variation read as
a confusion in Quentin's mind of two separate incidents, two
separate realities now conflated into one, a fusion of the admixture
of the real and the fantastic. Thus Faulkner, like Joyce, explores
in depth how the mind confuses reality and fantasy at the level
of desire, an echo of that intractable confusion which caused Freud
to abandon seduction theory as a positivistic misreading of his
patients' confessions of forced incest. Moreover, Faulkner explores
the confusion *in situ*, juxtaposing it to the external events, the
fights, arrest and court hearing, which would normally be
considered the incidents of an eventful day.

We find here also an important and distinctive departure from
Proust in Faulkner's treatment of memory. In place of Proust's
composed and at times artificial resurrection of memory as the
composed account of the past by a composed narrator, Faulkner
portrays the attempted ordering of memory by his first-person
narrator as a symptom of its very opposite – of fragmentation,
disorder and breakdown. For Proust's narrator, memory has the
magic quality of epiphanous sensation, but also the ordered structure of reason – the strategic reinterpretation and rationalisation
of past suffering. That use of rationalisation as a measure of reason
is itself a form of psychic survival, a sign of enduring. Quentin,
in a state of total disintegration, does not have such an option

open to him. The past devours all attempts to rationalise it and destroys him.

Faulkner's epiphany shows us the suicidal mind losing its grip on the world by vainly attempting to reshape a past it cannot alter. Absence – the absent past, the absent Caddy, the absent South – is the structure of feeling through which Quentin's consciousness composes and recomposes imaginary dialogues with compulsive repetition. The fixation with Caddy, with its intermingling of truth and falsehood, is the onanism of Quentin's desire eventuating in the climax of his death. Caddy consumes all the reality her absent figure can no longer touch:

> and i it was to isolate her out of the loud world so that it would have to flee us of necessity and then the sound of it would be as though it had never been and he did you try to make her do it and i i was afraid to i was afraid she might then it wouldnt have done any good but if i could tell you we did it it would have been so and then the others wouldnt be so and then the world would roar away[8]

Desire idealised is superseded by the wish to be thought incestuous, so that the mutual pact of which he had dreamed can come to pass through false accusation and without the act itself. Having been wrongly thought to commit incest, he and Caddy can ennoble themselves in the midst of hellfire by reclaiming the togetherness and innocence of childhood. But for Quentin himself there is something more. He knows that death is more actual than the fantasy which nourishes it. In giving himself to the act of dying he yearns for the pleasure of orgasm he never experienced in life.

The switch to the third section, narrated by Jason, fuses an alteration in the structure of feeling to the change in historical time. The difference of eighteen years, between 1910 and 1928, is the period when, historically speaking, the values of the Old South began to undergo a significant decline. In the same period, Jason's own jaundiced attitudes towards family and society begin to crystallise. Jason's narrative, however, not only reveals the rupture in family history but also its continuity. Jason has internalised the cynical commercialism of a new age, and is a rival in the scope of his petty, unscrupulous dealings to the infamous Snopes. This is exacerbated not merely by disgust with the demise of his family, but also because he inherits the cynicism of his father. In a new era he takes his father's cryptic cynicism to the point of no return, rescuing it from self-indulgent drunkenness and using it with a chilling sobriety. In Quentin's section, where Jason senior deflates, under the façade of a florid rhetoric, the idealist aspirations of his Harvard son, we have already a sense of the impending loss of value. The rhetorical tone echoes the traditional Southern aspiration to the ideal, but the substance of the paternal advice contradicts it, since it encourages Quentin to forget honour, love and Christian redemption and take a caustic, resigned view of life. 'Because no battle is ever won he said. They are not even fought. The field only reveals to man his own folly and despair, and victory is an illusion of philosophers and fools.'[9]

Jason's narrative voice strips his father's views of all their rhetoric and accommodates them to the commercial activism of the new South, echoing in that act of demolition the accommodation of the New South to a new America. With the collapse of one of Mississippi's great dynastic families, profitability is stripped of its rhetoric and wealth stripped of its cultural capital. Yet Jason's petty nihilism is not achieved *ex nihilo*. It is only made possible by the deterioration of a whole way of life. As such, it is the jaundiced revenge of a cynical survivor. But for the Southern Babbit the circumstances are somewhat different. The Northern rationalisation of the pursuit of profit accords easily with the individualistic premises of the American Dream, but the Southern stripping-down of a pre-capitalist system of value founded on slavery permits no facile optimism. The epiphanous style of the narrative here is fused thematically with that view of capital espoused by Marx in *The Communist Manifesto*, of capital as the constant subverter of tradition and myth. For Jason, capital, even in its meanest and pettiest form, has a palpable presence which rescues him from the family void. It also very conveniently accommodates desire. Jason disapproves of sexual intimacy unless he is paying for it, since any relationship only has meaning to him as a transaction:

Then she tried to buy a beer but I wouldn't let her. 'Keep your money', I says. 'Buy yourself a dress with it.' I gave the maid a five too. After all, like I say, money has no value; it's just the way you spend it. It don't belong to anybody so why try to hoard it. It just belongs to the man who can get it and keep it.[10]

Jason's contempt for women – 'Once a bitch, always a bitch, what I say'[11] – contrasts with the hopeless fixation of his two brothers. Naked hostility towards mother, niece and Dilsey, whom he treats with racist contempt, contrasts with the deluded paternalism of the gallant Quentin, who believed that he treated blacks well simply by 'taking them for what they are'. While his greatest contempt is reserved for his mother, who, like O'Neill's Mary Tyrone, has deserted the centre of the household convention reserves for her, Jason's fixation with his niece repeats Quentin's fixation with Candace. However, it also inverts it, transforming idealised desire into obsessive contempt. Thus Jason's misogyny is not the calm and composed attitude he would have wished. In his concern to keep Quentin imprisoned, to stifle her embryonic desires, he is as hopelessly self-defeating in his actions as his elder brother was in trying to defend their sister's honour. When reproduced as comic, petty and mundane, a fixation once sublime appears even more pointless, fixation itself as one of the central male failings in relationships with women.

As we have seen, the younger Quentin repeats the involuntary pattern of inheritance. But she enlarges the faults of her absent mother just as Jason enlarges the faults of his dead father. Forced into repeating the same cycle of female rebellion, she lacks Caddy's compassion, existing within the lovelessness against which she rebels. Though Jason hates her for openly violating the double standards he tries to impose upon her, her determined selfishness mirrors his own, and that of her grandmother. But it is a selfishness deprived of the freedom to choose which expresses itself in contempt for all around her, including Dilsey, whom her mother had respected, and Benjy, whom she had loved. Her departure with her fairground lover is predictable, her triumphant rescue of the money sent by her mother which Jason had kept from her a form of rough justice which reflects on the limits of Jason's petty obsessions. Obsessed by money, Jason finds he has no authority. Fixated on the share index, he throws away all hope of legitimacy. But in Quentin there is also a perceptible shift away from her mother in the nature of her sexuality. Any male is a potential sex object offering the chance of escape. While Quentin tried in vain to protect Caddy's honour, Jason runs around like a berserk jailer only to find that his intended prisoner is constantly escaping him.

The role of the black servants in the novel is seemingly peripheral, but actually central. They are seen, as Faulkner well knew, purely in their role within the white household, never in the cabins from which they come at dawn and to which they depart at night. But in that context Faulkner throws into relief through the device of Benjy's idiocy the definition of the normal which accompanies their work. The normal tasks of Dilsey, T. P. Versh and Luster involve caring for a mute, gibbering idiot because his own family and in particular his mother relinquishes the responsibility. And, in servicing the abnormal, the black role is to make it as unobtrusive as possible in the life of the white household. Faulkner portrays black–white relations here not merely in the context of domestic service, but through a dialectic which called into question the very rationale of that subjection – that is, through the interplay of the banal and the abnormal. At the same time, when the family has lost its entitlement to honour, Dilsey preserves the fading aura of its 'nobility' through a practical dignity which involves saving the household from complete collapse. Thus Jason, who would dearly like to get rid of her, clearly senses that she has become indispensable.

The most important role which Dilsey plays, however, lies in her defiant gesture of taking Benjy to a black service each Sunday when no white church would have him. The event links the impersonal narrative of the last section to the subjective grieving of the first. Benjy's inexpressible attachment to his sister and his voiceless grieving at her absence find their objective correlative in the nature of the black service on Easter Sunday. For, as the preacher speaks, 'the congregation seemed to watch with its own eyes while the voice consumed him, until he was nothing and they were nothing and there was not even a voice but instead their hearts were speaking to one another in chanting measures beyond the need for words'.[12] Through hope and striving the collective voice creates its own redemption for suffering and sorrow, so that amidst 'the voices and the hands Ben sat, rapt in his sweet blue gaze. Dilsey sat bolt upright beside, crying rigidly and quietly in the annealment and the blood of the remembered Lamb.'[13]

After Caddy's departure, the church is the only place where Benjy can forget her absence, forget his suffering, through the solidarity of suffering which is that of another race. The point here is not just to produce a suffering of analogous stature to match Benjy's own. The link is also an attempt by Faulkner to touch upon the black experience he deems largely beyond his scope. One reads back from the service in which both Benjy and the black congregation are offered redemption to the experience which demands it with such urgency and conviction. Benjy's sufferings are known, but those of the congregation can only, by analogy, be deduced. Thus Faulkner ends by shining a brief and flickering light on what is absent from his narrative, the deeper vein of racial tyranny beyond the shallow paternalism of the white household.

The movement back to Benjy towards the end has a deeper sense of turbulence and unease because he is no longer the single and isolated congenital idiot. His misery reflects a deeper misery, unseen and unspoken in the text, nominally absent, but indisputably there as lament is replaced by voiceless misery: 'Then Ben wailed again, hopeless and prolonged. It was nothing. Just sound. It might have been all time and injustice and sorrow become vocal for an instant by a conjunction of planets.'[14] Or again: 'He bellowed slowly, abjectly, without tears; the grave hopeless sound of all voiceless misery under the sun.'[15]

II

Though similar in style to *The Sound and the Fury*, Faulkner's next novel, *As I Lay Dying*, is also a new departure. It uses multiple first-person narrative, but this time exhaustively, dispensing with the impersonal narrative of the previous novel and its orchestrating final section. Though the story again centres on a single family, it is not a dynastic family of planters come to grief, but a family of poor tenants, Mississippi hill farmers, who have little in common, either socially or culturally, with the Compsons other than the colour of their skin. The switch in form which maintains its continuity is reminiscent of the Russian realists and the writers of the Irish Renaissance in their ability to move from the aristocratic to the demotic. The most immediate precedent here is not Joyce but Synge. Faulkner's design, in which he speaks exclusively through the narrative voice of his characters, recalls Synge's dramatisation of the peasant voices of the west of Ireland.

The demands and freedoms of the novel are, however, different from those of the play. In rendering the epiphany of the vernacular, Faulkner makes each individual voice a fusion of dialogue recorded with and between others and the imaginary thoughts of its narrator. These thoughts are almost but never quite spoken, close to the dialect and the rhythms of the public voice but also inwardly extensive, passing in monologue beyond the plateau of naturalistic speech. Morever, as the funeral procession to Jefferson gets underway, the interior point of view becomes palpable and immediate. Though the narrative sequence is asymmetrical, all the characters observe and are observed, each at some time a subjective voice and at others a figure in the landscape of another's vision, at one moment the seeing eye and at another the object of the eye that sees. The narrative is democratised and operates exclusively through the vernacular, through the epiphanous voice. Yet the method clearly creates a problem of relativism. Previously, the last section of *The Sound and the Fury* had orchestrated a unified field of meaning out of the disparate narratives of the three brothers which preceded it. But here, without any impersonal narrative, where is such an orchestrating perspective to be found?

The immediate answer is, of course, the voice of Darl, the most sensitive son, the most literate and perceptive member of the family. Darl, in fact, commands nearly half the narrative sections in the novel, and has no immediate rival narrator. But the narrative form produces a new and startling dialectic of thought and action. As the observer as self begins to see what the actor, as other, does, the power to sustain narration involves a relinquishment of the power to act. One vital form of presence within the story excludes another which is equally vital. The contradiction is made flesh and blood in the sibling rivalry of Darl and Jewel. The actions of the intemperate, headstrong Jewel are the constant obsession of his contemptuous yet envying brother. Thus Jewel, who has only one narrative section in the book, becomes a more imposing presence within the story than Darl, who provides the main external connection to the reader but who fails in his own actions to provide the necessary support for the absurd pilgrimage.

The reason why the novel could never be written off as a narrative of two levels, as a modernistic imposition upon the narrow, ingrown lives of country hicks, is that style and theme are so perfectly fused in the epiphanous form. The method of reading is to take all the sections as separate but related, continuous and discontinuous at the same time. The most important feature of Darl's famous questioning of his own identity, which begins, 'In a strange room you must empty yourself for sleep', is the context in which it occurs. It is the culmination of a passage in which Darl has watched his brother Cash labouring all night in the rain and darkness to finish his mother's coffin for a burial journey which he already considers unnecessary and absurd. It is followed by Cash giving a sparse inventory of reasons for making the coffin in the way that he did, and that in turn is followed by the startling claim of Vardaman, the confused and anxious youngest son, that his mother is a fish. Faulkner creates the lyrical continuity of the single narrative section along with the effect of montage, the strategic juxtaposition of narrative sections from whose subjective differences the reader has to construct an intersubjective meaning.

In this particular section we can see the contrast between the beginning and end of Darl's narrative.

> The lantern sits on a stump. Rusted, grease-fouled, its cracked chimney smeared on one side with a soaring smudge of soot, it sheds a feeble and sultry glare upon the trestles and the boards and the adjacent earth.[16]

The section ends,

> In a strange room you must empty yourself for sleep. And before you are emptied for sleep, what are you. And when you are emptied for sleep, you are not. And when you are filled with sleep, you never were . . . .
>
> How often have I lain beneath rain on a strange roof, thinking of home.[17]

The making of the coffin in rain and darkness for his mother's corpse, which Darl knows will start to rot because it has not been embalmed, undermines the surety of observing to the point at which the ego itself is in dissolution. Actions observed with exceptional clarity, a feature of most of Darl's narratives, have *less*, not greater, meaning for Darl as observer, because their context is absurd. The clue is already there in Tull's previous narrative section, where he claims, 'I have said and I say again, that's ever living thing the matter with Darl: he just thinks by himself too much.'[18] In the world of the absurd family, knowing is a form of transparency which becomes a deathwish. The world of the senses and the world of meaning hive apart. Darl's growing schizophrenia is echoed in the juxtaposed narratives of Cash and Vardaman which immediately follow, in Cash's factual inventory of the various stages involved in coffin-making and in Vardaman's confused and child-like metaphysic staring-out at the reader from a blank page, his puzzling, anguished claim that his mother is a fish.

Darl's epiphanous narrative repeats this sequence in most of the lengthier sections, moving progressively through the book from pictorial stasis to the vortex of dispersed energy. It thus progressively disintegrates the sense of the sense world it etches so clearly until, as in the wagon's disastrous crossing of the flooded river, nature itself seems totally unhinged. 'Above the ceaseless surface they stand – trees, canes, vines – rootless, severed from the earth, spectral above a scene of immense yet circumscribed desolation filled with the voice of the waste and mournful water.'[19] The alternation of fixity and turbulence is echoed too in the descriptions of Jewel and his horse, the contrast between the fixed and rigid posture of the rider on horseback and the scene of extreme violence where Jewel attacks the horse in the stable. The division reverberates as well through the other narratives. Those of Vardaman and Dewel Dell echo the process of dissolution, while those of Anse, Cash, Tull and Jewel restore the balance as naturalistic voices fiercely demotic, firmly rooted in the immediate world of the senses. Yet the division should not be seen as a harmonising force, a form of narrative balance. For the very actions of those who see harmoniously – because they do not see too much – create in Darl the turbulence which emanates from an excessive transparency of seeing. The practical absurdities of honouring his mother's wish to be buried in Jefferson, the overcoming of all the obstacles which lie in its path, give to the divided family a unifying but incongruous sense of honour which defies all rational judgement, and finally deprives Darl of his.

Like Caddy in *The Sound and the Fury*, Addie Bundren becomes the vacated centre of the novel, but this time literally. Her dying body lies in the bedroom through whose window Cash can be seen constructing her coffin. Thereafter her corpse in the coffin comes to have a hallucinatory presence. She is omnipresent in death and the metaphysical imaginations of Darl and Vardaman. That familiar sense of the ghostly presence of the recent dead, the unburied, is intensified by the uncanny device of placing Addie's sole narrative section – her reflections as she lies dying – at a point when she is already dead, just after her coffin has fallen off the capsizing wagon into the flooded river. Her narrative voice reveals her wish for burial in Jefferson, her original home, but also reveals how the wish is the outcome of deep domestic unhappiness. Not only does it give an edge to the family's difficult ordeal, undergone to satisfy her wishes. It also throws down a challenge to words themselves to give a meaning to her wasted life.

In Addie's narrative, absence involves both linguistic convention and social experience. It points to the sense of a life exhausted in failing to make the necessary connections between word and thing, signifier and signified. But the failure is not personal. The judgement is on the failure of adult life to satisfy any woman damned by marriage and unwanted pregnancy: 'When he was born I knew that motherhood was invented by someone who had to have a word for it because the ones that had the children didn't care whether there was a word for it or not.'[20] The absence of 'motherhood's' expected compassion, maternal love, is complemented by the absence of love in her marriage to the selfish and cynical Anse. Her narrative implies that 'love' is a word he uses without mutual meaning, as a synonym for his own desire: 'He had a word, too. Love, he called it. But I had been used to words for a long time. I knew that that word was like the others: just a shape to fill a lack; that when the right time came, you wouldn't need a word for that any more than for pride or fear.'[21]

In spite of its absurdity, perhaps at times through its absurdity, the burial journey fills in the void behind the words she utters poetically but without conviction – behind, that is, love and fear and pride. It gives renewed substance to all those things her dying voice has dissolved, so that by dying Addie induces all those things she could not induce in life. The plenitude is temporary, and it is too late. The pilgrimage turns out to be a minefield of disasters and tribulations which drive Darl mad, and enable him to see his train journey to the asylum at Jackson with the same transparent vision he has previously directed at other members of his family, narrating himself in the third person, jumping out of his own skin and turning back to look at his insane, laughing face, seeing himself finally as seen by others. 'Darl has gone to Jackson', Darl narrates. 'They put him on the train, laughing, down the long car laughing, the heads turning like the heads of owls when he passed.'[22] His voice becomes at the end the collective voice of the family he has distantly observed, now observing himself through their eyes, the absent other who mirrors the family void. 'Darl is our brother, our brother Darl. Our brother Darl in a cage in

Jackson where, his grimed hands lying light in the quiet interstices, looking out he foams. "Yes yes yes yes yes yes yes yes." '[23]

Inheriting his mother's absent selfhood, Darl takes it to the abyss while the rest of the family restores itself through the plenitude of pilgrimage, borne on by the grim, heroic absurdities of Jewel's fanaticism. By not inheriting, like Darl, his mother's scepticism, Jewel makes due expiation for the felt absences of her life. There is at the end, in a family where each individual has his or her own self-centred obsession, a reclamation of honour. The honour is flawed and provisional, a passing instant before the family is reconsolidated in emptiness by Anse's cynical resolve to find, at the journey's end in Jefferson, the second Mrs Bundren. But there is an expropriation of value none the less, an expropriation which only makes sense as that of the poor and the voiceless, of those beneath the level of middle-class respectability and public discourse. The expropriation is undoubtedly and deliberately eccentric, a snatching-back of the once ruling value of Southern society which is now in eclipse, and which therefore can be expressed in Faulkner's eyes only by those who do not rule. In that sense it is almost literally speechless, done in ways which have about them no overt consciousness of the genealogy of value at all. But it is something of which the Compson family, for example, would certainly no longer be capable.

The significance of the two family novels, in which Faulkner links interior monologue to the familiarity of encounter, is immense in the making of the twentieth-century novel. In a society where the family was traditionally honoured and traditionally associated with honour, Faulkner deconstructs the family in order to reconstruct realism as a literary form. The family gives to the epiphanous form that intensity of presence which comes from the recurrent nature of familiar encounter. But instead of solidarity he finds absence; instead of the nucleus of the nuclear family, he uncovers the extended family void. The the poor and oppressed he gives a provisional and heroic plenitude. But the privileged he casts, beyond all echo of compassion, into the hellfire of their internal damnation.

6 Faulkner II: Colours of Absence; Ubiquity of Desire

Faulkner lived in a society where colour was defined in absolute terms. The categories of black and white had been commandeered by one group of people for the explicit purpose of subjugating the other after slavery had been abolished. The segregation laws passed in most Southern states in the 1890s had deprived the heirs of the black slaves of their fragile and tenuous civil rights, spatially coralling them into limited sectors of civil society. In a society which by the 1920s was so uniformly oppressive, it was tempting for the white Southern artist to identify, as a rather different and more privileged victim, with the injustices of those who suffered from the brutal effects of segregation, a segregation accepted by that time as 'natural' by most whites. In discussing Faulkner, Ellison suggested that the white Southern writer was apt to associate any form of personal rebellion with the negro, who became a symbol not only of that rebellion but of the guilt and repression associated with it.[1]

In addressing himself to racial division, Faulkner's response according to Ellison was to dissolve the central distinction of white Southern stereotyping between the 'bad nigger', who is a potential rapist and murderer, and the 'good nigger', who is benign, complaint and deferential. Instead there is a different division in Faulkner's fiction, of deeper significance. This is the contrast between black characters such as Dilsey Gibson, Sam Fathers and Lucas Beauchamp, who emanate through impersonal narrative as figures of integrity, refusing to relinquish their selfhood or conforming to white stereotypes of what the negro should be, and those of mixed blood such as Joe Christmas and the mulatto chil-

111

dren of Thomas Sutpen, whose racial identity can never be firmly accepted or established at all. The protagonist of mixed parentage here moves to the foreground because he lacks the essential tie to the black community, whose internal life, away from their white masters, is in Faulkner's work a constant and deliberate absence.

Faulkner's narrative strategy here is to highlight the injustice of the fixed racial identities of white hegemony through the hypo- thetical absences of identity, through the raceless and selfless predicament of Joe Christmas, who can find no identity for himself at all. The injustice of categorisation is attacked not through didactic pleas for reform and false celebrations of hope, but by uncovering the absurdity of categorisation in action, by revealing the categories as metaphorical artefacts which are real in their consequences. In this respect Faulkner's critique of race is also a critique of Southern society. But that achievement in *Light in August* is foreshadowed by a deeper and more savage attack on Southern society in *Sanctuary*, where Faulkner achieves the extreme penetration of human evil through an impersonal and dehumanising narrative, which is then rehumanised in *Light in August* through the figures of Lena Grove and Joe Christmas. The achievement of *Light in August*, in fact, is inconceivable without the prior and still controversial example of *Sanctuary*.

The savagery of *Sanctuary* is so bleak, pitiless and impersonal that it continued to haunt Faulkner for much of his life, producing in the phase of his later artistic decline the rhetorical and guilt- ridden sequel *Requiem for a Nun*. At one level he felt the strong contrast to his previous novels, with their interior narrative and necessary echoes of compassion. In *Sanctuary* there was neither. Their absence impelled him to refer to his gangster novel as a 'cheap idea' written in order to make money. But these half-truths conceal a feature of the artistic predicament he had found himself in before he wrote *The Sound and the Fury*: how to avoid the unhappy marriage of Freudianism and bourgeois romanticism which had marred the pages of *Mosquitoes* and *Sartoris*. In the interior monologues of the Compsons and the Bundrens, Faulkner had used the familiarity of encounter in family life as the arena of intense, overlapping subjectivities. The technique assumed the ideological strength of the Southern family and the void within. But it would never enable him to renew in the epiphanous form the wider and societally more complex themes of *Sanctuary*, where he deals with the lateral cross-sections of society more familiar in Dickens, Balzac and Flaubert.

The model for *Sanctuary*, then, is not Joyce but Flaubert. It owes much in style and delineation of scope to *Madame Bovary*, to the style of an impersonal narrative written with a precise and dissecting exactitude and pitilessly depicting a provincial society. But the form of Faulkner's novel is more ambitious. Its cross-cutting montage contrasts not only the country and the city, but prosperous and poor, morality and crime, respectability and desire, and integrates them into a structure of feeling almost totally bereft of compassion and honour. The force of this savage departure from Faulkner's previous work can be seen by comparing the text with the original version, whose galley proofs Faulkner rewrote quite thoroughly and dramatically in 1930. He later cultivated the myth that the rewriting toned down the violence and extremity of the original, when in fact his real purpose was to etch them more clearly, to give them a more powerful and immediate resonance. The revisions were largely undertaken to depose the novel's Prufrockian hero, Horace Benbow, as its organising consciousness. The *Ur*-version used a Conradian narrative which thrust the major events back into the past and focused from the outset on its vacillating bourgeois hero, torn by guilt and desire, whose sensibility cushioned the impact of events which, as Faulkner well knew, had an intimidating savagery. He therefore tried through artistic compromise to vitiate the full force of the text and rewrote it when he realised what that compromise entailed.

In the first version of *Sanctuary*, Benbow, the lawyer, is reflective and distanced about the events which have occurred at Frenchman's Bend, more obsessed by the failure of his marriage and his quasi-incestuous attractions to sister and stepdaughter. But his consciousness is too weak to organise moral meaning, to suggest the residual honour of a concerned lawyer in a corrupt society. In deposing him from his artificial perch, Faulkner merely crystallised what was latent in his fictional conception, the total devaluation of honour in the public world of the contemporary South. The process of displacement is probably at its most ruthless in the transposition of Benbow's thoughts from reflective narrative into drunken dialogue. In the first *Sanctuary*, chapter 2 opens with Benbow's reflections on the sexual transgression of his stepdaughter, on the continuing tensions between his wife and sister. In the final version the latter is largely eliminated and the former is made the subject of a drunken confession by Benbow after he has left his wife and stumbled upon Popeye at the spring near Frenchmen's Bend. Back at the ruined plantation house, which has been turned into a bootleggers' den, his thoughts become confessions made incoherently to those of whom it is of no concern.

The transformation demonstrates the alienation effect which Faulkner achieved, the savage objectification of the weak, bourgeois hero. The first version begins,

At home, from his study window, he could see the grape arbor. Each spring he watched the reaffirmation of the old ferment, the green-snared promise of unease. What blossom the grape has in April and May, that is: that tortured waxlike bleeding less of bloom than leaf, until in the late twilight of spring Little Belle's voice would seem to be the murmur of the wild and waxing grape itself. She would never say 'Horace, this is Louis or Paul or whoever' but 'It's just Horace'. . . .[2]

Horace then goes on to remember the conversation in which he rebukes her for picking up boys on the train and bringing them home. She retaliates by mentioning the reason he later explains is the basis for his leaving home, the shrimp package he has to pick up from the train every Friday and bring home:

'But in the train, honey. If he'd walked into your room in a hotel, I'd just be enraged. But on the train, I'm disgusted. Let's send him along and start over again.'
'You're a fine one to talk about finding things on the train! You're a fine one! Shrimp! Shrimp!' Then she cried 'No! No!' flinging herself upon him in a myriad secret softnesses beneath firm young flesh and thin small bones. 'I didn't mean that! Horace! Horace!' And he could smell that delicate odor of dead flowers engendered by tears and scent, and in two mirrors he saw her secret, streaked small face watching the back of his head with pure dissimulation, forgetting that there were two mirrors.[3]

In order to radicalise Benbow's stifled consciousness of desire, and to give it social context, Faulkner has to dissolve its centripetal presence. Benbow's attack on Little Belle's boyfriends, which

barely conceals his own desire, echoes Quentin's imaginary
defences of Caddy on his last day at Harvard. In the final version
of *Sanctuary* he matches that radical absence by placing the sentiment as drunken confession in the bootleggers' den, where it
becomes the florid sensibility of a failed romantic confessed to
men who are barely literate and overheard by Ruby Lamarr, who
is eavesdropping on him from the other side of the door. The
alienation effect then wrenches the effete sensibility out of its
centred bourgeois context by a process of making strange in which
Benbow, surrounded by a people of a different class, becomes the
object rather then the subject of the text:

> She listened to him. 'From my window I could see the grape
> arbor, and in the winter I could see the hammock too. But in
> the winter it was just the hammock. That's why we know nature
> is a she; because of that conspiracy between female flesh and
> female season' . . . .

Ruby, still unnamed, is a filter for the reader's own consciousness as the overwrought images of nature and desire repeat themselves, 'the green snared promise of unease', 'a wild and waxlike
bleeding less of bloom than leaf'. We listen astonished with her
as Benbow vainly tries to explain the connection between the train
and the shrimp package and then ends with the convoluted image
of mirrored dissimulation:

> ' "You're a fine one to talk about finding things on the train!
> You're a fine one! Shrimp! Shrimp!" '
> 'He's crazy', the woman said motionless inside the door. The
> stranger's voice went on, tumbling over itself, rapid and diffuse.
> 'Then she was saying "No! No!" and me holding her and she
> clinging to me. "I didn't mean that! Horace, Horace!" And I was
> smelling the slain flowers, the delicate dead flowers and tears,
> and then I saw her face in the mirror. There was a mirror behind
> her and one behind me, and she was watching herself in the
> one behind me, forgetting about the other one in which I could
> see her face, see her watching the back of my head with pure
> dissimulation. That's why nature is "she" and Progress is "he";
> nature made the grape arbor, Progress invented the mirror.'
> 'He's crazy', the woman said inside the door, listening.[4]

Benbow's self-knowledge, cleverly achieved but romanticised and elaborate, becomes part of his pathology rather than its cure.

The image of the mirror is a pointer to Benbow's, and later Temple's, narcissism, and is echoed in the opening scene of the final version, the encounter of Benbow and Popeye at the spring. Not only did Faulkner take this scene out of chapter 2 to put it on the first page: he shows, in addition, each man from the other's point of view. This not merely equalises the lawyer and the gangster but also presents them as class doubles. Each sees the other as strange and inexplicable, Benbow carrying a book in the pocket where Popeye suspects a gun, since that is where he would carry a gun himself. But, in between the contrasting descriptions, Benbow sees the shattered reflection of Popeye's straw hat in the pool where he has just seen his own face. The meeting sets up the theme of doubling and complicity. As the lawyer later to defend Lee Goodwin against a false murder charge, Benbow has been to the scene of the crime before it takes place and met the actual murderer before he murders. The link is cemented when Tommy incessantly reiterates Popeye's hatred of the wilderness at Frenchman's Bend: 'I be dog if he ain't skeered of his own shadow.' To which Benbow replies, 'I'd be sacred of it too . . . If his shadow was mine.'[5]

But the central focus of doubling lies in parallel desire. Only later does Benbow find out that Temple was at the house when Tommy was murdered, then abducted to Memphis by Popeye. His horror of the events, after he has visited Temple in her willing captivity at Miss Reba's brothel, is understandable. Conscience, however, cannot subjugate desire. His wish to remove injustice from the face of the earth by liquidating all of them, perpetrators and victims alike, is linked to an even deeper desire he discovers on the journey home from Memphis. He glimpses a couple making love in the dark: 'In the alley-mouth two figures stood, face to face, not touching; the man speaking in a low tone unprintable epithet after epithet in a caressing whisper, the woman motionless before him as though in musing swoon of voluptuous ecstasy'.[6]

The sudden sight of the couple brings back to him what he is already trying to repress. He wishes for the annihilation of all the players in a tragic game because he himself has vicariously taken part, and if they remain, especially Temple, he cannot trust himself to be restrained. When he reaches home he sees the photograph of Little Belle, which gives way suddenly to images of Temple as he rushes to the toilet and climaxes, enacting out in fantasy his own version of the violation Popeye has perpetrated in the flesh. The hallucination, however, is narcissistic. He is both Temple's violator and Temple herself, penetrating the body he then fantasises androgynously as his own, the predator of erotic beauty and yet the incarnation of that savaged beauty itself. Benbow is horrified by Popeye's crime, yet his fantasies have gone the same route. At an even deeper level, too, Popeye's impotence, which results in the use of the corn cob and of Red as a surrogate stud, is Benbow's own. He can desire everyone and love no one.

The final version then gives both an individual and a social pattern to doubling and desire. Popeye and Benbow are class enemies both desiring the judge's daughter, while Goodwin and Benbow are class opposites who see a rather different sort of woman in Ruby Lamarr. By the end of the book Benbow has failed to take the opportunity which Goodwin has already seized before its beginning, of shacking up with a poor ex-prostitute turned domestic slave. In place of the vapid Freudian solecisms which are a hangover from *Sartoris*, Faulkner turns Benbow into an object of pathology in the wider context of class hostility and social injustice. There is no longer a cushioning voice of moderation, for there is no passing reflection of Benbow's which is not immediately replete with the irony of its own fragility and self-delusion.

The narrative form which Faulkner struggled to create was one which would allow the doubling-effect to work equally at the level of style. In his voyeurism and narcissism, Benbow is not only Popeye's double but also the reader's double, since the reader experiences through both the sudden polished surfaces of erotic sensation, shorn of depth or judgement. But the reader also finds in the narrative pattern a parallel bewilderment to that of the effete lawyer, a sense of delayed recognition born out of initial incomprehension. Faulkner finally dispensed with the Conradian narrative of flashback and reversed sequence in the first version of *Sanctuary* for straight chronology in largely impersonal narrative. Yet the narrative is anything but omniscient. The absences of knowledge through which Conrad obliquely backtracks are conveyed here instead by the techniques of montage.[7] Faulkner 'cuts' from chapter to chapter rather like a film-director cutting between scenes, but then using the process to forge a synthetic meaning. At times the chapter scenes involve baffling narrative leaps, gaps in narration which leave the reader, like Benbow himself, in a state of baffled suspense. Scenes with an intense pictorial immediacy come to have a fuller meaning later through juxtaposition, which is itself a kind of thematic doubling.

The text has numerous examples. Gowan Stevens and Temple Drake make the same journey out to Frenchman's Bend as Benbow and repeat in part the same encounters. The hilariously innocent trip of the country cousins Alonso and Virgil to Miss Reba's brothel in Memphis mirrors the earlier and horrifying abduction of Temple by Popeye as she continues to haemorrhage in the car. The injustice of the trial in which Goodwin is convicted of the murder Popeye committed is mirrored in the injustice of the trial in which Popeye is falsely convicted of a different murder. The story which doubles Benbow and Popeye, Popeye and Goodwin, Temple and Ruby, Benbow and Gowan Stevens is written in the doubling-style of montage. Such a technique adduces from the reader a prolonged uncertainty, a delayed recognition.

Though the doubling has a two-dimensional effect, it works because Faulkner does differentiate his characters with a high degree of social accuracy in observation and varying nuances of dialect. Doubling proceeds not from initial likeness, but rather the other way around. It proceeds to likeness through and in spite of the very fact of difference. In this context montage is highly appropriate to the epiphanous form. It provokes a delayed shock reaction to the theme of an evil which passes all understanding and a crime which nearly passes all detection. Its systematic elimination of motive on the margins of human pathology gives the novel the uncanny coherence of a relentless artistic purity. The reasons for this absence of conventional explanation of motive have to be seen in the context of the history of American realism. As Sundquist has pointed out, the closeness of *Sanctuary* to the new genre of hard-boiled detective story is linked to a wider literary impulse to escape from the complex naturalistic machinery prevalent in the works of Dreiser and Norris.[8] In Dreiser especially, there is an attempt to integrate a naturalistic theory of the determining fate of an urban capitalist environment into an evolutionary narrative of individual nemesis, of which *Sister Carrie* is the most perfect example. But, though absence of motive in Hammett, Hemingway and Cain oftens gives to the distinctively masculine hero a certain moral autonomy, Faulkner's baffled lawyer is already feminised and decentred, neither master nor victim of circumstance. A survivor by virtue of his privileged social class, he manages to come apart at the seams without actually going to pieces. Faulkner gives us a hard-boiled story without a hard-boiled hero – that is to say, without the recuperative power of masculine heroism which produced and thrived on its own ideology of the active and autonomous masculine will.

Faulkner then relegates heroism to the passive postures of Lee Goodwin scared in jail of the bullet from Popeye's gun which might find its way through the barred window, and of Ruby Lamarr nursing her weak and sickly child, a pariah among the respectable citizens of Jefferson. Lee and Lamarr, heroic Confederate names, symbolise the residue of honour beneath postures of extreme lassitude, the honour Faulkner bestows on the poor and the victimised when their unjust plight leaves them bereft of speech. Here the contours of class division are razor-sharp and savage. Tommy, Goodwin, Lamarr and finally Popeye all become victims, but Temple is rescued and finally returned to the fold, while Benbow is rescued from the gasoline mob who have burned Goodwin alive. The outrageous Senator Snopes gets his substantial bribe and District Attorney Grahame his big conviction. It then becomes clear that villainy, as opposed to heroism, operates at dual class levels, antagonistic yet also complementary.

It was not enough for Faulkner simply to invest Popeye with all the attributes of evil, alerting the reader to them largely at the level of appearance. The 'queer, bloodless face', the 'rubber knobs' for eyes that have 'the whorled smudge of a thumb on them',[9] the pinched figure with the 'vicious depthless quality of stamped tin' represent the emanation of evil at the level of sense experience, which Faulkner's writing then reduces rigorously to the level of pure sensation. But beneath appearance are the bloody deeds, the murders of Tommy and Red, the rape of Temple, whose nature is delayed in its recognition by the technique of montage. Beyond that, behind the narrator's frail omniscience, is the hidden conspiracy to pervert justice, a conspiracy which is seen only in fleeting glimpses and which the reader, like Benbow, can only piece together when it is too late and never conclusively know. Grahame, Snopes and the prosecuting Memphis lawyer are as evil in their chicanery as Popeye through his brutality. The link between the dual levels of evil, the one overt and proletarian, the other cryptic and bourgeois, is Temple Drake. Actively and consecutively she complies in both, collaborating with the second in order to extricate herself from the first, and to be led in pyrrhic triumph from the courtroom by her respected father. Benbow, the decentred lawyer, then discovers that he has made the wrong voyage of discovery. He realises that he has learnt too much about the evil of his class enemies only to discover that he does not know enough about the evil of his own kind.

Popeye's evil has a resonance beyond appearance which is none the less predicated on it. The visual quality of the novel, at times comparable to the synaesthesia of *Nightwood* and *The Sound and the Fury*, projects in its multiplying similes of staring eyes the notion that the figures of its narrative are actually staring back at the reader of the text. But even this is outrivalled by the evocation of colour in physical description. Because of Popeye's black, tight-waisted suit, Temple frequently refers to him as 'that black man'. His face is said to have 'a dead, dark pallor', and in the brothel at Memphis Temple confesses to Benbow that she has imagined herself as a middle-aged schoolteacher rebuking Popeye as a tiny negro child. Lee Goodwin is also described in court as having 'a black head and a gaunt brown face'.[10] As gangster and bootleggers, Popeye and the inhabitants of the Old Frenchman place would be seen by the respectable bourgeois of Jefferson as 'white trash'. But Faulkner's visual images of evil are also surrogate images of race.

The context for this remarkable doubling of colour is the Old Frenchman place itself, 'a gutted ruin rising gaunt and stark out of a grove of unpruned cedar trees', its 'cottonfields and gardens and lawns long since gone back to jungle'.[11] As a city gangster, Popeye is scared of its undergrowth and its animal inhabitants. But, as Tommy recounts the foibles of his city boss to Benbow with a mixture of awe and derision, something deeper is hinted at: 'I be a dog if he ain't the skeeriest durn *white* man I ever see.'[12] The italicised *white* jars the reader into realising that he is already conceiving Popeye subliminally as black, the black overseer of a ruined and masterless plantation house surrounded by a jungle like 'a lake of ink'. The white bootleggers are both white trash and the phantoms of black plantation slaves who once inhabited the jungle of the ruin in its brief reign of ante-bellum glory.

This ghostly invocation prepares the way later for the climactic visit of Quentin and Rosa Coldfield in *Absalom, Absalom!* to the ruin of Sutpen's Hundred, where the figure of Henry Sutpen is still cowering, shadowed by the howling mulatto figure of Jim Bond. In *Sanctuary*, of course, the echoes of the past have a less pronounced resonance. For its events to be credible in a segregated society, Popeye and Goodwin are white proletarians, since it is their whiteness which permits them their dubious, symbiotic contacts with Benbow, Gowan Stevens and Temple Drake. But, after Temple has perjured herself and incriminated Goodwin, there is added, in the final version of the text, a further imprint of blackness. Goodwin is burned alive in gasoline by an angry mob, a fate more redolent of a convicted black, and echoing that of the wrongly accused negro, Will Mayes, in 'Dry September', which in many ways it parallels. The social difference between violator and violated evokes not only class but also race. The epiphanous form from which blacks are figuratively absent evokes consistently this mirage of double seeing. Goodwin's death is an imprint of a deeper racial injustice which Faulkner often felt he could not explore except in passing, because he felt speechless before its immensity. His technique here has the same intensity of the soundless stutter on the lips of the falsely accused Billy Budd before he strikes Claggart dead. Though Popeye and Goodwin are not black, *it is as if they were*. In reading and rereading the text, their faces seem to flash into photographic negative before reverting to normal monochrome.

Blackness here becomes a destination of what is formally absent but present by default, what can be alluded to, pictured and evoked but never actually named. Yet the extended metaphor of absence is not an isolated conceit. The colours of absence meld and fuse with the ubiquity of desire. The incarnation of Popeye as Benbow's double contains within it his oscillating and metaphorical blackness. Both desire Temple, and Benbow's own desire is catalysed by Temple's evasive description of her violation by the man whose reflection has already shattered his own on the surface of the spring. Temple's desire is the focus for male doubling, but her desire for desire has a radical promiscuity founded on the alchemy of danger and vanity, and this can only be referred back to a deliberate transgression of the conventions of her class. Her 'grimace of taut, toothed coquetry'[13] is a catalyst to deeds she both craves and fears, that strange cyclical sociometry of terror and desire at the Old Frenchman place, where, stricken with fear, her vanity will not be assuaged until all men there have finally desired her. Both Van, who openly wants to rape her and beats up Gowan to better his chances, and even Goodwin and Tommy, who try to prevent Van from raping her, end up trapped themselves in the contagions of desire, to which Popeye, lurking distantly, has himself also submitted and to which end he proves himself willing to kill in cold blood.

Temple then represents the centring of desire through her desire to be totally and ubiquitously desired. All the men who know her become prey to her as she in turn becomes prey to them, as they constantly reverse the roles of hunted and hunted. Above all, she provokes desire narcissistically in order to respond to her successful provocation. In giving herself to what she has provoked she gives herself to herself. Desire is then evoked, in a social context, as a Hobbesian transaction, a dehumanising consequence of class relationships at every symbiotic level and, at a more subliminal level, of the relationships of race. Even at the end, the linking of Benbow to Goodwin in the mind of the mob is made through Temple, an extension of the guilt by association which already exists in Benbow himself. But their false attribution of guilt derives from the reputation of the beauty of the violated Belle they wish to avenge, since by implication they desire her too:

> 'Here's the man that defended him. That tried to get him clear.'
> 'Put him in, too. There's enough left to kill a lawyer.'
> 'Do to the lawyer what we did to him. What he did to her.'[14]

The doubling is thus extended in the mutual narcissism of Benbow and Temple, but their respective gender roles produce completely opposed consequences. Both revel in the duplicating and reduplicating of the love object, but, whereas Benbow secretly desires what he cannot force himself openly to try and possess, Temple tries openly to provoke the desire which will provoke her own. But in the end Popeye's sexual failure cuts deeper than the lawyer's. Benbow can always take refuge in masturbation as the source of duplicating fantasies, but Popeye, physically impotent and finally failing to keep possession of Temple, senses his own doom. The absence of motive in the final scene, where he submits as fatalistically to the injustice of his imprisonment and conviction, places the onus on the reader to fill in that absent motivation by reconsidering the story along with all its strategic absences, so that the unanswered questions – what happens to Temple after Red's murder? what deal does Popeye's lawyer strike with the corrupt prosecutors of the innocent Lee? – have to be answered by the reader's own conjectures, conjectures which can never be arbitrary but which must fit into the coherent frame which Faulkner has created around them.

This procedure, which is a feature of the montage style, also throws into relief the chapter which Faulkner saw fit to add to the final version about Popeye's deprived childhood. At one fell stroke, in the space of five pages, it adds everything and nothing. Socially and psychologically, it makes his propensity for evil partly credible, but appears in narrative form as a mere afterthought, an addition which confirms in its sparse accuracy the intimation of a fundamental emptiness. It does not so much explain evil as explain its lack of explanation, taking 'explanation' to the very point at which it appears powerless, if not redundant. There is thus an ironic play upon the nature of Popeye's deprivation in which he is deprived not only of manhood but also of that plenitude of personality within which motive signifies. Popeye's lack of family, postulated on the rootlessness of transient encounter, suggests reflexively that the traditional forces of determination can no longer be mustered. What determines by default is the absence of any substance to determine. By giving the illusion in the final version that he is finally revealing what has hitherto been withheld – an illusion, since the chapter was never in the first version anyway – Faulkner also reveals that nothing in that sense can be revealed at all. Spiralling like the Compsons down the family void, Popeye lacks even the substance of their experience of loss. In the colours of his absence he remains a volatile imprint on the eye, an imprint that will continue to reappear as constantly as it vanishes.

II

If *The Sound and the Fury* was a challenge to the solidity of the Southern family, *Light in August* throws into question the solidity of the white Southern community. Historically in the children of black servants and white masters, culturally in the pages of the Southern romance, its central trauma was that of miscegenation. The hero of *Light in August* embodies that trauma more powerfully than any of Faulkner's fictional creations. Joe Christmas is an orphan of mixed blood whose ambiguous racial identity threatens the received stereotypes of a segregated society. His pigmentation, the colour of 'parchment', removes him from the fixed recognitions of race and pushes him into the arena of 'passing' where he alternates between feeling himself to be an invisible negro in a white man's world and feeling himself a white man with the invisible taint of coloured blood. In this, superficially speaking the most Dickensian of Faulkner's novels, family for Christmas is an artefact, the unreal torment of a puritanical upbringing under the Calvinistic McEacherns. Yet the community is an even greater artefact. Instead of juxtaposing Christmas against the hostile community, *Light in August* is a set of overlapping stories of isolated individuals all of whom are in some respect absented from society. The life of Christmas is preceded by the stories of Lena Grove, Byron Bunch and Gail Hightower. It is superseded by those of Doc and Mrs Hines and Percy Grimm. Each character's story is constituted separately, not organically, so that instead of one consensual narrative there are several fragmented narratives, instead of a unified field of meaning the spasmodic use of narrators within the story who are strategically juxtaposed against the impersonal narrative itself.

The mode of narration is the most conventional of all the major novels, a third-person narrative which re-creates the viewpoint of the individual protagonist within the framework of authorial description. But it is in no sense classic, since Faulkner switches continually between past and present tenses, and it is no way consensual, since the novel is a series of overlapping stories, in which characters themselves become narrators and in which the 'community' of townspeople, recounting the exploits of Christmas, comes to have its own anonymous narrative voice. The fictional narrators, the tale-tellers within the tale, are generally the ones who disperse the reality of Christmas's tragic life into racial myth. All of them, and particularly Hightower, strive for a closure of meaning, but all the attempts eventually rebound as a series of rationalisations over which there constantly hang a series of unanswered questions.

Faulkner encloses the epiphanous form within a series of layered narratives, and when it emerges most fully, in the story of Joe Christmas, it reads as an abrupt departure into an intense and irrevocable tragedy of false recognition. Others who share his separateness echo it, but have individual fates which are recuperable. Christmas does not. The orphan cannot make good in a hostile society by striving to find his own forms of acceptance and compassion, because at the back of his lost identity lies the trauma of mixed blood. Without the shadow of race, desire would have been a series of transient encounters in Christmas's life ensuring his sexual survival. But in meeting Joanna Burden, for whom he has such an extraordinary importance, desire becomes the source of a tragic bitterness. The murder of his mistress transports him back into the realms of racial mythology as the brutal black murderer of a pure white woman.

The theme of doubling which pervades *Sanctuary* is sustained less overtly. Not only is Byron Bunch mistaken for Lucas Burch; Burch is in turn mistaken for Christmas as Joanna Burden's murderer. When Lena Grove's baby is delivered by Hightower, she mistakes Burch's alias, Joe Brown, for Joe Christmas, falsely identifying the father through a slip of the tongue, while Christmas's grandmother falsely identifies the child with her illegitimate grandson, Christmas himself. The doubling-strategy is made clearest at the beginning of chapter 2. The reader is made to anticipate a description of Burch, the disappearing father, when Bunch describes the arrival of a complete stranger at the planing-mill in Jefferson, which appears to provide the missing piece of the jigsaw in Lena's search for the father of her child. But the stranger Bunch describes turns out to be Christmas instead. The puritanical Bunch, who appears to be describing his hedonistic *alter ego*, Burch, describes instead the parchment shadow which is the double of both of them. The Bunch–Burch–Christmas relationship echoes the mirrored doubling Benbow–Goodwin–Popeye in *Sanctuary*, but balances with the lighter, comic aspect of mistaken identities the deeper trauma of race.

Absence rather then alienation seems the keynote of Christmas's predicament, because there is no *prima facie* evidence of a community from which he has been estranged. 'He did not look like the professional hobo in his professional rags, but there was something definitely rootless about him, as though no town, no city was his, no street, no walls, no square of earth his home.'[15] The plight of absence is intensified by the whole paradox of passing, in which the question of race is never instantly invoked by the glance of the eye but is raised by a deeper half-truth, the proclaimed knowledge of genealogy. It is no accident that Christmas's brutal executioner is the Nazified Percy Grimm, for Joe in passing as white can be compared to those German Jews who could pass for Aryan but were for that reason hysterically rooted out by the Nazis in pursuit of a racially 'pure' society. Genealogy perpetrates the mythic division of appearance and reality, in which Christmas is stereotyped as not being what he seems, as if he is personally responsible for the failure of others to realise the truth, which is mainly rumour and hearsay. He in turn is forced by degrees to internalise the false division between appearance and reality until it dismembers his own identity and he no longer knows for sure either who he is or where he has come from, so that years later he returns to his town of origin without realising at first that that is where his wanderings have led him.

As a youth, Christmas experiences a wider conflict than that of race but one which the confusions of racial identity draw into the arena of disaster. His meeting with Bobbie Allen, the prostitute in the town diner, occurs by chance. His attraction to her is part of his rebellion against his authoritarian foster father. But the Dickensian attempt at compassion occurs for this parentless child in non-Dickensian circumstances. In his determination to take away Bobbie and marry her we see the double humanisation of male and female, self and other. But in Faulkner there is a harshness, almost an aridity, in the encounter which defies all sentimentality. The harshness is a quality of environment which is all-pervasive in its contrariness. Christmas can escape neither from the Southern rural society which produces among the God-fearing a fanatical repression of sexuality, nor from the corrupt modernising influences of the city which expand prostitution as a way of life. He experiences the contradiction at its fullest because he has no place in either of these habitats, nor the power to break them. When he strikes down McEachern at the dance, he merely destroys the delicate balance between them, the conspiracy of silence which is broken when McEachern calls Bobbie a 'harlot'.

It is thus an irony that Christmas, even after he thinks he has killed his foster father for the insult, cannot see the depth of Bobbie's resistance to him. Nor is he to know that, when he rides back to town after her on horseback, her animosity will make public the secret doubts he has confessed to her about his mixed blood. The hysteria expressed in her cry 'Bastard! Son of a bitch! Getting me into a jam, that always treated you like you were a white man. A white man!'[16] is destined to follow him right through to the moment of castration and death. He hears the men echo the question of his colour as he lies on the floor, beaten and semi-conscious. But the point has been made. Bobbie Allen has no heart of gold and her hatred sets the racial myth in motion. When he later leaves the town alone to lead a life of drifting, to walk 'a thousand savage and lonely streets', he takes prostitutes at their face value, as the means of paying for the satisfaction of desire. Having failed to prise a waitress prostitute from her style of life through first love, he gives up the idea of love and spends his time instead with prostitutes, white Northern women who do not mind his mixed blood and black ones whose colour shows its true darkness next to his light skin. Escaping into a shiftless freedom for fifteen years, and thus escaping retribution for McEachern's murder, he lives in a world of absence and spasmodic desire. Love and compassion are irrevocably behind him.

When he returns to Mississippi and comes back, unwittingly, to Jefferson, the circle of youth and maturity is almost closed. When he meets Joanna Burden, the lone descendant of New England abolitionists ostracised by the town, his fate is reawakened by a theology of terror which strangles its supposed compassion. In her attraction to Joe as part-negro, the solitary and frustrated woman who is detested as a 'nigger-lover' revives the nightmare of Calvinism and desire which Joe had fled fifteen years previously. But in Burden the contradiction he could not resolve and which had aborted his first love has been grotesquely overcome. Burden's personality strangely unites the two extremes in one body without ever dissolving the polarity. Christmas is shocked by 'the abject fury of the New England glacier exposed suddenly to the fire of the New England biblical hell'. Burden embraces the obscenities of desire 'to attempt to compensate each night as if she believed that it would be the last night on earth', and as if desire 'would damn her forever to the hell of her forefathers'.[17] Christmas watches 'the two creatures that struggled in the one body like two moongleamed shapes struggling drowning in alternate throes upon the surface of a thick black pool beneath the last moon'.[18]

Burden's divided self echoes earlier Faulknerian images of the double, but goes deeper to resurrect the extreme Calvinist polarities of James Hogg. While Darl and Jewel Bundren, sons of the same mother by different fathers, one of them a priest, echo the uncanny relationship of George Colwan and Robert Wringham, Joanna Burden comes closest among all Faulkner's characters to the demonic possession of Wringham himself. Yet, while Hogg's concern is with moral absolutes, Faulkner's concern is with the secular relationships between murder, morality and desire. For

Christmas, the trauma of murder is never far away. He has to confront again the spectre of Calvinism, which he has *never* internalised but which continues to haunt him through the medium of desire, along with the other nightmare, which he *has* internalised and which equally haunts him through the medium of desire – the spectre of race. Just as Joanna fuses two opposing creatures in one body, that very fusion also fuses Joe's two recurring nightmares. The consequences are fatal. Having 'killed off', in part by chance, the Calvinism of his surrogate father, Joe deliberately murders the Calvinism of his schizophrenic mistress.

The affair with Burden is the culmination of Joe's whole life, in which absence has moulded the genealogy of desire. In the first traumatic instance – when as a child in an orphanage he hid to eat the toothpaste and was an involuntary witness to the copulation between the intern and the dietician – he could not understand the stigma of wrongdoing because he did not understand the act. He was as much a voyeur as he was a nigger – namely, neither. But the distraught dietician deemed him both together, setting up the future associations which occurred and reoccurred as nightmare in his later life. Desire in the first instance came to symbolise the absence of compassion, the lack of affection in the act, the hostility directed towards the reluctant and uncomprehending witness. Later with Bobbie Allen, he was finally unable to translate desire into love or compassion, for his embryonic passion was aborted by circumstance. Thereafter desire accorded with the rootlessness of his own life, a series of acts which no longer expected love or compassion, and were willingly committed in their absence. In retrospect all compassion has come to seem a false solution, the act of bad faith which Mrs McEachern committed every time she conspiratorially tried to soften the worst aspects of her husband's methodical tyranny. When Joanna Burden eventually offers Joe compassion in a new form, which opens up rather than closes off the nightmare of colour, it is more than he can bear.

In a sense Joe has already failed as a love object of Joanna Burden. Despite the racial titillations of desire which he offers and satisfies, he cannot enable her to supersede her divided self, the day-time self of cold austerity, the night-time self of wild desire. Rather he is the catalyst to the division, precipitating the latent into the actual. Though Joanna goes through the imagined jealousies of the incensed lover, there remains in the demonic division of self a voiding of all love and genuine compassion. Instead of making compassion personal, she tries to make it institutional, wanting Joe to be her assistant in the business affairs she conducts with negro schools, wanting him to act as go-between in the stage management of false compassion. His refusal and her reaction to it show the ultimate absence of connection, of true contact between them: 'He tried to argue with her. But it was like trying to argue with a tree; she did not even rouse herself to deny, she just listened quietly and then talked again in that level, cold tone as if he had never spoken.'[19]

What is 'remote and fanatic' is the abstract formulation of compassion, which results, through a supreme stroke of irony, in dehumanising Christmas altogether. The mission Joanna offers him is to minister unto those with whom he feels affinity but with whom his light skin denies visible likeness. It is an unintended insult but deeply insensitive, merely confirming the deep pain of his voided identity by embroiling compassion in a nightmare of repetition. To make public his secret confession to her would be the ultimate act of humiliation, of deference to an inhuman fanaticism for humanity. Though he does not yet fully know it, the impulse is growing in Christmas to murder his lover.

Sundquist has suggested that, in the light of racial stereotyping, the effect of the novel is to make Christmas a figure rather than a person.[20] He is, in the final analysis, how he is defined. This becomes apparent when the metaphor of the photographic negative suggested by Popeye in *Sanctuary* becomes actual in *Light in August* on the night of Joe's return from the town to murder Joanna. When he darts naked into the full glare of the headlights of an oncoming car, his body grows white out of the darkness like a photographic print emerging from the liquid. Then he proceeds to taunt the car's white occupants with the exposure of his 'black' nakedness, deliberately attempting to realise their worst fears. But he is never totally a mere figure, a projection, a self-fulfilling prophecy of racial guilt and fear. In flight and torment, as in murder, he is, like Bigger Thomas in *Native Son*, a definitive presence, human, all too human. Despite configuration of other stories of other characters, the epiphanous force of the narrative centres around Christmas, around his recurrent and inescapable tragedies of absence and desire. As the epiphanous style forces the essence of his humanity out of the repeating cycle of his transgressions, Faulkner makes him a person beneath the figure he becomes, and this is what makes him a more enduring artistic creation than Popeye, who is little more than a pictorial figure of evil. Without ever being completely evil, Christmas becomes evil in spite of his potential goodness, and does so because he has been dehumanised in spite of his humanity.

The transition from person to figure is a gradual process, a movement in the story which radically distances us from Christmas, after his arrest in Mottstown, by narrative overloading. The Joe Christmas we have come to know intimately is made almost to disappear before our eyes. From chapter 15 onward we are into the story of Doc Hines and back to the overlapping stories of Lena Grove, Hightower and Joe Brown, all linked, sometimes gratuitously, through the movements of Byron Bunch. At this point Christmas gradually turns into a figment of the collective imagination of the community, figuring as an exceptional villain in a kind of instant folk-lore which is beginning to be invented even before he dies. The distancing is at first sight a disappointment, a dilution of the narrative's force, of the compulsion which the reader previously felt in following Joe's fate through to the moment of arrest. But this is neither creative exhaustion nor a failure of nerve on the author's part. For Christmas mythologised is Christmas dehumanised, dehumanised this time through notoriety when previously he had been dehumanised through anonymity. Faulkner shows us how he comes to have the wrong name after having had no name at all. He is thus a living legend cast in the mould of other people's fears and wishes rather than his own, a person once in pain and flight but now a figure congealed in legend and fantasy.

The irony lies in the act of reading. As his reputation grows in the story, his presence dwindles in the text, almost to the point of insignificance. This is not only a means of denying the reader a premature idealisation of the novel's hero, but its more pitiless obverse, a dissection of the social process by which the essence of his tragic heroism, too explosive for public consumption, has to be extinguished from public knowledge. He becomes in legend the cut-throat black murderer and rapist of a pure white woman, a murderer who gets uppity and tries to escape but finally turns 'nigger' and gives himself in without a fight. Thus the reader's view of Christmas from the inside is made to clash dramatically with the subsequent judgement upon him of the white community. And the community which is itself fragile and divisive, as the various stories of Lena, Brown, Burden and High-tower have shown, finds a precarious unity in banding together to extinguish through notoriety the very figure whose racial ambi-guity threatens to expose its own weakness, and possibly its fundamental emptiness.

Two contrasting passages exemplify the loss of Joe's humanity when his figure still remains central to the story. In the first we see the link between the social and psychic levels of absence, the dramatic movement through the black and white sections of the town, in which he oscillates between the two colours which constantly elude him – the tragic prelude to a tragic murder. The second is the explanation for his final surrender given by lawyer Gavin Stevens, later to cast a blight over much of Faulkner's fiction and crudely to flaw *Intruder in the Dust* with his unacknowledged racist rhetoric. Steven's single intervention in this novel presents a succinct yet false closure of public opinion which appears at first sight to be decisive but whose dubious pedigree casts into doubt the whole nature of community. First the electrifying epiphany of flight toward disaster:

> Then he found himself . . . and before he knew it he was in Freedom Town, surrounded by the summer smell and the summer voices of invisible negroes. They seemed to enclose him like bodiless voices murmuring, talking, laughing, in a language not his. As from the bottom of a thick black pit he saw himself enclosed by cabinshapes, vague, kerosenelit, so that the street lamps themselves seemed to be further spaced, as if the black life, the black breathing had compounded the substance of breath so that not only voices but moving bodies and light itself must become fluid and accrete slowly from particle to particle, of and with the now ponderable night inseparable and one.[21]

Joe is among blacks but not of them, feeling as fluid sensation the elective affinity of the distant figures and his own light-skinned body, feeling the movement inward from the outside as an almost religious experience.

But, as he moves back into the prosperous white section, a different feeling seizes him. He desires to belong to the race of which he no longer feels himself a part, desires the label pinned upon him without equivocation:

There were people on the porches too, and in chairs upon the lawns; but he could walk quiet here. Now and then he could see them: heads in silhouette, a white blurred garmented shape; on a lighted veranda four people sat about a card table, the white faces intent and sharp in the low light, the bare arms of the women glaring smooth and white above the trivial cards. 'That's all I wanted', he thought. 'That don't seem like a whole lot to ask.'[22]

The nocturnal sensation of opposites, black and white, briefly projects outwards a division which has already been internalised as the two poles between which his still unformed self is fated to bounce back and forth in perpetuity. Feeling incestuously close to the black life he rejects, he feels equally distant from the white life he wants, which he craves with a certainty he knows he can never have.

In the judgement of Stevens upon the dead, castrated Christmas the polarity of the tragically divided self is congealed into false metaphors of blood, of opposing forces which have a biological fixity. Stevens's mannered contrast appears to complement Joe's own feeling of division, but it is in fact the opposite. It suggests that Christmas is the servant of two masters when we already know that he is unable to attach himself to either. The terrible freedom of the hero's void is replaced in Stevens's explanation by a mythic dualism of biological fate. As the lawyer tries to explain why Joe failed to kill Hightower before he was murdered by Grimm, we have a brilliant example of the racist mythologising of racial difference:

> Because the black blood drove him first to the negro cabin. And then the white blood drove him out of there, as it was the black blood which snatched up the pistol and the white blood which would not let him fire it. And it was the white blood which sent him to the minister. . . . It was the black blood which swept him by his own desire beyond the aid of any man.[23]

Two things challenge the false closure of Stevens's judgement. The first is the barbaric act of Grimm in castrating Christmas after he has shot him, raising the question of who is the real monster the community has allowed to run amok. The second is in the failure of Christmas's fate to have any power of healing. The narrative appears to move toward sentimentality with the delivery of Lena's baby and Bunch falling in love, but then draws back. Hightower can learn nothing from the brutal murder of the man who nearly killed him, because he is still fixated on the past, on the phantoms of his family's life and the glory of his grandfather's death, trying to resurrect honour through 'the wild bugles and the clashing sabres and the dying thunder of hooves', when the age of lynching has ground it into the dust. Lena is still fixated on Burch, the biological father of her child, while ignoring the devotion of Bryon, who travels with her loyally in her quest to find him. Burch continues to run from her. The pattern of a dispersed, decentred life continues. The tragic fate of Christmas has provided it with a false and fleeting unity.

Without doubt, Joe Christmas emerges in this novel as the major lower-class figure of Faulknerian tragedy. Including even Thomas Sutpen, he is the most tragic figure that Faulkner ever created, combining what had germinated in the previous writing, in contrasting ways, into a single and unified being. He has the figural presence of Popeye Vitelli, the lacerating and self-lacerating percipience of Darl Bundren, the pitiless victimisation which besets Lee Goodwin. The previous demotic figures are fused and deepened in the figure of a working-class hero who fights a losing battle to retain his own humanity. But it is not just that. Unlike the other working-class figures of Faulkner's fiction, Christmas has no trace of a community to which he belongs, no possibility of a shared fate, and, on the bitter landscape of a Jim Crow South, no accepted race. He is thus the peripheral figure of a peripheral landscape, the embodiment of living tragedy at its furthest margin. And that margin, for Christmas, is the point of no return.

7   Faulkner III: Abstraction

The gap between figure and person, history and myth, accrues a deeper dimension in Faulkner's historical novel *Absalom, Absalom!* In *Light in August* Faulkner came to terms with the Jim Crow South of his own lifetime.[1] The later novel is his attempt to come to terms with the history of the Old South. Yet Faulkner does two highly unexpected things. First, he sets the novel in the inter-mediate past of 1909, when Quentin Compson, along with his father, Rosa Coldfield and Shreve, his room mate at Harvard, all take turns at narrating events which span the years between 1817 and 1870 and end, dramatically, in the December of the year of narration. Second, the demonic hero of Faulkner's story, Thomas Sutpen, does not embody the idea of honour which had been part of the prevalent ruling-class ideology of the Old South. Sutpen is a transgressor, his life a challenge to that ideology at every turn, and the rise and fall of his short-lived dynasty cuts the ground dramatically from under his feet.

As a poor white of Scots–English stock from the mountains of West Virginia, his creation of a plantation in Mississippi with West Indian slaves violates the mythical code of Southern honour, as does his subsequent running of the plantation. Instead of evoking that 'honour' nostalgically, Faulkner evokes its opposite, its absence, its negation. Sutpen's trangressions are in fact a reality which has been repressed beneath the myth of the Old South. As a poor boy turned away from a Virginia planter's house by a negro butler, he makes his fortune by emulating his social betters in every way except their paternalistic compassion and code of honour. His ambition is transformed into an abstract design for total success which takes no account of human fallibility, his own included, and ends in disaster. The fascination of the abstract design for Quentin and his co-narrators is that it was paradoxically more substantial in nature than the conventional goals of the

Compsons or Sartorises, the revered families of the aristocracy. For they soften the ruthlessness of their expropriations of land and human flesh through individual acts of mercy and rituals of honour. Sutpen dispenses with both because they do not fit into his design. The substance of his life is predicated entirely on his ruthless desire to create a plantation dynasty out of nothing. The forms of ideology which softened the first impact of brutal domination in a slave society are conspicuous by their absence. Sutpen differs because he continues to act with the same dishonourable ruthlessness which he had shown in bringing a group of half-naked slaves from Haiti and founding Sutpen's Hundred.

Through a narrative about Sutpen which is composed almost entirely of a series of acts of story-telling, Faulkner deconstructs the ideology of the Old South. Sutpen is both a challenge to that order and, as the subject of a set of complex, interlocking, tales also a phantom of history whose nature his various narrators can never quite grasp. For one thing, all the narrators attempt with growing frenzy to read their own obsessions back into history. Sutpen and his sons, who are the victims of history, also become the victims of myth-making, seemingly at the mercy of those who try in retrospect to pin Sutpen down. Yet they never actually can pin him down. The urgency of the quest for knowledge thrives on the very absence of any absolute and definitive truth. In the event speculation has its partial reward. For, in the ruin of Sutpen's Hundred, Quentin and Rosa discover the aging Henry Sutpen and the mulatto grandson of his brother, the howling Benjy-like Jim Bond. But the discovery, though dramatic, is not a resolution. It can only intensify speculation rather than end it, and speculation in that sense becomes endless.

The interwoven narratives themselves constitute the epiphanous narrative of the form because the narrators are themselves important characters in the story. Rosa Coldfield was once engaged to Sutpen and mortally insulted by his suggestion of trial copulation before marriage to see if she could bear him a son. As Irwin has shown in his brilliant study of Quentin Compson, act and narrative are involved in a complex process of doubling which is temporal as well as spatial. Sutpen's two sons by different marriages, Henry and Charles, are for Quentin historical images of the two dimensions of his split personality, the favoured son who decently defends his sister's honour and the dark shadow of Charles Bon, who threatens his half-sister's virginity in a demonic fusion of incest and miscegenation. At one point, when Bon is rejected by Sutpen, he taunts Henry's acceptance of him as brother with the remark, '*I'm the nigger that's going to sleep with your sister.*'[2] The fear is Quentin's, a fear which carries over from his protective-ness towards Candace in *The Sound and the Fury* but also from his desire for her. History enables him to idealise his divided self as simultaneously protector and violator. The narcissism of interpret-ation here accords with the narcissism of imaginary incest in the earlier novel.

Yet it is still important to treat the two novels as separate texts, in no way as origin and sequel. To do otherwise leads to a reductive Freudian position in which Quentin is seen at the centre of both of them, transferring the Oedipal structure of his infantile sexuality first onto his own life and then onto history. But Faulkner does not offer us any evidence for this deeper structure of desire regressing back into childhood. What he does is to place incest and miscegenation, narcissism and doubling, within the deeper structure of society. The double identification with Sutpen's sons is integral to Quentin's ambivalent attitude towards Sutpen himself. For Quentin, he is without origin or lineage, without the embroidered genealogy of the other planter families. It is precisely this quality which makes him so daunting, his emergence out of nowhere with a cluster of West Indian slaves with whom he seems to share his reckless adventures and disdain for material depri-vation, with whom he will wrestle half-naked in front of his watching children.

Behind his astonishment at Sutpen's lack of social grace and lack of compassion, Quentin suppresses an attraction towards someone who is powerful enough to be worth resisting, who is awe-inspiring in his most monstrous actions. In resisting him out of secret admiration he could therefore strongly identify with Charles Bon's wish to be accepted at Sutpen's Hundred. Confronted by the weakness and cynicism of his father in the next generation, he searches back, without fully realising it, for someone whose patriarchal authority is worth craving and rejecting at the same time. Sutpen offers the challenge of destiny. But it is an imagined challenge, the vicarious challenge for someone who cannot act decisively in his own life. Quentin has good psychological reasons for projecting himself back into history, yet Sutpen is not merely a surrogate father; he is also, as Quentin senses, the *alter ego* of the short-lived planter aristocracy of the Deep South, its unacknowledged dimension, the *arriviste* without birthright or credentials who establishes his dynasty in a wilderness. Since in Mississippi his rise *was* historically possible, the subsequent mythologising of honour becomes an even more pressing issue in the Deep South than among the slave-owners of Virginia. The figure of Sutpen rends the veil of mystification in two, but for that reason his demonic attraction cannot be explicitly acknowledged. He must be seen as an individual destroyer, an overreacher whose fate is to be destroyed in turn, even when his own fate could be seen as emblematical of the Old South itself.

His sin of abstraction is to deny the forging of a cultured life with which to accompany conquest and depredation, in order to ensure that the fruits of depredation survive. He is at once more and less substantial than the De Spains or the Compsons. He can make no attempt to erect a smokescreen of honour, because he does not know what honour is. But he has a stronger material presence, in his closeness to the land and to his slaves. Paradoxically, his means of implementing the abstract design make his life more sensuous and more tangible, but also impervious to the feelings of others, including his own family, whom he treats as mere pawns in the design. For the design implies an exercise of power, public and private, which makes no concessions to legitimacy. At times Sutpen treats women worse than he treats his slaves. He regards his first marriage as little more than a property transaction and repudiates his wife when he learns she has negro blood. The subsequent women in his life he treats as no more than the potential bearers of a male heir. The outrage in Rosa Coldfield's rhetoric in a 'dim hot airless room with the blinds all closed and fastened for forty-three summers'[3] comes from her fixation on Sutpen's insult after the war, when he suggests to his young fiancée a trial run at bearing a male child as a precondition of marriage. His violation of family honour in a society where the extended family was so strong accentuates in Quentin's eyes the promise–threat of the demonic planter. The man whose contempt for family ruins his design for dynasty is discussed fervently by a youth who already senses that he will not continue his own. Quentin, imbued with paternalism, cannot but condemn the man who seemed to have acted without any shred of paternalism at all.

Ironically enough, there are indications in the story that Sutpen's faults will be redeemed in the next generation. Both Henry and

Judith are acceptable models of their class – Judith the young home-loving Southern belle stricken only by external misfortune, and Henry the awkward but sensitive and educated provincial gentleman. As Brooks has pointed out, there is a strong sense in which the honour, decency and etiquette of Southern upper-class ideology will be upheld by the next generation.[4] But the arrival of the war and the arrival of Charles Bon at Sutpen's Hundred both destroy that promise. Yankee soldiers destroy Sutpen's plantation and Henry is forced to flee after killing Charles to uphold his father's wishes and his sister's honour, thus depriving Sutpen of his male heir and forcing him, in the interest of his design, to attempt conception with the nearest suitable woman at hand. After the refusal of the wounded Rosa, he uses the grand-daughter of the destitute Wash Jones, only to have her bear him a daughter. When he insultingly offers Milly a stable instead of marriage, Jones, the poor white who is laughed at by Sutpen's black slaves, exacts the class revenge of white trash – which Sutpen once was – in the interest of family honour which Sutpen can never understand: 'I'm going to tech you, Kernel.'[5] He kills Sutpen with a scythe when the design is already in ruins. The process of revenge, which started when Sutpen was turned away by a black servant from the Big House, ends with Sutpen being murdered by his own *alter ego*, his class double.

For all his narrators that is a kind of tragic but divine retribution, the price of his demonic transgressions. But, though that demonism contains the unacknowledged ruthlessness of his class as a whole, Sutpen is not a typical slave-holder. We never see his slaves at work, or the plantation in operation. The slaves remain shadowy figures like Sutpen himself. His demonic image should be seen not as the extensive historical reality beneath appearance but as an almost literal inversion of stereotype by Sutpen's narrators. The inversation is itself an idealisation, just as much as the plantation stereotype of the paternalistic master which it stands on its head. Sutpen wrestles with his slaves, treats women like animals, and simply uses the family as an instrument in his 'design'. The lack of compassion is invoked as part and parcel of the sin of abstraction. For, according to stereotype, the typical planter should be firmly rooted in the concrete concerns of daily living. He should keep a dignified distance from his slaves, treat his women with courtesy, and respect and revere his family.

Abstraction is the connecting term between absence and desire.

But in the history of contemporary realism this is probably the most complex and intricate literary form which it is has taken. The demands upon the reader of a narrative rhetoric which strains towards truth with an almost unrelieved frenzy are exceptional and at times show the crisis of form which threatened to engulf *Ulysses*. But the comparison does not end there. Faulkner had been clearly influenced in *The Sound and the Fury* by the hallucinatory gaps in narrative of the present which Joyce used in 'Circe'. The past, in the form of dream or memory, erupts within the present entirely without warning. Here Faulkner takes that eruption a stage further. The past is always more than the sum of its parts, more than the aggregate knowledge of its questing narrators, who often second-guess the nature of particular events through empathic understanding with their fellow narrators. As in Joyce, there is no continuous thread of omniscient narration. Quentin seems to know more than either Rosa Coldfield or his father tells him, and Shreve seems to know more than Quentin in turn could possibly pass onto him. Knowledge goes beyond overt communication, so that at times the act of narrating, and internarrating, becomes as hallucinatory as the history they are trying to recapture. Thus the Civil War section concerning the two half-brothers and Sutpen is told in impersonal narrative as a shared vision of the two Harvard students very much like a sudden cinematic dissolve from the present, in which both simultaneously project onto a moving screen their view of the past.

In this context, absence is the central and ubiquitous feature of the text, where desire remains latent and never fully acknowledged. Absence is the dovetailing of Sutpen's lack of compassion and his lack of substance, a lack of substance which, as we have seen, certainly does not lie in history itself but lies in the act of recapturing it. The timespan here between the act of writing and the period the story is roughly the same as in *War and Peace*. But Faulkner's multi-layered narrative subverts the classic confidence in the power of the historical novel to recapture the past. In *Absalom, Absalom!* it becomes as hallucinatory as Joyce's nocturnal Dublin. For, though Sutpen dominates the narrative – Rosa Coldfield has also known him in the flesh – he has presence as a figure on a black stallion, not as a distinctive voice. He seems uncannily to be present to all the senses except that of hearing.

His absence of a voice is made clear when Mr Compson tells Quentin of his grandfather's conversations with the 'demon' about

his great design. Here is one of the very few passages in the novel
in which Sutpen has a voice:

> ' "You see, I had a design in my mind. Whether it was a good
> or bad design is beside the point; the question is, Where did I
> make the mistake in it, what did I do or misdo in it, whom or
> what injure by it to the extent this would indicate. I had a
> design. To accomplish it I should require money, a house, a
> plantation, slaves, a family – incidentally of course a wife. I set
> out to acquire these, asking no favor of any man." '[6]

But the reader learns of this during Quentin's conversations with
Shreve after the narrative episodes of Rosa and his father. He is
thus telling to Shreve the story his father told him of his grandfather's remembered conversations with Sutpen. Shreve responds
caustically by pointing to the obvious difficulties of mediation:

> 'Your old man', Shreve said. 'When your grandfather was
> telling this to him, he didn't know any more what your grand-
> father knew what the demon was talking about when the demon
> told it to him, did he; And when your old man told it to you,
> you wouldn't have known what anybody was talking about if
> you hadn't been out there and seen Clytie. Is that right?'[7]

The only absolute confirmation of anything comes from Quentin's visit to Sutpen's Hundred with Miss Rosa, which, as Shreve
astutely realises, is the necessary precondition of his act of
historical reconstruction, the only context within which their joint
and frenzied speculation could have any substance at all.

The rolling, withheld, backtracking and accelerating narrative,
which only pauses for breath when it is tantalisingly postponing
its purported truths to a later page, therefore has good reason for
its convoluted rhythms. It imposes on the reader its own rhetorical
tyranny, a rhetoric which, arising out of the Southern tradition it
lays bare, is both the subject and medium of the novel. In addition,
all speech is filtered through Quentin's consciousness, which is
why Sutpen's figure never comes to have a clear, autonomous
voice. Shreve and Quentin finally achieve the union of their
competing narrative voices at the price of their elusive subject. As
Shreve imagines the dandified life of Charles Bon, the union of

voices is achieved at the expense of the truth of the events it recounts:

> it might have been either of them and was in a sense both: both thinking as one, the voice which happened to be speaking the thought only the thinking become audible, vocal; the two of them creating between them, out of the rag-tag and bob-ends of old tales and talking, people who had perhaps never existed at all anywhere, who, shadows, were not shadows of flesh and blood which had lived and died but shadows in turn of what were (to one of them at least, to Shreve) shades too, quiet as the visible murmur of their vaporizing breath.[8]

Shreve and Quentin have resurrected Sutpen as the 'absence' of the Old South in a way antithetical to that of Rosa Coldfield, for whom in memory he could never be anything else but always present. While she is fixated on the tragic sterility of her repudiation – on what might have been, were Sutpen honourable and compassionate – for Quentin Sutpen is the return of the repressed in an altogether different form, not as mere echo or repetition, but, in his relationship to Shreve, as the potential cathexis of desire. The fiercely competitive nature of their story-telling and their close identification with each of Sutpen's sons intimates the surfacing of a concealed homoeroticism. To tell in frenzied sequence, then tell together with one voice, to identify with Charles and Henry in turn, and then to become them in the telling, suggests, in its elaborate ritual of doubling and reversal and intertwining, an erotic jostling for position, an imaginary journey into desire. In the absence of Caddy, who is not mentioned in the book, Judith, the surrogate Candace of history, is not the vacated centre of desire but merely the pretext for the homoerotic, for the incentuous attraction of the half-brothers predicated in part upon the promise–threat of miscegenation, an attraction earlier planted in Quentin's mind by his father's narrative. Thus Sutpen, the absent hero of the text, is indirectly the catalyst to his younger narrators' suppressed desire as they switch their attention to his equally elusive sons. The accelerating *dénouement* of Sutpen's story *qua* dynasty brings in its wake the accelerating impulse of his narrators' desires. The struggle for control of the history which has become myth, in which they are fused with each other, with one of the two brothers and with each brother's double, opens through its rhetoric onto the unconscious and brings forth a struggle for erotic domination which is no longer repressed.

Yet, if it is no longer repressed, it is not yet fully part of consciousness, for it is based on a virgin passion, a sexual innocence which echoes the mythical innocence it invokes of Sutpen setting up house and plantation in a virgin wilderness:

> There was something curious in the way they looked at one another, curious and profound and quietly intent, not at all as two young men might look at each other but almost as a youth and a very young girl might out of virginity itself – a sort of hushed and naked searching, each look burdened with youth's immemorial obsession not with time's dragging weight which the old live with but its fluidity: the bright heels of all the lost moments of fifteen and sixteen.[9]

The virginity is crucial. The effort of Shreve to catch up and overtake in the act of narrating is the frantic motion of the virgin seducer trying, without fully knowing, to pin down his virgin prey. His identification with Henry, the masculine defender of family honour, is as crucial as Quentin's identification with Charles Bon, the dark, feminised shadow of the repressed self. Faulkner completes the polarities of repression and desire, which begin with Rosa Coldfield in the 'dim hot airless room' of a Mississippi summer, by ending with the ice-cold night of a New England winter. The radiators switch off in the college room, and, frozen, the two young men retire to the same bed under an open window, their breath vaporising, their bodies rigid with cold but their blood secretly warmed by their hothouse rhetoric of another country, of what Shreve calls 'a kind of vacuum filled with wraithlike and indomitable anger and pride and glory at and in happenings that occurred and ceased fifty years ago'.[10] The ending thus brings the book back full circle. What had begun with Rosa's fused opposites of heat and sterility ends with the fused opposites of ice and desire.

The key moment in the book's dual climax is the one where Shreve leans up in bed on one elbow and watches with apparent solicitude as the clash between cold air and warm blood sends Quentin into a sudden convulsion. The scene is a masterpiece of erotic understatement. It is the one moment when all the narrative fusions might find their echo and completion in the fusion of the two male bodies, in the folding of the active Shreve over his passive brother in spirit. But then Quentin chooses to tell instead the climax to the story, his witnessing of the events out at Sutpen's Hundred which Shreve never witnessed, his dramatic discovery of the aging and cowering Henry Sutpen.

As part of the ceaseless play upon ruined innocence, Quentin defends his virginity with an exclusive knowledge, the secret confirmation of all that has been told. Truth becomes a function of the will-to-truth, and the will-to-truth a last ditch defence against the will-to-power. As Shreve speaks of all the mulatto Jim Bonds conquering the Western hemisphere, Quentin defends his honour by defending the honour of the South he denies hating. The struggle remains open, its resolution as unresolved as Sutpen's story is elusive, in which, by a process of stylistic doubling, the reader is in the same position *vis-à-vis* Shreve and Quentin as Shreve and Quentin have been *vis-à-vis* Thomas Sutpen. All one can infer is that on this particular night the climax of narrative will not be echoed in the climax of desire. At least for the moment, the rape of the South will not be repeated.

II

The nature of abstraction in *The Wild Palms* is less significant and more secondary than in Faulkner's historical masterpiece. But it is none the less the key to the relationship between absence and desire. The novel, with its dual alternating narrative, veers outside Yoknapatawpha in the story of Harry Wilbourne and Charlotte Rittenmeyer, and is in many respects one of the least Southern of Faulkner's novels. For that reason he breaks new ground, but there is also a dilution in the strength of the writing, evident in the juxtaposition of a partly allegorical to a highly realist narrative. The influence of Hemingway and Hollywood is evident in the dialogue and the characterisation. The geographical openness of the United States as a whole is evident in the couple's flight north to Chicago and Wisconsin, then west to Utah. Absence here is not constituted through the South-as-periphery but in the escape of love from the South. Desire is embellished as a new variant of Flaubert's love of love. For the love of Harry and Charlotte is intensified by flight, by springing the trap of provincialism and exploring a more open world.

The novel subsequently unveils the illusion of that openness, which is itself a constituent element in the American Dream. But it does so from the point of view of an abstract design which, like that of Thomas Sutpen's, finally comes to grief. The architect of that design in the great gamble on passion is not, however, the man but the woman. It is Charlotte Rittenmeyer who leaves her husband and children to live out the utopia of everlasting honeymoon with a man chosen not so much for himself as for his contribution to the design. Not only has it got to be, for Charlotte, 'allhoneymoon, always'; love itself is an impersonal principle. 'So it's not just me you believe in', Harry queries, ' . . . it's love. Not just me any man.' Charlotte replies that love never dies between two people: 'it just leaves you, goes away, if you are not good enough'.[11] The lovers have to live up to the principle which guides them but is yet beyond them. In harnessing her lover almost literally to that abstractness, she boldly tries to go where Emma Bovary never dared. In subordinating her specific man to the general principle, in choosing him because of love instead of choosing love because of him, she also does what Catherine Barclay never dared either. She, in a sense, is the abstract instigator, as Birkin is in *Women in Love*, while Harry, with no small sense of irony, charts the consequences.

Escaping to the North with a sudden windfall is easy, but continuing to live on it is difficult. Faulkner uses the need for money to subvert the elegy of romance. The rural idyll in Wisconsin is finally interrupted. They go to Chicago to earn a living, Harry writing pulp romantic fiction, Charlotte dressing mannequins in department-store windows. The very nature of the acts involved in surviving, parodies the reason for doing it. In order that they can afford to be romantic, their work travesties romance. Wilbourne senses not only that love is nearly always for sale, but also that, except through a deliberate strategy of starving, the material blandishments of the city will prove to be too tempting. Living in Chicago becomes a prison, so that Harry thinks of *'winter and city together, a dungeon; the routine even of living an absolution even for adultery'*.[12] The condition of purity, of refusing to succumb to either the comfortable or the respectable, is flight. In the middle of winter Harry and Charlotte head for an ore-mining camp in the wilds of Utah, where Harry lands a job as a doctor. But there is no escape from the depredations of civilisation, which merely continue by other means. The workers of the mine are all immigrants who are neither paid nor fed by the company. The couple find themselves unwittingly tangled in a vicious system of concealed exploitation. Nor do they have any personal freedom, being forced to sleep in a single-room cabin with the mine's manager and his wife, consciously inhibiting their own desires while the other couple, with no attachment to any love ideal at all, are quite open about theirs. Harry and Charlotte can deliberately suffer in order to escape comfort and respectability, but they cannot escape the system which offers it. Rather they merely find themselves trapped in the system at that end of the spectrum where it offers no comfort at all. Hypothermia and starvation are as much a product of its ubiquity as, so they find out, comfort and respectability.

It is not merely that the abstract ideal proves impossible to sustain. It is the pitiless detail of that impossibility which is the strength of the novel. In that sense it tests the untested assumptions of Flaubert and Hemingway, indicating that, when the illusions of passion remain untested by extended circumstance, then and only then can they be sustained. Charlotte refuses Emma Bovary's option of retreating back into the security of marriage, and Catherine Barclay's romantic idyll of bearing her lover's child. And Faulkner himself begs the question of a passionate intensity which is purely temporal, such as the romantic three days of Maria and Robert Jordan, by putting to the test the length of time which such an abstractly conceived passion can be sustained.

Charlotte's ideal founders on the unwanted pregnancy which challenges her identification of passion and childlessness. 'I remember somebody telling me once', she confides to Harry, ' . . . that when people loved hard, really loved each other, they didn't have children, the seed got burned up in the love, the passion.'[13] She is explaining that her douche bag froze in the Utah winter and then burst when the stove was relit, but also explaining why she was happy to dispense with it. The reader knows by this time that Charlotte's fanaticism precludes pure rationalisation of a *fait accompli*. Though Faulkner exploits the ironic subversion of ideals by the practicality of everyday life, this alone cannot explain Charlotte's downfall. It is not that she choose a ruthless utopia, but that she chose the wrong man to accompany her, a man who is medically incompetent and without previous sexual experience, whose weakness allows her to dominate him almost at will. '*She is not only a better man and a better gentleman than I am*', Harry thinks;

'she is a better everything than I will ever be.'[14] He proves himself
right when he abjectly fails to arrange a proper abortion for her,
tries it himself and kills her. The pain of the infection echoes the
pain of Catherine Barclay giving birth but also inverts it. It is the
pain of sticking to the ideal by not giving birth. But, while Frederic
Henry looks on helplessly, Harry connives through his incompetence in Charlotte's death.

After his arrest for manslaughter, Wilbourne rescues himself
from ignominy through the last-ditch vestiges of honour. Charlotte's husband offers him first the money to jump bail and leave
the country. Later, when Harry, having refused, is in jail, he
makes a second offer of a cyanide capsule with which to kill
himself. But Wilbourne chooses grief instead of nothingness,
hoping through the grievous fusion of punishment and memory
to keep alive Charlotte's fanatical and at times arid chivalry. But
the chivalry is not hopelessly Quixotic. It is a considered gamble,
in its own way calculated and ruthless, replete with its own irony.
In escaping geographically from the South, Charlotte's crusade
exhibits the residue of a Southern obsession. In making his belated
response to its memory, Wilbourne resurrects the honour which
Faulkner's work had systematically denied to those who claimed
to embody it, and given cryptically to those who never claimed it
but showed instead in the face of adversity a basic and unshakable
dignity.

It is significant that *Absalom, Absalom!* and *The Wild Palms* were
written while Faulkner was working in Hollywood, a fact which
unfortunately contributed during the following decade to his
artistic decline. These two novels are significant not only because
they postpone that decline but because they contrast very clearly
with the work of the Hollywood director who was closest to him
– Howard Hawks. The two screenplays Faulkner helped to write
for Hawks, consecrating the famous partnership of Humphrey
Bogart and Lauren Bacall, have an importance far in advance of
Faulkner's contribution to the finished screenplays. The persona
of Lauren Bacall was largely something new in the Hollywood
cinema, a very young woman with extraordinary self-confidence
and independence of spirit. In *To Have and Have Not* and *The Big
Sleep* the Bacall persona possesses much of the brittleness and
pride of Charlotte Rittenmeyer. Where the new Bogart could easily
be fabricated out of the fictional heroes of Hemingway, Hammett
and Chandler, these same writers never provided Hawks with

anyone as active or as positive as Bacall. With Faulkner it was the other way around. Conspicuously lacking in tough-boiled male heroes, his female characterisations had radically altered the direction of modern fiction. Masterly synthetic, Hawks succeeded in fusing alternate literary sources and harnessing them to the administered spirit of Hollywood optimism, directing his two *film noir* classics with triumphant lovers.

A second comparison is possible between *Absalom, Absalom!* and Hawks's epic western *Red River*, even though Faulkner never wrote for it. Both concern the ruthlessness of the exploiting patriarch in the history of American capitalism and the resistance of the rejected son. Whereas the refusal of Sutpen to recognise Charles Bon results in his own downfall, the basis of the conflict in *Red River* between the ruthless cattle baron Tom Dunston and his adopted son never results in the tragic finale towards which it appears to be moving. Crucially, Hawk's Western myth lacked the Southern dimension of miscegenation, and the director, as if sensing a vital lack of tragic intensity, effects a reconciliation between father and son at the last moment. Such an ending had of course a familiar place in the scenarios of Hollywood morality and its use of myth. The ruthlessness of the robber barons in the West is reconciled with the more civilised future through the more sensitive and humanised heir. Thus the optimism of the American Dream is maintained.

Hawks worked mainly within the limits of popular genres where constraints were externally imposed. These three pictures remain, significantly, three of his best. But they also point to the fact that Faulknerian tragedy could never be accommodated in the popular cinema, for Los Angeles is no more the New South than the Wild West is the Old South. Faulkner's career thus shows us how strong tragedy can be in the modern American novel and how non-existent it is, by comparison, in the modern American cinema. Faulkner's work, ironically enough, had already destroyed those myths of Southern honour which *Gone with the Wind* showered in sentimentalised form on cinema audiences all over the world. Before it was even conceived, he had already filled in its gross omissions. Deep in the cauldron of a racial tyranny which had appeared in his own lifetime to be resting on its laurels as a triumphant instrument of repression, Faulkner remoulded the elements of tragedy out of absence and desire.

8 Lowry: The Day of the Dead

I

In Joyce and Lowry past-time narrative is subordinated to the needs of the diurnal present. Yet, even then, *Under the Volcano* daringly halves the already daring timespan of *Ulysses*. Both start with the dawn – if we discount Laruelle's prelude – but Bloomsday survives through darkness until the following morning, and by implication many mornings to come. Geoffrey Firmin, however, does not even have to wait, like Faustus, for the dark of midnight. He dies at seven in the evening amidst the darkness of thunder-clouds. The different narrative strategies highlight the different fates of similar heroes. Both are impotent cuckolds haunted by the traumatic shadow of decayed marriage, but, as the shadows grow longer, the options differ. Bloom remains faithful by default. His psychic survival is ensured by masturbation and fantasy. Firmin breaks the dread of his sexual anxiety by more literal means. Drenched in mescal, he is willingly ravished by a young prostitute. But the conscious act of debasement is far from being a renewed sign of health. It portends imminent murder and death. While Bloom ends up in bed asleep with the wakeful Molly, Firmin unwittingly sets free the horse which will trample Yvonne to death before being shot himself and tossed into a ravine. While Joyce endorses life's troubled and affirmative cycle, Lowry embraces tragic finitude.

Bloom's thematic absences are basically affirmative because they are absences within the familiar, the known, within the frag-mented community in which he has always lived but to which he has never really belonged. Firmin's Quauhnahuac, which Lowry places in the mountains fifty miles to the south of Mexico City, is, by contrast, a mirror of the hero's strangeness, providing him with a pure and perverse reflection of his troubled soul. Yet, as the external imprint of a tragic psyche lost to the world through alcohol and dread, it is also a landscape with its own autonomy, with an identity which goes beyond the interloper who inhabits it. This, of course, is part of the literary topography of exile. Firmin finds the landscape which complements his being only on the condition that it can never be his own. It is appropriate, therefore, that Lowry sets his novel on the Day of the Dead, when the indigenous culture celebrates the universal predicament which is soon to become the fate of its infirm English ex-consul. In his study of Mexican culture Octavio Paz has suggested that death is a mirror of life because the Mexican ignores both of them.[1] This disdain for life, which the Consul shares, ironically becomes his link with the life around him. For that indigenous life explodes publicly through the fiesta into a symbolic celebration of death. Yet Firmin must also be different. For in his final hour of degradation he still strives to find in death a transcendent meaning – and make it a gamble with desire – in a country where, according to Paz, death is often empty of meaning and devoid of erotic emotion. He thus imports the illusion of fecundity into a ambience of sterility.

The mood and the rhythms of the novel match those of *Ulysses*, but also differ. The absences of marriage and adultery, the things from which Bloom willingly escapes, are converted here to sudden and unexpected presences. Yvonne returns when Geoffrey least expects her. She meets his brother, Hugh, who has been her lover, when she least expects him to be there. In its incestuous and familial way, circumstance creates its own parody of the return of the repressed. The Consul is ambushed by what he drinks to forget, but it soon becomes clear that those same things for the degraded ego are what it also drinks to remember. To cap a day of surprises, all the three of them bump into Jacques Laruelle the film-director, who has introduced the story to us a year after the events it recounts, and who is as uncertain about Hugh's relationship to Yvonne as Hugh is about his. Only Geoffrey, as the drunken cuckold, can grimly rejoice over the chance pairing of his two betrayers. Absence thus co-exists with an interlocking set of presences, or perhaps it would be truer to say that, in the Consul's deteriorating psyche, presence must constantly be dissolved into the absences, which are artificially stimulated by tequila and mescal.

The novel can be read as a variation on the Faust theme with tragic consequences for its stumbling hero. For Firmin the goal is no longer cosmic infinity in the unbounded external sense. It is the unconscious, that elusive metaphor of the deep without literal topography, the minefield of hidden secrets and forbidden truths, that craved unknown which lies under the volcano. The volcanoes, of course, are actually there on the landscape of southern Mexico. Firmin's fateful journey to the Farolito *cantina* in Parián is an ascent towards them which parallels the descent within, a descent which is both a form of self-willed psychic derangement and a desperate, failed quest after truth. Yet the search after truth is also based on truth's abandonment. In reaching down through intoxication beneath the layers of the conscious mind, Firmin decisively disorganises his own ego, dissolving it into the splintered fragments which can no longer be recognised and no longer reorganised. His senses impaired, his powers of perception lost, his conscious assault on the unconscious soon looses its own consciousness. In trying to penetrate under the volcano, Firmin provokes the eruption which is soon to engulf him.

Yet the quest is also an escape from the conscious mind, from the truths of actual circumstance which are too degrading to confront and too terrible to bear. The quest is a flight, and in part therefore an exchange, part of a demonic temptation to swap the truths that Firmin does not want, because he knows them all too well, for others that he imagines in his alcoholic self-delusion have a primal innocence, are apples still unplucked from the tree of knowledge in the Garden of Eden. But, agonisingly, painfully, Firmin discovers there is no such thing – though it is really the reader who makes the discovery on his behalf, leaving Firmin in that classic state of *anagnorisis* where he has failed to discover that he has discovered nothing. On the way, throughout the day, the quest leads Firmin to forsake feeling and disassemble meaning, and finally to abdicate from life. The only begetter of his own analysis, he swaps the couch for the bottle, translating all errors of language into Freudian slips, making all associations disassociate, and accepting accidents of translation as truths of desire – or, more accurately, truths of the absence of desire.

The absence of desire is the novel's connecting thread, where alcohol, its cause and consequence, recurrently disconnects. It is also the gloss on love which makes a mockery of all love's conventions. It is prefaced by Laruelle's discovery, exactly a year after Firmin's death, of a letter he had never posted to Yvonne. The letter is a powerful statement of the lover's – in this case, the jilted husband's – despair, the desperate plea for help amidst 'the nightly grapple with death', the 'howling pariah dogs' and the noises of the night, which are like 'the unbandaging of great giants in agony'. In anguish Firmin declares that 'love is the only thing which gives meaning to our poor ways on earth' and finishes by begging Yvonne to come back 'if only for a day'.[2] The irony of the letter, as the reader is soon to realise, is that, without having read it, she does return for precisely that length of time, only to discover that the statement of love she has not witnessed is a fabrication which Geoffrey can produce only in her absence. Firmin's love may be fickle and sporadic, but his desire is permanently repressed. Quauhnahuac is the purgatory in which he punishes himself, but also the strange place whose landscape upholds the identity he is trying to disintegrate, upholding it in its constant state of dissolution. It congeals into a static and immobile image, 'the horror of an intolerable unreality', where space and time no longer seem to be co-ordinates and where mescal dissolves the material world into its constituent atoms.

Soon after Yvonne has come back to find him in the Bella Vista bar they come across the window of a printer's shop in the town where Yvonne sees 'some touched-up prints of extravagantly floriferous brides', a mirrored image of her own nostalgia. But Geoffrey then points out the picture of the landscape beside it, which contradicts: 'with a murmur of "Strange", peering closer: a photographic enlargement purporting to show the disintegration of a glacial deposit in the Sierra Madre, of a great rock split by forest fires.'[3] Set above the spinning flywheel of the presses, the picture is called *'La Despedida'*, 'The Parting'. The landscape reflects back symbolic images of their separation, which is still continuing now that she has returned: though she still longs 'to heal the cleft rock', its other half, standing beside her, proposes to disintegrate how he pleases. They cannot escape from the strange, almost estranged, symbolic reflections of their own predicament. The Spanish language and Mexican landscape constantly contain the lineaments of their continuing absence, of the truth of absence which for Firmin co-exists so painfully with the world's absence of truth.

Yet Lowry's narrative could not retain its strength were it to rely on the mirroring of landscape and the subjective rendering of images alone. If the world is seen through the eyes of the Consul, the Consul too must be seen from the outside. Yet to put him completely at the mercy of the other's point of view might merely make him pathetic and insignificant. He has to be objectified from the inside, become the 'outside looking in' that Yvonne already helplessly is, but remain within the interior which she can never reach. The first onset of *delirium tremens* that morning, when, after failing to make love to Yvonne, he has a hallucination on the patio of a man dying by the side of the pool, is one catalyst. It involves a radical decentring of self in which Geoffrey is both sufferer and witness of his own suffering, himself and not himself, a body without a mind and mind which is disembodied. Yet before they even reach the house it is clear that the Consul's voice is not merely a metaphorical presence in the novel. It literally exists in his own ear. His voice is both thought and speech, thought when it is never actually spoken, and speech when it is spoken to someone in particular or no one in particular or no one at all. The reader is cued into thought-speech by inverted commas, but they are no more a guarantee for the reader than for Firmin of any clear boundary between sound and silence.

Not only does Firmin not always know when he himself is speaking, or when others are listening: he also does not always know at first if the words uttered by others are actually said by them, often realising after some delay that they are merely the projections of his own wishes or fears:

> The Consul was beginning to shake again.
> 'Geoffrey, I'm so thirsty, why don't we stop and have a drink?'
> 'Geoffrey, let's be reckless this once and get tight together before breakfast!'
> Yvonne said neither of these things.[4]

Firmin's consciousness breaks down the conventional distinctions of realist narrative, the divisions between direct and indirect speech, and between thought as consciousness and voice as speech. Lowry's narrative expresses the decentred world of its hero by externalising his thoughts as voices, but not merely as a function of innovation in style. For the hallucinatory world of Firmin itself puts all such distinctions into disarray. Permanent intoxification has already broken them down. Epiphanous narrative then gives expression to the process of decentring which gravitates around the world of desire. It is the absent structure of feeling, the failure to 'rediscover' Yvonne when she comes back and presents herself to be rediscovered, that precipitates the dissolution whose medium is alcohol. The narrative, as decentred narrative, must capture simultaneously the structure of feeling and express the primacy of the anguished voice over the composed thought. Firmin's consciousness often appears to him as a reified product, as the demonic voice of the other which in reality is the disembodied voice of self. Thus, as he and Yvonne return to the house: 'The tragedy . . . the Consul thought distantly, seemed to be reviewed and interpreted by a person walking at his side suffering him and saying: "Regard: see how strange, how sad familiar things may be." '[5] Or, again, as Yvonne demands breakfast instead of a straight whisky, the voice this time not the attribute of another body but a sound in his own ear:

' – She might have said yes for once', a voice said in the Consul's ear at this moment with incredible rapidity, 'for now of course poor old chap you want horribly to get drunk all over again don't you the whole trouble being as we see it that Yvonne's long-dreamed-of coming alas but put away the anguish my boy there's nothing in it', the voice gabbled on, 'has in itself created the most important situation in your life save one namely the far more important situation it in turn creates of your having to have five hundred drinks in order to deal with it', the voice he recognised of a pleasant and impertinent familiar, perhaps horned, prodigal of disguise, a specialist in casuistry . . . .[6]

With its varieties of unexpected hallucination, alcohol is the demonic correlative. But the process of doubling that it intimates within the self is echoed outside it in Geoffrey's relationship to his two betrayers, Hugh and Jacques Laruelle. Both are tentative doubles, projections of self which never materialised in Firmin's life, the childhood friend become film-director, the younger brother politicised by fascism yet stable in his sporadic subversion. When Hugh and Yvonne, after meeting at the house, go riding together in the valley, the idyllic scene is the homecoming she would have ideally desired with Geoffrey. Only towards the end of the ride, after the pair have conversed with a natural and spontaneous ease, does the figure of the absent Geoffrey cast, almost by default, the shadow of a doubt. Hugh is the normal, natural potent *alter ego*, the wrong person with the right personality just as Geoffrey is for Yvonne the right person imprisoned in the wrong personality.

Yet the stability of Firmin's *alter ego*s, which fix his disoriented terror of the world, also reveal his importance and, to adopt the Freudian slippage, the importance of his impotence. Their normality is weak and vacillating, vain and banal. They are bereft of the necessity to repress because they have no terror of truth. Yet that very distance from truth is what makes them shallow. The Consul's constant evasions are, by contrast, emanations of tortuous perspicacity. He refuses to see because of what he can, already. His cabbalistic pursuit of the subterranean is an evasion of its overt manifestations in his own life – almost as if, in plunging down to the deep, he fails to see what is coming in the opposite direction to the surface. His search for what is repressed is a form of repression of what is available to his own senses about his own relationships. The impotence which could be a literary weakness is never allowed to be so, because it is part of the wider evasion which is the source of Firmin's fictional strength. That strength lies in the paradox of chthonic repression, where the Heideggerian resonances of thereness and presencing in Firmin's imagination co-exist with the forced absences which decentre and fragment his ego. Because he is nowhere the Consul is everywhere, and his doubles appear, by harsh comparison, as characterological *idées fixes*.

The criticism of Lowry that Hugh's way of thinking is too close to that of his brother to indicate differences in personality conse-quently misses the point. In the case of both brothers the point of view is governed by stream of consciousness. Neither accords with the composure of classic realism. But Lowry's narrative does not accord stream of consciousness the status of an undifferentiated given. He makes it work at *different* levels, Hugh's reminiscences a compendium of surface impressions, Geoffrey's spiral disso-lutions a sign of the limitless depths of terrified evasion. At one level, Hugh is the Consul potent and sober, the portent of a discarded normality. At another he is above motive where Geof-frey is beyond it, blithely failing to reason why where the Consul painfully and cunningly refused to do so.

In contrast to the sobriety of the *alter ego*, drink is the surrogate passion of the decentred self incapable of passion, whose greatest love is mescal. Yvonne returns in hope only to find that she is not really there, that Firmin's surrogate mistresses of the bottle render

her chimerical each time that she tries to make her presence felt.
Love remains as strange as the landscape of the cleft rock, and in
seeing it estranged Firmin degrades Yvonne to a person without
qualities. On the balcony of Laruelle's house, she pleads with him
to escape together, to drink '*after*'; but love itself has escaped and
left them both behind – an estrangement, terrible in its inevita-
bility, which presents itself, occupying only one of the senses, as
a voice in his ear, 'a droning or a weeping':

> 'Haven't you got any tenderness or love left for me at all?'
> Yvonne asked suddenly, almost piteously, turning around on
> him, and he thought: Yes, I do love you, I have all the love in
> the world left for you, only that love seems so far away from
> me and so strange too, for it is as though I could almost hear
> it, a droning or a weeping, but far, far away, and a sad lost
> sound, it might be either approaching or receding, I can't tell
> which.
> And a moment later:
> 'But I'm back', she was apparently saying, 'Can't you see it?
> We're here together again, it's *us*. Can't you see that?' Her lips
> were trembling, she was almost crying.
> Then she was close to him, in his arms, but he was gazing
> over her head.
> 'Yes, I can see', she said, only he couldn't see, only hear, the
> droning, the weeping, and feel, feel the unreality. 'I do love
> you. Only – ' 'I can never forgive you deeply enough': was that
> what he had in mind to add?[7]

Not only does the Consul repress love and tenderness: he also
withholds the *lack* of forgiveness of her betrayals which impels
him to repression. Though it is hard to forgive, he holds back
from articulating *unforgiveness*, an act that is even 'harder still'. His
withholding of hate as well as love perpetuates the vicious circle
of impotence and betrayal, absence and desire, where their
relationship is captive to an infinite regress they seem powerless
to alter. The distance from Lawrence could not be greater. The
power of hate to re-equilibrate, to sustain through the intensity of
opposites the waning power of love, is an instinctual vicissitude
no longer available to lovers who cannot love. Yet it is Firmin,
not Yvonne, who cannot love, their life an eternal recurrence of
repetition and revenge in which the victim of life is ever wounding

the victim of life's victim, who in turn, without intending to, wounds back.

The heroism of Firmin, so unlikely for so much of the book, yet in the end inexorable, is predicated on his lost illusions. He stifles passion and ignores compassion, his most compassionate encounter of the novel being, as Day has pointed out, with a starving pariah dog in Señora Gregorio's *cantina*.[8] Yet at every point in the day he encounters their trace. Besides passion's distant droning in his ear, there is the haunting sign in Laruelle's room – *'No se puede vivir sin amar'* ('One cannot live without love') – he cannot bear to look at. In his political arguments with Hugh, which grow increasingly more incoherent, he appears to want to leave the world to the fate of barbarism and scorns all political causes. Yet he senses more clearly than Hugh or Yvonne the significance of the dying Indian they see on the highway, and the later threat that will be posed by his official persecutors. The loss of *eros* and *agape* are made tragic by their latency, by the sense that what is repressed can never be extinguished, by the hope shared by Yvonne, Hugh and Laruelle that such qualities can be prompted into returning. Their possible return under impossible circumstances is made to constitute in him a fate which is that of all humanity. Thus Firmin, who in his own eyes represents no one but himself, comes to represent in the eyes of others, including the reader, everyone. He is the embodiment of universal suffering and the repository of universal hope.

Yet Firmin's heroism would be empty if it had no political dimension. His Mexico is governed by a socialist president, Izara Cárdenas, who has enlisted trade-union support in the pursuit of agrarian reform, and in the expropriation of foreign oil companies, which has prompted the breaking off of diplomatic relations by Britain and left the Consul without a job. Cárdenas is also supporting the Loyalist government in Spain against Franco's military uprising. Mexico becomes Spain's New World double, taking sides in the Civil War as other countries remained neutral. As he was writing the novel, Lorwy was well aware that the Civil War had prefigured the world war then engulfing the whole of Europe and most of Asia. He thus gave the Consul's determination to die an indirectly global significance. Firmin places himself at the mercy of the Unión Militar at the Farolito in Parián, knowing that in true Francoist style they are paramilitary rebels, the unofficial arm of the military police and currently fighting the government's policies of agrarian reform with the aid of rich landowners and German spies. Mexico is thus revealed as a potential arena for fascism in the New World, and Firmin's murderers prefigure the shadowy death squads of post-war Hispanic America. In the dialectic of centre and periphery, Lowry's periphery signals its warning to the centres of civilisation, a retrospective warning which, as Lowry was rewriting the novel, he knew had never been heeded in the first place. Complacent about the world's politics, as his own country was until the invasion of Poland, the Consul none the less reveals his adversaries as figures of evil by offering himself up as a sacrificial victim. The novel's political perspective thus has a retrospective clarity. While those figures of evil in Mexico are still thin on the ground, their European counterparts are poised to conquer a whole continent.

The link between the personal and political levels of narrative is one of the most necessarily complex features of Lowry's text. But it is also of the main sources of its extraordinary power. That power can best be seen through comparison with *For whom the Bell Tolls*, a novel of similar period and theme. In his more conventional treatment of passion and politics, Hemingway attempts to fuse Robert Jordan's passion for the victimised Maria with his hero's distinctively American combination of hard boiled scepticism and practical heroism. Both both the passion and the scepticism are substantially artefacts. Jordan's criticism of the government and the communists is penetrating but preformed, *too* controlled and clever, while his passion is a celebration of pure libido, openly narcissistic, Maria little more than a passive admirer mingling adoration and gratitude. Even though his death is as sure as Firmin's, Jordan's heroism has the thrust of the romantic revolutionary skating lyrically across the surfaces of experience and using his scepticism as a defence against penetrating any deeper. As opposed to this idealised fusion of scepticism and passion, Firmin offers the implausible if not impossible combination of paranoia and impotence. Neither quality is classically heroic. Neither seems a viable contender for the formidable tasking of fusing the personal and political levels of epiphany. Yet on that fusion hinges a substantial part of Firmin's heroic stature – on the forging, that is, of a heroism which is neither idealism nor romanticises its tragic subject.

In his famous letter to Cape defending the novel, Lowry acknowledged the Consul's mania of persecution but pointed out that, objectively speaking, the Consul *was* being followed throughout the book, without aware of being so.[9] It is the reader instead who watches him being watched and is haunted by it where Firmin remains largely oblivious. Moreover, the watching figures are seen not only by the Consul but also by Jacques, Yvonne and Hugh. Edmonds has noted in detail the frequent reappearances of the man in dark glasses, the bare-footed man with the patch over one eye, the lounging peon, the bald boy with earrings, and has also noted the Consul's familiarity with his future persecutors.[10] In looking up the phone directory in Laruelle's house for the number of Dr Guzmán, the Consul finds staring out at him as he flips the pages the names of Zuzugoitea and Sanabria, the police chiefs who will eventually order his murder in the Farolito. In prefiguring the Consul's fate, Lowry cleverly fuses the uncanny and the familiar, as if the different figures, including the dead Indian who appears several times earlier in the novel, are premonitions of what is already known.

At the same time, Lowry steers a clear passage between the Scylla of a purely paranoid state of mind and the Charybdis of actual conspiracy. The story is consistently ambiguous. As Lowry pointed out, it is the reader, not Firmin, who is directly haunted by the recurrent intimations of watching, which are shared and mediated, anyway, by Firmin's various doubles. Yet the resonances of watching extend beyond the level of political suspicion. In light of Yvonne's return and the abject failure of the Consul's passion, the paranoid affliction, ingeniously objectified, suggests the classical Freudian locus of sexuality.[11] It is almost as if the spies who are spying on Firmin's spying would witness, if Firmin's house had no walls, the failure of the sexual act. What they cannot see, but could, is what the reader already knows, yet, because the watchers haunt the reader rather than the Consul, the act of reading itself provides the locus for the intersection of paranoia and desire. For, in witnessing the abject failure of the Consul's desire, the reader is in part a voyeur, seeing a drunken cuckold being exposed, poignantly and pathetically, at the point of greatest weakness.

The Consul's failure is also connected, however, to his own unforgiveness, and by extension to his paranoia about Yvonne's infidelities, which recur as Hugh accompanies them on the trip to Tomalín. The failure that is witnessed is in turn the outcome of the suspicion, which involves witnessing and the subsequent failure to forgive. Amidst the deepening phantasmogoria of mescal, the Consul himself watches more closely, inverting the process of surveillance which begins the novel and ending up, in a stroke of supreme tragic irony, being accused as the spy he has become. He is indeed an observer of what is meant to be concealed, but not a spy in the sense meant by his fascist accusers. The motor of his suspicion, which they cannot know, is not political opposition, but sexual betrayal. Once in motion, it translates itself from the level of paranoid impotent cuckoldry to the level of political acumen, to the astute revelation of a conspiracy to murder and oppress. The Consul's seeing is a futile and self-destructive act of retaliation against those whose 'watching' he had not previously been fully conscious of, which by implication he had previously repressed.

As his mind disintegrates, it can never become an act of revenge. Even though he is too paralytic to try and escape and report his suspicions to sympathetic authorities, there is a sense in which the reader never expects him to. Self-destruction is his first priority. Phantasmagoria and sexual guilt over his copulation with Maria also confuse in his own mind even further the separate levels of suspicion. He is too far gone consciously to disentangle the sexual and the political. As he drunkenly seizes a machete and accuses his accusers, the different levels confusingly merge:

> The Consul didn't know what he was saying: 'Only the poor, only through God, only the people you wipe your feet on, the poor in spirit, old men carrying their fathers and philosophers weeping in the dust. America perhaps, Don Quixote – ' he was still brandishing the sword, it was the sabre really, he thought, in Maria's room – 'if only you'd stop interfering, stop walking in your sleep, stop sleeping with my wife, only the beggars and the accursed.'[12]

Paranoia stumbles by chance upon a sinister truth which uncannily, has appeared to be there all along for the knowing. Yet knowledge of it is not indicative of either enlightenment or salvation, only of damnation. In a way the Faustian pact has been met. The proof that the *fascistas* have killed the Indian and stolen his horse and money lies in their willingness to kill the Consul too. Of all the Consul's doubles, the most ubiquitous and yet most shadowy now comes into focus. The anonymous Indian is the messenger of goodness, carrying money from the agrarian credit bank to the agrarian collectives in the area, embodying the potential goodness the others have seen in the Consul but which he has constantly failed to display. The Consul compensates for his failure to be like the Indian in life by sharing the same kind of death. The messenger ambushed at the roadside is the universal victim of fascism, and the Consul mimics his fate, so that, without himself being one of the damned of the earth, he can, none the less, also be one of the accursed. Unable to save the oppressed, he joins them by default.

Mexico is the transatlantic double of Spain, the arena of one man's private obsessions which also stages a prologue to the conflagration which is soon to rage across the Old World. Lowry deepens the tragic import of periphery by doubling it. The political divisions which eventually emerge in the novel are emblematic of wider ones but at two stages removed, remote, obscured, with a significance which at times seems more farcical than formal. For that reason, Hugh, the nearest equivalent to Robert Jordan, cannot be a genuine hero. To be heroic is not to have left Spain in its hour of defeat and become an 'indoor Marxman' complete with cowboy dudes. It is, rather, never to have been there, and tragically to deny its experience by experiencing it, but experiencing it remotely, and even then, like the Consul, not fully realising that one is experiencing it at all.

Having done nothing of political value, Firmin none the less attracts all the political insults his persecutors can muster. On the basis of no real evidence, they decide to kill him, only to find mistaken evidence to validate their arbitrary decision. For the *facistas* Firmin is a '*Cabrón*', 'Trotsky', 'Al Capón', an '*antichrista* prik', 'a Jew *chingao*'.[13] Try as he might, he cannot escape from Spain. Passing himself off to the police as William Blackstone, after a New England settler who disappeared to join the Indians, he is caught with Hugh's syndicalist trade-union card in his pocket: '*Federación Anarquista Ibérica*'. The scene is set for the simultaneous abomination of language and truth. Magically unreal, paranoia is pidgin-Englished back into his own face:

> 'What for you lie?' the Chief of Rostrums repeated in a glowering voice. 'You say your name is Black. *No es* Black.' He shoved him backwards towards the door. 'You say you are a wrider.' He shoved him again. 'You no are wrider.' He pushed

the Consul more violently, but the Consul stood his ground. 'You are no a de wrider, you are de espider, and we shoota de espiders in Mejico.'[14]

Mexican English simultaneously distorts and deepens the truth, making a black farce out of paranoia but doubling as an amusing Freudian commentary on the abortive journey into drink and desire. In the morning, as Firmin walks with Yvonne through the town, they come across the 'milk shop under its sign *Lecheria* (brothel, someone insisted it meant, and she hadn't seen the joke)',[15] while moments later an invisible voice in the street inquires, 'Who is the beautiful layee?'[16] Later Dr Vigil attempts to pin down the Consul's fragile and precarious soul: 'The nerves are a mesh, like, how you say it, an eclectic systemë. . . . But after much tequila the eclectic systemë is perhaps *un poco decompuesto* . . .'[17] The Terminal Cantina El Bosque prompts the Consul to recall the opening lines of Dante's *Divina Commedia* – *Mi ritrovai in una bosca oscura* – while inside Señora Gregoria tells him, 'Life changes, you know, you can never drink of it.'[18] At the door of Los Novedades, Yvonne cries in front of the little man who has just told them it 'was half past three by the cock'.[19] The slip is echoed three hours later at Parián when Maria's pimp welcomes Firmin after his exit from 'the calamity he was now penetrating' by telling him, 'it er ah half past sick by the cock'.[20] Hope destroyed becomes a visual image vivid in its slow motion angle, time the metaphor for a literal phallic fall. And throughout the day the Consul's fate is echoed in a bauble of strange accents speaking his language more truthfully through their assorted errors than his decomposing cabbalistic consciousness through its deluded claim to the absolute.

Taken in conjunction with Lowry's method of sentence construction and his externalisation of the tragic psyche, the constant slippages of mistranslation and miscommunication form the basis for the distinctive use of the epiphanous form. The elongated sentence is itself a lynchpin of the form. O'Kill has convincingly demonstrated how Lowry uses the sentence unit to link the specific to the universal through syntactical digression and expansion.[21] For a sentence unit which withholds through a series of mellifluous digressions the eventual linking of subject, verb and object imitates linguistically the simultaneity of experience in everyday life, where the past recurrently merges into the present as instantly retrieved memory. Lowry's characters seem more strongly rooted in time and place because, paradoxically, of the ease with which the epiphanous form can traverse the here-and-now to reproduce in the same sentence or paragraph a series of significations which go beyond what, in strictly naturalistic terms, would be available to it. The depth and resonance of Lowry's method compares favourably with the histrionic exoticism in *The Plumed Serpent*, which, for all its eloquence and stunning set pieces, is always straining to evoke a sense of place, let alone endow it with universal significance.

In its withholding and digressing idioms, the style has many similarities with *Absalom, Absalom!*, whose extraordinary use of technique Conrad Aiken was one of the first fully to appreciate during the period of his close friendship with Lowry.[22] The style dictates, as in Faulkner's novel, a unilateral flow of narrative which carries along with it the individual voices of the characters. In Faulkner the novel consists of a series of multiple spoken narrations; the similarity of voice among the narrators is predicated on their discussion of identical historical subjects in their separate narratives. But in Lowry, writing a contemporary novel, the merging of past and present implies a more impersonal narration in which the method of digressing and withholding has greater fluency and, since it is no longer a calculated act of first-person rhetoric, wider resonance. The Consul is as objectified as Sutpen yet thinks and speaks with the emotional intensity of Sutpen's narrators. What Faulkner conceived of as a new and challenging form for the historical novel – since he was intent on challenging history itself – is reabsorbed here, through the elision of speaker and subject and use of the third-person past tense, into contemporary narrative.

The novel possesses a central feature which only a contemporaneous narrative can achieve – the breathtaking gaps in time which run through Firmin's consciousness. Besides loss of memory, discontinuity of consciousness erupts directly out of the excess of alcohol. One moment the Consul is looking for Yvonne on the porch; the next he is 'guiltily climbing the Calle Nicaragua'. The gaps in time are not the narrator's gaps in time but the Consul's gaps in time. The gaps in his consciousness determine the omissions of narrative. At one moment he is sitting with Yvonne and Hugh in the Salón Ofelia while Cervantes offers them from the menu 'Onans in garlic soup on egg'; 'Vol-au-vent à la reine', which he translates into English as 'Somersaults for the queen'; 'poxy eggs, poxy in toast' and 'spectral chicken of the house'.[23] The next moment the Consul is sitting in the stone toilet with a lemonade bottle of mescal unable to account for his absence from the table, reading tourist brochures of Tlaxcala while he hears Hugh and Yvonne discussing the assault on the Indian lying by the roadside. The time leap is a crucial feature of the narrative strategy of absence. The Consul finds himself elsewhere because he is unable to account for the time between, in which, without knowing it, he has made his escape from the others. Absence of time entails absence of communication. Thus the irony of the simultaneous experience in which, while the Consul reads the brochures about the Tlaxcalans who betrayed Mexico to the Spaniards, Hugh and Yvonne, unaware that he is also listening to them, continue their discussion about Mexico's contemporary betrayers. The separations of simultaneous being are embedded by narrative montage in the hero's tragic loss of time.

II

Like all the epiphanous writers, Lowry portrays the problematic intersection of presence and the unconscious, absence and being, Heidegger and Freud, but with a sustained intensity which is only rivalled by *The Sound and the Fury*. Firmin, like Quentin Compson and Leopold Bloom, fuses in his fragmented self the absences of what he represses with the immediacy of what is present to the senses. This is achieved through the form of a 'presencing' to which memory, as the source of release from the unconscious, also belongs.[24] Since there is no strict ontological separation of past and present, being, in the Heideggerian sense, incorporates time, while absence, as the fused, voided form of the social and the self, engenders impossible desire. The epiphanous novel constructs an imaginary unity out of the major polarity of twentieth-century thought, an extraordinary fictive resolution of the enduring analytical antinomies of Freud and Heidegger, which go far beyond the simplistic juxtapositions of existentialism and psychoanalysis. It does this not as an addendum to abstraction but through the invention of an imaginary world of imaginary persons which exists beyond discursive thought. At its most powerful it reveals, through an imaginative rendering of particular dimensions of culture, psyche and the time–space edges of Western civilisation, the world of us all.

Freud's revolutionary account of the self, with its threefold division of id, ego and superego, calls into question the whole nature of human agency as much for his own theory as for those which preceded it.[25] For the Freudian self is fragmented into internal agencies of will which exist alongside its own, a philosophical absurdity which none the less derives physically from the actual forms of the destabilisation of the personality. *Das Ich* is at times part of self, at other times self itself. But this contrary usage, which is ultimately self-defeating, comes from a practical recognition of decentring which undermines the Cartesian convention of the perceiving subject as well as the rounded character or stable ego of nineteenth-century realism.

In this context the epiphanous novel reconstructs what Freud omitted – or simply made reference to in a cursory manner – the social dimensions of the decentring of the subject. Fictional evocation of the absence of self within the social, which runs through Joyce and Faulkner, Barnes and Lowry, and later through Wright, Ellison and Styron, establishes absence as constitutive of the relationship between the self and the social world. Yet the very decentring of the subject is dependent in the epiphanous novel on the author's power to evoke the subject's constant ontological presence, a paradox whose literary resolution affirms the subject's significance rather than vindicating the structuralist illusion of the subject's elimination. While Freud and Heidegger both fail sufficiently to theorise the social, the more conventional discourses of social science have remained largely blind to the decentring of the subject within advanced capitalist societies, a decentring which is mediated through various forms of individualism and its modes of presencing. It is thus fiction, rather than social science, the language of the realistic imagination rather than discursive consciousness, which has attempted to forge a resolution. In imagining the real, epiphanous narrative places that resolution in worlds which are imagined rather than real. In so doing the transformed mimetic form preserves the dialectic interplay of the real and the imagined which characterised the nineteenth-century novel, but in transformed historical circumstances.

The literary resolution of the polar extremes of theorising cannot be achieved within the unified field of experience which constitutes the consensual basis of nineteenth-century realism, or its

peripheral alternative, the impassioned tragedy of social alienation. As we have seen, the nineteenth-century English novel
became through its typical ending an imaginary reconciliation of
belief and experience, life and ideal, after the telling of a story
which reveals their disjunctions in the lives of characters with
stable and intelligible selves.[26] The decentring of self in the
epiphanous novel is largely a response to the crisis of value which
convulsed Western civilisation before, during and after the First
World War, when the self ceased to be seen as the centre of gravity
for reconcilable disjunctions between evanescent value and lives
in disarray. As we have seen, Freud and Heidegger responded in
opposed and separate ways to that crisis in value, but their antithetical responses were unified by the scope and depth of its
identification. Beneath the level of discursive consciousness
deriving from both thinkers, the epiphanous novel has transmuted
that recognition into an imaginary unity, but only by transmuting
the previous figural dimensions of narrative perspective into a
form which, in the wake of civilisation's perceived loss of value,
could incorporate the manifold contusions of absence and desire.

Absence of motive is an integral part of that response to loss of
value. In the novels of Joyce and Faulkner, Barnes and
Hemingway, it is both a thematic suppression and a literary tran-
scendence. It affirms Freud through its intimations of that which
cannot be spoken, yet it repudiates him through its chthonic resonances. For in the constant presencing of the subject in everyday
life motive itself can become an artefact, an extrapolation, at times
an illusion. Since continuous action is grounded in intention and
practical reasoning, the ascription of motive can degenerate into
a fetish. Where it becomes indispensable is not in the delineation
of presence, but in the delineation of absence, in the explication
of action which has been suppressed. *Under the Volcano* provides us
with an ironic and reflexive gloss upon this particular predicament
when its narrator translates, through tragi-comic intent, accidents
of language as parapraxes of desire. Because the unintentional is
made intentional, accident is rendered as necessity.

Yet the analytic recourse to motive cannot easily be swept aside.
The vast and devastating scope of Freud's account of rationalisation has suggested the vulnerability of the accounts of action
which are taken for granted in the impersonal narrators of nineteenth-century fiction, and which are predicated on the intelligible
self of the rounded character. Discursive analysis denudes twenti-

eth-century fiction of the authority of motive as a constituent part of narrative by simultaneously sanctifying it and calling it into question, by reforming analytically what lies beneath the rationalisations of the erring subject. But the epiphanous novel in turn evades the pitfalls of discursive language by escaping from the reflexive trap in which constant analysis of motive fails to avoid the ubiquities of rationalisation it detects, thereby seeming at times in contemporary culture to be hoist on its own petard. For the labile presencing of the human subject often causes the compulsive ascription of motive to congeal into the fetishism of over-analysis, of seeking out or finding motive where none exists.

Absence of motive also explains, in part at least, the ubiquity of doubling in the epiphanous novel, where it clearly goes beyond the Gothic tradition of demonic projection. Its importance is best seen in comparison with the developmental self of the rounded character in classic realism. Here, in the course of experience, the major character undergoes changes of attitude, makes discoveries of concealed knowledge and demonstrates growth of personality in response to events. All are constituent elements of the linear path of realist narrative, part of an internal evolutionary scheme by which the narrative perspective is eventually fused with the structure of feeling we have called compassion. Conversely, however, the process of doubling, which deconstructs the intelligibility of self, is a challenge to evolutionary narrative. The potentialities of self are not projected forward through experience but are projected outward and laterally through other selves, offering imprints of the original in altered form.

Of all nineteenth-century writers, Dostoevsky is clearly the one who most powerfully incorporates the demonic tradition in his own work and who from his peripheral position in Western literature transmits the doubling-procedure to his twentieth-century successors. But in Joyce, Faulkner and Lowry the simultaneous presencing of the doubled self in its own person and its various personas, who have to be constituted in the realist continuum as persons in their own right, links the fragmentation of self to the simultaneity of experience in a startling and revolutionary form. Here narrative can be neither rationalising nor wholly evolutionary. The kind of eventuality which Ermath claims is latent in nineteenth-century realism, where shared information and the unearthing of buried secrets may be enough to avert disaster, does not obtain.[27] The projections of the different, better or more fortunate person the hero could become already exist through doubling in forms of otherness, other selves, where simultaneous presence and intractable otherness shatter the whole fabric of shared communication and consensual possibility. While consensus is often predicated on the growing harmony of different subjects, epiphany reveals the disintegrating world of similar selves which are shattered by their necessary differences.

Themes of periphery in Lowry echo those of the Southern novel. The overcoming of distances, the closer proximity of region to centre is part of the historical movement of centralisation on the American continent, by which differences between North and South, the United States and Mexico, are diminished by time, culture and capital. In Southern writing after Faulkner, the next phase of the epiphanous novel incorporates the movement north, which is both a pattern of migration and an elision of cultural differences. *Native Son*, *Invisible Man* and *Lie Down in Darkness* all capture this dialectic of differences within the time–space continuum of American history. In Lowry it is the same. *Dark as the Grave wherein my Friend is Laid* is the autobiographical return to Mexico, thinly fictionalised after the years spent in British Columbia writing *Under the Volcano* in that idyllic coastal spot of which Yvonne, in the novel itself, constantly dreams.

When Lowry returned at the end of 1945 to the scene of the Inferno which had haunted his imagination, the Oaxaca he had transformed into the sinister Parián in his absence was no longer the sinister place he had imagined it to be. By changing and obliterating familiar landmarks, place had outlived imagination. Instead of evoking ghosts, it more or less erased them. This explains in part the literary weakness of the autobiographical centre to the writer's return. Recentred on the hero's visiting and traversing self, the novel is too reflexive, manacled by self-aware-ness, overwrought by anticipation, and ends up displaying all the egotistical urgency of travelogue masquerading as fiction. If *Under the Volcano* had been magnificent expiation for *The Plumed Serpent*, *Dark as the Grave* seems at times a self-indulgent sequel to the more incisive and evocative *Mornings in Mexico*. Yet the deficiency of the project is not merely that of its author. It is also the passing of time which has unhinged the spatial epiphanies of *Under the Volcano*. Giddens has suggested that 'all social life occurs, and is constructed by, intersections of presence and absence in the "fading away" of time and the "shading off" of space'.[28] In Lowry it is a process which cuts across national boundaries, across the expanse of the United States which divided him from his literary landscape, and which cultural differences diminish. It was a fallacy on his part to think that in a changed Mexico periphery could be easily recreated as a work of art, for the margins of periphery had themselves changed.

His return to Cuernavaca shows him it is no longer – if it ever was – the Quauhnahuac of his novel, just as Oaxaca is no longer the infernal Parián, the City of Dreadful Night. It too had altered out of all recognition. Not only had the Banco Ejidal changed its location, but Lowry could not even find the Farolito, which had also been removed from its original place, and he finally gave up.[29] At the end, Oaxaca had become for Lowry's fictional persona, Sigbjorn Wilderness, a paradisal Eden, the rich lush granary of a new Mexico. But in the narrative it is a place without resonance. There is no mirroring of psychic fusion, where in the previous novel there had been a sustained mirroring of psychic estrangement; there are few authentic paradisal signs of landscape, where previously they had been infernal and abundant. Because the richness of *Under the Volcano* was constructed out of poverty and terror, the later novel, with its pastoral idylls, seem peculiarly vacuous. But to put this down to literary deterioration is to miss the point. It seems rather that in the space of a few years, a mere decade, the historical moment of Lowry's tragic periphery had passed, and nostalgia could put nothing in its place.

9 Completion: Wright and Ellison

The epiphanous novel finds its completion in a movement in Southern writing which runs parallel to *Under the Volcano*, the migratory movement north which celebrates difference of place just as history is ending those differences and challenging the myth of the South as a nation-within-a-nation. There are separate but parallel phases. In black fiction, Richard Wright and Ralph Ellison bring into the modern novel the heritage of slave and blues narratives, the folk culture and vernacular idioms of Afro-American life. Among white novelists, Thomas Wolfe and William Styron stand out as the elegists of a metaphorical confrontation between Southern town and Northern city, while Flannery O'Connor's *Wise Blood* dissolves finally a traditional vision of the South as an arcadian repository of Christian value. All five echo and at times prophesy the erosion of historical differences between North and South as centre and periphery of modern American life. Though epiphanous fiction outlives them in, for example, John Updike's *Rabbit, Run* or, more recently, Toni Morrison's *Song of Solomon*, there is here a sense of climax and completion, particularly in *Native Son*, *Invisible Man* and *Lie Down in Darkness*. Along with *Wise Blood* they capture the decentring epiphanies of absence as if for the last time – the last time, that is, where there is a full uncompromising fusion of periphery and the repressed, demotic voice, and, consequently, of absence and desire.

I

As Southern writers, Wright and Ellison were heirs to Faulkner but also to the Afro-American folk tradition. Though Faulkner was one of the few white writers to penetrate beneath racial stereotyping, the black Southern experience was, despite Dilsey Gibson

169

or Lucas Beauchamp, at times a significant absence in his work, at times separated from him by an abyss which he rightly judged impossible to cross. But Richard Wright's reclaiming of Afro-American life as enduring cultural presence, personified by the titles *Black Boy* and *Native Son*, observes a double dialectic. *Black Boy* is an outstanding literary memoir which recentres the self through an autobiographical account of Southern upbringing. *Native Son*, however, is a fiction of the Northern city in which Southern identity is ostensibly suppressed, only to dominate the narrative through its haunting absences. And *Invisible Man* is a novel balancing Southern countryside against Northern city only to throw, as the title suggests, all identities into confusion. The black–white oppositions in Wright and Ellison, as with the male–female oppositions in *Lie Down in Darkness*, are catalysed by the movement South–North. It is as if, in art, the American South finally falls into place through being vacated.

The initial designation of *Native Son* as a 'protest novel', a simple exposure of racial injustice in Chicago, suppressed recognition of its Southern nexus. In terms of its literary genealogy there is here one clear parallel between Bigger Thomas and Joe Christmas. But, as a black Afro-American, Bigger cannot 'pass' like the parentless Christmas for being white. The intolerable ambiguities of identity rest not on ambiguous pigmentation but on the unspoken differences between Chicago and Mississippi, in which Bigger has lived in ways that the white communists who befriend him can neither know nor share. Formally, Bigger only makes fleeting mention of his Southern background to Mary Dalton and Jan Erleone. But the South is there all along, there and not there, a phantasm, a ghost from which Bigger cannot escape, forcing him into a double life with a double identity which threatens to destroy all identity. Beyond the poverty of family life in a rat-infested tenement, beyond the spatial enclosures of the Black Belt, which fuel the brutal uncertainties of gang life, is a structure of feeling in which claustrophobia and escape co-exist, the sense of having eluded Dixie being undermined by a deeper fear and horror of never having got away from it at all. Stepto has pointed out that the Hyde Park mansion of the Daltons, barely a block away from the Thomas tenement, contains more than an echo of the Big House as the story of Bigger's employment there as chauffeur unfolds, at times with the resonance of a plantation romance.[1] But the explicit suppression of signifying actually strengthens Wright's narrative. After the edgy and aggressive encounters with his black friends, in which Bigger is a dominating figure, the hero is reduced by the shock of entry into the Dalton household to a sullen silence which goes far beyond conventional expectations of difference and deference. The deeper trauma in his speechlessness intimates an unsignified return of the repressed, echoes of his childhood which are, however, more than a mere regression into childhood, since they are also a regression into the deeper history of the Deep South.

The inexpressible trauma becomes an interior absence underlying the narrative rationalisation of motive, which Wright borrows, rather uncertainly, from Dreiser. At one level the murder of Mary Dalton is a tragic miscalculation. But what gives it such extraordinary power is the unwitting role the blind Mrs Dalton plays in her daughter's death. Were it not for her presence the incident might recall the elided slaughter of Joanna Burden or the elided rape of Temple Drake. But it differs fundamentally from both. For Bigger's impulse to smother Mary as the blind Mrs Dalton enters the room is less a culmination of desire than a desire to suffocate desire, to obliterate the transient and momentary evidence of wanting. The luminous presence of the blind mother dressed all in white evokes by default the absent, white and 'watching' father, the Master of the Big House. Murder is the outcome of Bigger's paranoia, his fear of the transparency of his previously repressed desire filtered through the mother who cannot see, to the absent Master, whose watching is ubiquitous. It is no wonder that Dalton's failure to decipher Bigger's guilt through interrogation the following day seems uncannily unnatural, as if his inquiring mind had failed to identify the evidence of his watching eyes.

The imploded Oedipal motif provides us here with an inverted perspective on the racial trauma of the white South which Faulkner had illuminated – the fantasised link between incest and miscegenation. It is as if Dalton, in not recognising the culprit, had failed to witness his rival and adversary – rival in the double sense of rival for his power and rival for his daughter. Bigger invokes miscegenation by bearing no overt trace of it. He can be safely 'adopted' by white philanthropy into the household because there seems no chance of his being, like Charles Bon, the real miscegenated son. But the surrogate son is still an Oedipal rival, as Bon was for Sutpen, his rivalry for the daughter evoking the quasi-double-incest of patriarchy (white) and surrogate siblinghood (black). The latter then inverts as unsignified fantasy the actual historical pattern of miscegenation between white master and black servant which constituted for Faulkner one of the many dooms of slavery, the patriarchal rape of the black woman, the plantation's unspoken *droit de seigneur*. Dalton's refusal to recognise, which Wright reiterated critically, after writing the book, as a failure of responsibility, is a metaphorical snub to Bigger's identity – Bigger's murder of the sister–daughter being the inexpressible tie which binds, yet also the act of historical revenge.

Thereafter the landscape of subterfuge and flight takes on for Bigger a threatening iridescent whiteness. In her memoir of Wright,[2] Mary Walker recalls his ecstatic response to *Sanctuary*, and it is of *Sanctuary* one thinks when Wright creates a landscape dominated by a single colour, this time inverting Faulkner's 'jungle' that is 'a lake of ink' by creating a print from the photographic negative and finding his own optic purity to act as a metaphor of oppression. As Bigger tries to shove Mary's dead body into the furnace, the latter's redness is overcome by a different colour, which finds feline rather than human embodiment. 'A white cat and its round green eyes gazed past him at the white face hanging limply from the fiery furnace door.' Its eyes are 'two green burning pools – pools of accusation and guilt' which 'stared at him from a white blur'.[3] The next morning, when he wakes in the tenement, there is now snow falling past the window; and that night, when he returns to the Daltons with his fake kidnap note, the snow is 'falling as though it had fallen from the beginning of time and would always fall till the end of the world'.[4] Its oppressive ubiquity echoes the earlier image in Bigger's mind of white people as 'a sort of great natural force, like a stormy sky looming overhead'. When he reaches the Dalton's house, it is 'white and silent'. Later, after being questioned by Dalton and Britten – Dalton's private detective, an updated plantation overseer – the snow has turned into a blizzard which 'moved in no given direction, but filled the world with a vast white storm of flying powder'.[5]

The oppressiveness of the white landscape subvert's the hero's constant rationalisations of identity. The pride which Bigger tries to acquire by imagining the outrage the murder will cause among his white adversaries is undermined by a narrative form which transparently relegates its hero's consciousness below the level of the novel's author. This is the sense, perhaps, of Ellison's remark that, while Richard Wright could imagine Bigger Thomas, Bigger Thomas could never imagine Richard Wright.[6] For Bigger's re-created identity thrives only in the transient moment between murder and arrest. Thereafter it clearly founders when Bigger transfers his newly won sense of pride onto Max, his white attorney, who defends him through the skills of official discourse which Bigger lacks. The hero's voice is thus suppressed beneath the level of an articulate political consciousness which is itself equivocal. Smothered by the rhetoric of the white articulate other, Bigger's sense of self-renewal remains a brief and burning illusion. It is a recentring of self which cannot be sustained.

It was perhaps this difference of levels which fatally flawed the ending of *Native Son*, the bifurcated consciousness which Ellison wanted to transcend through first-person narrative in *Invisible Man*. In charting the historical survival of the Afro-American in the northern city, Ellison extends the unity of the narrative voice to be found in the writings of Frederick Douglass and James Weldon Johnson. Equally, he fuses it with the imagistic modernism of Joyce, Eliot and Jean Toomer's *Cane*. For his unnamed narrator, the very act of narrating becomes a means of mastering experience. The narrative, of course, is retrospective yet always captures the living instant of social encounter. Even when bewildered by the ubiquitous absurdities of his journey north, his perilous ascent, the narrator constantly articulates without losing his vernacular idiom. Ellison's epiphanous style produces a fluid continuum between author and narrator, narrative and speech, knowledge and experience. To that extent the many rationalisations of anxiety are eventually overhauled by the cutting edge of inquiry. In a world where all values are subject to betrayal, improvisation becomes the source of adaptation and the key to his survival.

Murray has seen this dimension of Ellison's writing as a literary extension of the blues, a twelve-bar blues scored for full orchestra, a form so consistently open and existential that it turns meaning inside out without offering clear-cut solutions.[7] In the constant presencing of Ellison's hero, the blues voice unifies speech and narrative. The decentring of self implicit in Toomer's fragmented multiple narration is here retained in the single unifying voice. In Proust the retrospective rationalisations of the narrator are measured and controlled. But Ellison's hero lives and reflects upon living at the same time. Confronted at every turn by figures in authority, black and white, who conspire to betray him, he dons the mantle of a trickster, a huckster, a confidence man echoing Melville's novel of the same name. Yet in seeking the confidence of others, where mental alertness is the key to survival, he never compromises his own integrity. He learns to fake appearances, but he never fakes the truth.

Yet at the start Ellison's hero is, with obvious parodic intent, like Bigger Thomas. He too is recruited as a young and anxious black chauffeur, but with a difference. He drives the patriarch himself rather than the patriarch's daughter and her boyfriend. Norton, the New England benefactor of the hero's black college, is similarly a source of danger for the nervous chauffeur keen to get through the performance of his duties without blemish but predictably blazing a trail of disaster. Ellison's Trueblood chapter then becomes an ironic and grimly humorous gloss on the initial motif of *Native Son*. Just as Bigger is forced into taking Jan and Mary slumming to a black South Side diner, so the narrator drives Norton past the run-down cabins of poor black sharecroppers, where the benefactor insists on stopping to talk to Trueblood, thus initiating the set of amusing and macabre events which will lead to the hero's expulsion from his beloved college. Just as we realise that, unlike Bigger, his crime of malperformance will soon be discovered, we sense too that, as Bledsoe sends him packing, his 'pre-invisible days' will soon be over.

Through his parodic use of difference and repetition, Ellison tightens the screw in two opposing ways. The scene *is* the South, the confrontation with the Northern patriarch immediate and not indirect. At the same time the meeting with Trueblood produces the reflexive narrative of a tale-within-a-tale made doubly reflexive by the dream Trueblood recounts at the crux of his tall tale. While the evidence of his incest with his daughter, Matty Lou, is there for all to see, the dream is invisible, a stated cause of transgression which its teller knows has no trace. As a teller of tall tales whose tale is pure demotic performance, Trueblood is the authentic model and double for the young narrator. More ominously, he becomes, through the substance of his tale, the seduction of his daughter, the involuntary double of the white philanthropist who has funded the narrator's college as a memorial tribute to his own daughter, whom he had deeply loved. Since the nature of that love is left unspoken, its immediate contrast with the carnal love of Trueblood for Matty Lou, received by Morton's listening ear in a state of morbid compulsion, suggests that the tale becomes for him a showpiece desublination of his own sublimated affections, desublimated in his white eyes, that is, by the fact of race. For him, Trueblood is truly beyond the pale, but Trueblood is also his own ugly 'black' reflection in the mirror, the worst of his wish dreams come true.

In his account of his daughter's seduction, Trueblood attributes it to unfortunate propinquity, husband, wife and daughter sleeping three to a bed in a freezing cabin. But the nub of the tale is the strange dream which he makes an excuse for his actions. In the dream Trueblood finds himself in the hilltop house of a white philanthropist, Mr Broadnax – a Southernised version, perhaps, of Norton himself – and proceeds to a bedroom where he is sensually embraced by a white woman in 'a nightgown of soft white silky stuff and nothin' else'.[8] He tries to break her hold by throwing her onto the bed and nearly smothering her, escapes into a grandfather clock, and then through a long, dark tunnel towards a bright light which bursts over him as he catches up with it. He awakes to find himself having intercourse with Matty Lou.

In a masterly analysis of the Trueblood chapter,[9] Baker has suggested that the fusion of dream and incest constitutes a historical regression in which the sharecropper's dreamed violations of Southern taboos, both sexual and social, contain a desire to slaughter Broadnax the white patriarch who dispenses the 'fat meat' of the land. In its linking of the dreamed seduction of the nameless white woman, the meat of the totemic animal and the slaughter of the patriarch, there is a parodic echo of the Freudian version of the origin of the incest taboo. But the dream can also be seen as Norton's nightmare, since it links incest and miscegenation – taking incest out of the black family, where it is treated by local white stereotyping as an acceptable illustration of the horrors of black promiscuity, into that dimension of the double challenge, sexual and social, to white power itself. The listening Norton knows he could be Broadnax just as the astute reader can see in the unnamed woman in white a parodic version of Mary Dalton. By taking desire from reality into dream, where violation should be a lesser threat, Ellison lets the fervent imagination of the philanthropist conceive it as an even greater threat, since Trueblood, the tall-tale-teller, presents the dream as the reason for his transgression. Discovered, he protests to his wife, 'Naw, Kate. Things ain't what they 'pear! Don't make no blood-sin on accounta no dream-sin.' But Kate, unlike Norton, is resolute. 'Shut up, nigguh. You done *fouled!*'[10]

Amidst his fascinated horror, Norton clearly does feel guilty – witness the $100 bill he gives on departure to the astonished Trueblood, who has sold his story with a vengeance. Ellison cunningly merges Northern liberal guilt with Southern racist fear – the fear of black male miscegenation. Norton's previous euphemisms of philanthropy duly catch him out. In the car he has confessed to the hero the deeper reason for helping the college, 'more passionate and, yes, even more sacred than all the others'.[11] It is the trauma of the terminal illness of his pure and beautiful daughter to whom he has been devoted. Everything he has done has been a 'monument to her memory'. With the training of black students for the skilled tasks of life, 'I also construct a living memorial to my daughter. Understand? I can see the fruits produced by the land that your great Founder has transformed from barren clay to fertile soil'.[12] The hero, and the other Great Black Hopes of his college, are progeny born, metaphorically speaking, out of the benefactor's love for his daughter. In an instant Trueblood will make the metaphor frighteningly real.

In the following chapter at the Golden Day, where the trail of disaster hilariously and gruesomely continues, we are given more clues to suggest that we should believe the evidence of our eyes. One of the shell-shocked black veterans who start harassing Norton claims that the white-haired white man is Thomas Jefferson, his own grandfather, and he himself a grandson 'on the "field-nigger" side'. Before the drunken mêlée which culminates in an attack on Supercargo, the whoring attendant, another pockmarked vet suddenly slaps the bewildered Norton hard on the face. The blow echoes that which Kate has struck Trueblood with an axe as punishment for his crime. For, when Norton sees the sharecropper, the wound on his cheek is still 'raw and moist', assailed by gnats. Later, as the crazed vet hits the benefactor, 'five pale red lines bloomed on the white cheek, glowing like fire beneath translucent stone'.[13] The slap is a shallow imprint of the deeper wound, the skin unbroken. But the vet's sudden movement 'pinching the chin like a barber about to apply a razor' echoes the downward swing of the blade which marks Trueblood's face. The doubling of Trueblood and Norton through the 'mark' of incest, incest that in one case is actual and in the other metaphorical, strengthens the impact of the black inversion of white miscegenation brought to us in Trueblood's dream. In *Sanctuary's* doubling, Benbow's orgasmic fantasy puts Temple's image in the place of Little Belle, his stepdaughter, but, later at the dance hall, Temple's plaintive whisper is 'Popeye, Daddy.' What is imagistic in Faulkner becomes reflexive in Ellison, yet the outcome is the same. Norton, like Benbow, becomes a broken man.

When the duplicitous Bledsoe sends the hero to New York City, the journey is an escape into freedom but also into invisibility, the *rite de passage* into black manhood. The previous pattern of absence and desire is somewhat reversed. The sublimations and desublimations of desire largely precede the absences of self experienced in the North. The hero's own erotic encounters with white women are sardonic and demythologising. Not that he eludes all sexual stereotyping, but rather that his existential presencing allows him to get under its skin, enabling him in his own fleeting and muted manner to fulfil a version of the desire embedded in Trueblood's dream.

In New York City, the visible nonentity becomes an invisible somebody, a paradox which Ellison teases out in a series of extraordinary episodes where the epiphanous evocation of the metropolis is equal to anything in Joyce or Dos Passos. As a worker in the Liberty Paints factory, his narrator stands out as a black man who cannot mix 'optic white' without leaving an undertow of grey. In the streets of Harlem he stands out as an impromptu spokesman for group anger at a brutal eviction, and later for the collective grief and rage at Clifton's funeral after his murder. The hero is not invisible because, as one false convention has it, he tries to assimilate or blend into white culture. He is invisible because he ultimately resists all forms of assimilation and rejects all reified labels of identity on offer to him. Since those offers have only been made because of the impact he makes in the first place, he can decide to become invisible only because he is so visible, opting for a life of subterfuge rather than submitting to false stereotype.

Ellison's view of the radical politics of the period evokes the conflicting loyalties of class and race – exemplified most strongly in the clash between the Brotherhood and Ras the Exhorter. But the strength of his evocation lies in the visible and nightmarish absurdities such conflicts create in the daily life of his hero. The author's power to place collective agency between individual and society lies in his hero's self-image as an invisible man, which in turn spurs in him a close identity with all those in history on whom no name is bestowed. This impulse lies in his Afro-American roots. For him the American way of life spurs that frantic search for a name which is an integral part of identity, only to withhold it. For black Americans that withholding also highlights the conventions of false naming which have their origin in slavery.[14] The constant unnaming of the hero has its roots in his collective past. But, in the elusive search for identity, it also raises one vital issue of the present for the hero and his migrating Southern brothers – 'us transitory ones', he calls them, 'birds of passage too obscure for learned classification' – for whom the life of the city gives no answers:

> Yes, I thought, what about those of us who shoot up from the South into the busy city like a jack-in-the-box broken loose from our springs – so sudden that our gait becomes that of deep-sea divers suffering from the bends? What about those fellows waiting still and silent there on the platform, so still and silent that they clash with the crowd in their very immobility; standing noisy in their very silence; harsh as a cry of terror in their quietness.[15]

This loyalty to those 'outside of historical time' separates the hero from his new double, Rinehart, the trickster with a variety of disguises for whom the hero is sometimes mistaken but whom he never sees, who has a name and no voice just as the hero has a voice and no name. Benston has pointed out that Rinehart is an Emersonian poet in a world of limitless possibilities but also, like Melville's confidence man, a social parasite undermining the stable forms of life he exploits.[16] In the life of the city, improvisational freedom dissolves the few forms of stability out of which an identity can be formed. The actual men outside historical time to whom the hero refers are seen walking along a subway platform, fashionable in dress and ostentatious in style but still 'men of transition'. Observing the fast and volatile life of the city in motion, the hero has the impression of persona being reduced to a series of passing shadows, while Ellison himself deconstructs that cherished myth of American sociology, the looking-glass self.

The most memorable instance is in the scene where the hero is given a dressing-down by the Brotherhood for his eloquent oration at Clifton's funeral. The white leader and organisational villain, to the allure of indiscriminate narcissism, the narrator stands to lose, through the gamble on his strategy, any substance of any ego ideal he may have created for himself. The forgotten basement of a white tenement to which he finally retreats, an underground refuge flooded in light, is a kind of ironic closure for the self which life above ground can no longer give him. The pattern of his existence, from the traumatic moment in Emerson's office when he reads Bledsoe's letter of betrayal, to the existential moment when he confronts the wrath of Ras the Destroyer amidst riot and insurrection, is a pattern of picaresque absences of self running through a kaleidoscope of perennial motion, a motion hinging on the movement north. Out of the specific and unique experiences of Afro-American life, experiences which lie beneath and beyond facile Anglo-Saxon conventions of rational intelligibility, Ellison pinpoints a universal predicament of American and twentieth-century society. At the end of the book, the narrator poses the question, 'Who knows but that, on the lower frequencies, I speak for you?'[19] He does.

II

The movement from country to city and South to North in Thomas Wolfe's novels is embodied in the *rite de passage* of his duplicated hero, first Eugene Gant, then George Webber, a doubled autobiographical self whose alteration of name implies no difference in egocentric identity. The key work here, in Wolfe's rambling odyssey, is *The Web and the Rock*. Attentive readers will note that Webber's journey from Libya Hill in North Carolina to New York City is similar to the expansive journeys undertaken by the country-boy heroes of Goethe and Tolstoy, Balzac and Dickens, Fielding and Twain, their provincial innocence soon deflowered by enthralling and enlarging experiences. They will also realise that Webber's journey north in the mid twenties is symbolic of the historical shattering of the provincial insularity of the South since the days of Reconstruction. They will know because the author explicitly tells them so in his text. No kind of motive in character or explanation of society in history that Wolfe can think of seems to have been left out. His explicating momentum infuses his lyrical narrative with an encyclopaedic compendium of endless reason and self-definitions. In its bid to embrace the whole world, his social pantheism rescues narrative from the significant silences of his epiphanous contemporaries. To read Wolfe is to marvel at times at the extensive lyricism of breathtaking hyperbole. But it is also to experience a regression into the nineteenth century, to feel the pantheistic extension of the small-town self into the depthless metropolis as pre-Freudian and pre-existential, to be offered as absolute truth the experience and hyperbole of the self-regarding self.

In comparing Wolfe with Ellison, the deficiencies are soon apparent. Ellison sees blues narrative as a vehicle for putting questions, for exploring encounters by taking inquiry into new dimensions. Narrative runs existentially in counterpoint to his hero's experiencing of the multivalent here-and-now. In Wolfe, narrative explication raises itself ethereally above the immediate and the quotidian into what at times is a miasma of generality, providing vague answers before it has even found the precise questions to be asked. His technique of occasional grandiose distancing, in which he attempts to merge his hero with the cosmos, can be sublimely myopic, a form of not-seeing which comes from not-asking at the centre of a formally enlarging discourse. The spasmodic myopia seems curiously enough to be an extension of genealogy, the modest privilege of a sensitive white, male Southerner seeking advance and accomplishment in the Northern city. If not exactly born with a silver spoon in his mouth, the duplicated hero is none the less sufficiently cushioned and centred by his momentum to exude a radiant confidence of being and anticipation amid the life of the city. It is a luxury that the black heroes of Wright and Ellison could not afford.

It is of course gender, not race, which provides the crucial distinction between Wolfe's doubled hero and Peyton Loftis in *Lie Down in Darkness*. The distinction is made even sharper by the social advantages of family which Styron's heroine holds over Eugene Gant or George Webber. For, in her journey north, the double standards of sexual convention outweigh the legacy of family privilege through the reproduction of the legacies of familial disintegration in a Northern city which is another country, where the decentring dimensions of home become irrevocable once home is abandoned. In choosing a biographical setting, Styron himself was well aware of the difference between his Virginian milieu and Faulkner's small-town Mississippi.[20] The upper-middle-class families of his fictitious Port Warwick, a small but expanding city whose industrial vitality and effluent make it a trope for progress, are not scions of the old Virginian aristocracy but *nouveaux riches*, distinctively Southern but endowed with what Faulkner would have seen as a more affluent version of Snopesian vulgarity.

The New South in wartime, its insularity evaporating, its new affluence that of the wider prospering American nation, provides an apt thematic basis for the reconstruction of realism. For much of its narrative, that appears to be the novel's achievement. For here is the naturalistic delineation of middle-class life whose solidities of recurrent experience testify to a new social stability and confidence, whose largesse and powers of expansion can absorb the individual crises in its midst – even, indeed, reproduce them as comic melodrama. The novel initiates the concern with sexual intrigue in everyday life which goes beyond Sinclair Lewis and paves the way for its deeper exploration in the decades to come, in Updike and Cheever, Murdoch and Lessing, Bellow and Roth. The marital conflict of Milton and Helen Loftis offers us predictable opposites – the alcoholism and comic adultery of the erratic lawyer, the lack of forgiveness and dependence on priestly advice in his fretting domesticated wife. We are moving perhaps towards the staple diet of post-Freudian suburban realism, for none of Styron's characters are large enough or transgressing enough to be genuinely tragic. None, that is, except for Peyton Loftis. True, her father's drinking disrupts and destabilises in poignant ways, evoking that deadly combination of amnesia, absent-mindedness and reverie to be found in Geoffrey Firmin. But Milton is still too cushioned by affluence and community to experience total self-destruction. That is the fate of his daughter, to which he acts as the involuntary catalyst.

The Freudian family, which Lowry failed to tie together in the earlier drafts of *Under the Volcano* and which he liquidated from the later ones, is reborn here in a purer form. For if in Lowry Yvonne the daughter rightly became Yvonne the estranged wife, then in Styron she is rightly turned back into Peyton, the loving estranged daughter. In New York, married and compulsively unfaithful, Peyton becomes the distant conjunction of her parent's internecine vices, of Milton's drunken inconstancies and Helen's debilitating refusal to forgive. Thus she tries to punish her disbelieving husband for imaginary copies of her own transgression while punishing herself through transgression, mimicking the pleasures of desire which bring her no pleasure and dragging

down the conventions of sensual joy into the abyss of pain and misery. The double sexual standard Freud discerned in the *fin-de-siècle* bourgeoisie is updated to wartime New York, where repression and constraint have given way to conditional acknowledgments of desire. Just as the constraint and repression was greater for Freud's women patients, so Peyton's freedom is more conditional than that of her male contemporaries. Instead of being the passive victim of ruthless seduction, and so a pardonable sinner, Peyton is both instigator and active victim of desire, victimised not by others but by herself. The ironic coda is that on the last day of her life the analytic understanding of her fashionable Freudian acquaintances cannot save her. What is absent is the compassion which goes beyond its cerebral aridity and which is lodged in the South and in childhood, in the love of the absent father who has helped to destroy her.

Styron, like Faulkner in *The Sound and the Fury*, uses the South and childhood as tropes for the impossible co-existence of compassion and desire. The mutual affection of Milton and Peyton which has borne Peyton through childhood is, like Candace Compson's affection for Benjy, a love which cannot last for ever. Styron takes us breathtakingly to the point where, at Peyton's wedding, which is the sign of her parting, affection almost transforms itself into incestuous desire. In drunken anguish, Milton passionately kisses her in view of her husband, in the absent realisation of 'irrevocable loss' just before bride and bridegroom begin the ritual of carving the wedding-cake:

> *Now don't be such an ass*, his conscience said, but she seemed to be fading from him, vanishing in a powder of crushed-up dreams, and he found himself beside her, kissing her in front of everyone, much more than a father.
>
> 'Don't smother me' she whispered, and pushing him away angrily. 'Don't *smother* me, Daddy! You're crazy! What will people think! Daddy, don't!' Beads of champagne rose up between them, a green smell of grapes, and she had indeed pushed him away furiously, where he stood witless with horror and desire, his heart pounding, a smear of red grease sticky across his lips.[21]

Minutes later, Loftis is sunk in reveries of Peyton's childhood, remembering the 'little girl with clear pink legs, a pink ribbon in

her hair', recalling how 'she looks at her book, says "Tiddley-
pom", rubs her head against his own, gently musingly, her long,
soft hair falling on his knees'. The memory is one of the protection
and compassion of the father still feeling wounded as a jilted
Oedipal lover. That same day, he recalls, they go on to enter the
belfry of a church to see the bells and he clutches the weeping
Peyton to him 'as the timbers shudder' and the bells' hammers
'descend on the bell throats as swiftly and wickedly as birds of
prey'. Amidst 'the fury of her weeping', 'sparrows scuttle in their
nests and fly off with a raucous sound'.[22] Years later in New York,
having fused the image of bells and sparrows, Peyton is pursued
by imaginary birds of prey, whose imagery now is overtly sexual
and from whom her absent father can no longer protect her. The
predation which both attracts and frightens is personified in the
figure of her casual lover Tony Cecchino, (*cecchino*: bird), whose
macho advances embody the pain of desublimated desire. And
yet in that metaphorical flight from childhood to womanhood,
where the birds are now like pigeons and not sparrows, the role
of Loftis himself has changed. Not only is he no longer a protector:
he himself is an incestuous bird of prey, the primal bird of prey
remembering with compassion and nostalgia the incident she later
transforms after his abortive predation into an indelible image of
terror and desire.

On Peyton's last day in New York, there is a significant echo of
the belfry scene in the women's room high up in a Harlem loft
building where she escapes to die. In this memorable climax,
where Styron suddenly and powerfully decentres his heroine by
introducing first-person narrative, fixing the 'I' when the 'I' is in
process of dissolution, the previous grain of a reconstructed narrative is finally effaced. Not only is the stability of exterior identity
called into question. The switch in epiphanous narrative convinces
as the authentic culmination of all previous dangers, now
presenting themselves in retrospect as the harbingers of destruction. It means destruction not only for Peyton but also for the
family itself, shattered through her in a way that is withheld from
the reader until the last moment, but which is just as decisive as
the shattering of the Compsons after Quentin's death.

Before taking her own life, Peyton echoes the Oedipal longing
of her father which she had repulsed on her wedding-day, an echo
which both confesses loss of self and yet expresses the authentic
nostalgia of desire amidst the craving for death. Her voice suggests

both Quentin Compson and Molly Bloom: an unvirgin and materialised Quentin; Molly made tragic by the failure of reverie to escape suffocation, to elude an experience of desire shorn of all pleasure and narcissism where desire becomes a synonym for despair. As Peyton sheds her clothes and prepares to die, the novel's recurrent images of absence and nostalgia, compassion and desire suddenly coalesce:

> Something hurries me through memory, too, but I can't pause to remember, for a guilt past memory or dreaming, much darker, impels me on. I pray but my prayer climbs up like a broken wisp of smoke: *oh my Lord, I am dying,* is all I know and *oh my father, oh my darling* longingly, lonesomely, I fly into your arms! *Peyton you must be proper nice girls don't. Peyton.* Me? Myself all shattered, this lovely shell? Perhaps I shall rise at another time, though I lie down in darkness and have my light in ashes. I turn in the room, see them come across the tiles, dimly prancing, fluffing up their wings. I think: my poor flightless birds, have you suffered without soaring on this earth. Come then and fly.[23]

The tragic power in Peyton's final moments comes from the narrative switch, the sudden move from the exterior to the interior of the heroine's mind. Up to that point the reader has followed Peyton's childhood, her adolescence, the *rite de passage* into womanhood, with a belief in the basic solidity of her character. The switch is astonishing, yet with it the death and funeral of Peyton, which Styron has introduced at the beginning of the book, finally falls into place, is no longer the chance occurrence it appeared at first sight. With its confessional and lyric intensity, Peyton's expiring monologue points forward to the later poetry of Sylvia Plath, where the image of birds in flight finds equivalence in the image of Ariel, Plath's horse whose swiftness 'hauls me through air'. Milton finds his more sinister double in the Aryan 'Daddy', 'A man in black with a Meinkampf look' whose cruelty makes his daughter, lost in confused adoration, think she 'may well be a Jew'.[24] The parallels are never exact, but the haunting images of forbidding father and ceaseless flight reverberate through both the novel and the poems. Peyton's despairing, interrogating 'Me? Myself all shattered, this lovely shell?' is echoed and inverted in 'Lady Lazarus' by

The second time I meant
To last it out and not come back at all
I rocked shut

As a sea shell
They had to call and call
And pick the worms of me like sticky pearls.[25]

Plath's Lady Lazarus has used up the third of her nine lives, but Peyton Loftis does not rock shut and wait. On her first attempt, she opens the window instead and jumps.

In *Two Strange Ladies*, Jane Bowles uses the opposite strategy for conveying the disintegration of the female self in a world bereft of value. She censors the language of motive so stringently that dissolution is given no process of recognition, no form of naming at all. The women of her novel's title are conveyed through the forms of proper address of the period, 'Miss Goering' and 'Mrs Copperfield'. But the respectable titles, which are also titles of constraint, end up being as honorific as that of 'the Consul' of *Under the Volcano*, who is no longer a consul at all. Bowles's two figures are unspoken pathologies propped up by titles suggesting a propriety and decorum which are redundant in their everyday lives. While their speech and gestures are genteel on the surface, both drift through parties, bars and restaurants with an unacknowledged openness to sexual encounter with both men and women which makes nonsense of the formal proprieties governing their lives. Bowles's very spare narrative has all the signifying features of moral decorum. What is actually signified is the promise of sexual encounter. The gap between signifier and signified reproduces the hiatus between moral value and daily life. In that hiatus, that silence of unmotivation which lies between thought and act, the reader discerns, very gradually, the processes of psychic disintegration.

In Southern fiction another woman novelist has produced a different vision of disintegration. *Wise Blood* appeared in the same year, 1952, as *Invisible Man* and nine years after *Two Strange Ladies*. It is often similar to Bowles in its refusal of explicit referencing but more firmly within the Southern and Faulknerian vision of the disintegration of value. O'Connor highlights the Protestant evangelism which had an integral part in Southern culture but only found a secondary place in Faulkner's fiction. In *Wise Blood* she charts the disintegration of Christian compassion and belief in the same way that Faulkner charted the disintegration of honour. There is, though, an important difference. Faulkner's poor and oppressed attain honour by default, but O'Connor's proletarian believers destroy the values they embrace. In *Wise Blood* the street-wise evangelists are demotic and demonic at the same time, their speech patterns indistinguishable from their sacrilege. Hazel Motes with his grand and absurd 'Church without Christ' proves the point. To democratise is to demonise. Religion by the people, as opposed to religion for the people, is not an opiate but a self-administered poison.

The name of the hero, Hazel Motes, invokes the biblical parable of the mote and the beam but also the haze out of which he appears both to see no one and to look through everyone. On the streets of post-war Tennessee, religion as conceived by O'Connor in a state of Protestant dissolution, mimics the marketplace. Motes competes with rival preachers for the ears of the late-night cinema crowds, haranguing them from the nose of his battered car. The strident pitch of Haze's sacrilege, of his lyrical and colloquial blasphemy, echoes the sectarian insularity of the Bible Belt. But the world of cinemas and automobiles in which it has to operate is a world of commerce and technology to which it has to accommodate itself, a world outside the arcadian Southern tradition which for O'Connor is a kiss of death. When Motes finally rubs quicklime in his eyes and blinds himself, it is a terrifying but appropriate doom. The fixated prisoner of his own blasphemies, he cannot exorcise the Christ he hates. As in Faulkner, doom in O'Connor's work becomes a metaphor for the fate of the South itself.

10 False Composure: Durrell and Fowles, Bellow and Styron

I

The epiphanous novel runs its historical course through war and revolution, depression and fascism to the Second World War and the Cold War which followed it – a period, all told, from 1914 to the early 1950s. During this time the West is spasmodically in crisis but becomes neither fascist for communist. It eventually surmounts the threat of Nazism and the realities of economic collapse through Keynesian recovery and Allied victory. In dissecting his reasons for writing *Native Son*, Richard Wright pointed out the unspoken affinity between his restless and volatile hero and the collective convulsions, at that time, of classes, races and nations. It is that affinity which Ellison follows through on an American plane in the later sections of *Invisible Man*. Yet the epiphanous novel has always tried to match the historical schisms of the social to the schisms of the self. It is an imaginary chart of the price of the West's survival as a liberalistic and capitalistic entity with all the drawbacks that such a survival has entailed. During an age when liberal versions of progress have been under attack, epiphanous fiction has focused the price for that survival upon the decentred self in its precarious world of absence and desire.

The restabilising of the West during the Cold War, within the fixed boundaries of the 'Iron Curtain', is matched in the modern novel by the two-pronged movement away from epiphany – by, on the one hand, the reconstruction of a more conventional realism, and on the other, the proliferation of forms of writing, fantastic, science-fictional and meta-fictional, which go outside realism altogether. Historically, the nightmare of the nuclear-arms race, which anticipated the space age but also provided a retro-spective on the war against fascism, is a catalyst to that literary abandonment. Yet, in the secondary form of naturalistic detail, traces of realism substantially persist. Orwell's dystopia of *Nineteen Eighty-Four* is a hypothetical extension of war-blitzed London, while more recently Kurt Vonnegut and Thomas Pynchon have reconstructed the mechanics of that same war with a mixture of naturalistic precision and transcendental fantasy. After the universal nightmare of such mass slaughter, microscopic focus on the presencing of decentred selves gives way to macroscopic fabulation, where characters are pawns in an omniscient game. The self-dramatising author intersperses the text with extravagant post-Joycean displays of empirical minutiae to sustain the illusion of having a finger on the pulse of history. In addition to Vonnegut and Pynchon, one can think of J. G. Ballard, whose teenage experi-ence of wartime Shanghai led him in the serenity of post-war England to seek fictional equivalents in the freer realms of fantasy and science fiction. Forty years later, however, he reproduced in his fictionalised memoir of the war, *The Empire of the Sun*, a highly riveting, naturalistic fiction of his experiences, the disturbing and nightmarish experiences which had prompted him into seeking out a *non-representationalist* fiction in the first place.

The creation of real worlds in fiction, of imaginary figures consti-tuting persons in history has, however, persisted through to the present day. Above and beyond the abortive efforts of Norman Mailer and Truman Capote to establish 'faction' or the non-fiction novel as a dominant genre, there is a reconstructed realist form which has resisted, unlike Mailer, the electronic media's cult of the fact. The putative distinction suggested by Lodge between empirical and fictional narratives in writing cannot, therefore, really be sustained.[1] Certainly, the twilight of epiphany has inten-sified the novel's crisis, but in a more stable West the new realism has adopted a more stable, accessible form. Reconstructed realism is both empirical *and* fictional. But it forsakes the intense and luminous epiphany for the techniques of fabulation. Scholes is surely right to point out the close contemporary relationship between fabulation and meta-fiction, but also right to see other fabulations as a reworking of the texture of reality.[2] For in the work of Durrell, Fowles, Updike Bellow and Styron, as well as many others, it has been used to reconstruct realism itself.

The crucial post-war text in this respect is *The Alexandria Quartet*.

As a novelist of exile, Lawrence Durrell inherits the legacy of Joyce and Barnes, but, unlike them and unlike Lowry, his fellow Englishman, exile and periphery are not the key to absence and desire. Durrell certainly extends the Joycean world of desire through a self-conscious exploration of modern love. But the mode of that knowingly Freudian exploration results in the stabilising of the self through a distanced and analytical narrative. In Durrell's novel, the objects of narrative, Justine, Nessim, Melissa and the Alexandrians, constantly slip through the fingers. But the act of discoursing through narrative, which is the province of Darnley, Arnauti and Pursewarden, is meant to lead the reader to be infatuated with the superfluities of signifying, especially where Alexandria is a trope for the exotic, and its erotic promise a constant spur to Anglo-Saxon speculations on the nature of Mediterranean desire. Thus we get the paradox that, even when the act of narrating turns out to be factually in error, as it often is with the naïve Darnley, it still has the aura of the authoritative European voice stabilising an elusive Eastern reality. The signifying voice, highly sophisticated and post-Freudian in its exploration of love's secrets, uses the vantage point of analytic discourse to colonise its signified, to fabricate versions of desire around those, such as Justine, who remain so elusively other that they appear to have no nature at all.

For Durrell, fabulation is the key to false composure. He lures the reader into a sense of well-being by matching the analytical confidence of the psychoanalyst to the traditional echoes of self-confidence in the British coloniser. It does not matter that the most analysed and dissected object, Justine, finally eludes all analysis and has no substance at all. For the hollowness at the core of her narcissism is filled by deception, a deception which moves desire into the realm of political intrigue, thus explaining it away as a series of elaborate deceptions performed in a higher cause. Justine comes perilously close to the *femme fatale* of the formula spy thriller, female desire eroticised only through the mechanics of deception. In that sense the emptiness of desire constitutes for Durrell the hollowness of personality in the world of desublimated desire where the manipulations of pure narcissism prevail. It is a hollowness not of humanity but of the beautiful people of his own imagination, whom he joyfully punishes through disfigurement or painful death. And the reader too can gloat in fascination because held at arm's length by the impressive intricacies of

Durrell's fabulating. The disfigurements of the desiring and the once desirable are seen largely from afar, so that the reader who is now a spectator views them with a morbid curiosity. He or she is meant to regard those same subjects, in all their endless erotic intrigues, with a mixture of fascination and envy. It is an envy, however, which always stops short of empathy. The Alexandrians remain the elusive creatures of a foreign world. That they slip through the narrator's fingers is permissible only because, in the post-colonial age, the worlds they inhabit, Egypt and Palestine, will come to elude the tentacles of British rule. In Durrell's mode of fabulation is already contained the echo of recent history.

In Durrell's world of dissembling beautiful people, the didactic claims he makes for art, or for the artist as fabulator, are largely fraudulent. Since to be mortal is to be hollow, the artist achieves significance in the way that he or she, like Pursewarden or Clea, can portray that hollow narcissism, making the narcissistic artist sublime by showing just how hollow narcissism is among the posturing and the mundane. Art then becomes a salvation which results from a knowing exposure of human emptiness. At the same time its narrative form which is fabulation must be analytical as well as lyrical, closer to Freud than to Cavafy. The fetishising of motive by Durrell's narrators strikes one as the foolish shortfall of an author whose characters are often nothing more than a series of charades, a set of posturings and hollow selves. Durrell sets up the illusion of plenitude in the pursuit of a glittering emptiness. The plenitude of the narrator as the lyrical, discoursing voice atones for the vanishing character, who is neither the rounded intelligible person of classic realism nor the decentred self of the epiphanous novel. Unlike the characters of Barnes or Faulkner, who are decentred within the text, those of Durrell are displaced from it, literally taking their selves with them. Their fate becomes an off-stage tragedy which the narrator fabulates centre stage. But the narrator is no longer the impersonal device of classic realism. It is the self-dramatising extension of the author's ego, there for all to see.

II

Three of the outstanding English-language novels of the last fifteen years inherit Durrell's legacy; John Fowles's *The French Lieutenant's*

Woman, Saul Bellow's *Humboldt's Gift* and William Styron's *Sophie's Choice*. Their fabulations, which, like Durrell's, luxuriate in the pleasures of story-telling, are part of an artistic response to the crisis of modern fiction. Where the age of the global village and the documentary cult of fact has cast increasing doubt upon the rationale of writing fictions, any story-telling which does not dramatise itself, any unsignified signifying, has appeared fragile. As a challenge to the growing hegemony of documentary knowledge and its cultural sureties of actual rather than invented lives has arisen a self-advertising fiction in which narrative can no longer be taken for granted. But these changes also complement the internal changes within the novels' form, where the tragic intensity of Faulkner and Lowry has proved too difficult to sustain in post-war metropolitan fiction. Where tragedy threatens to degenerate into melodrama, or where, in *Rabbit, Run*, its environmental fabric is eventually too small in scale to sustain tragic catharsis, the response has been to distance the reader from tragic events and make the act of a story-telling a central part of the reader's experience. In Updike's later work, this has entailed a fusion of Joyce and Sinclair Lewis, an elaborate embroidering of naturalistic and psychic detail in the daily affairs and sexuality of suburban life. But in the three novels of Fowles, Bellow and Styron fabulation has been more significantly intrusive, being used to reinstate tragedy where the post-epiphanous form has failed to generate the classic dimensions of tragic intensity. Their heroic subjects are tragic in a way that Durrell's are not, tragic both because of the greater substance to their being and because of the ensuing loss of substance. Fabulation provides a modulated and controlled version of the self's decentring in which narrative is stabilised by analytical commentary and made conventional by its distance from the heroic subject. It is the narrator, not the hero, through which the author reintroduces into realism the convention of the ordered and intelligible self.

Through fabulation the decentring of the heroic self is made subordinate to narrative displacement within the text. In diverse ways, Sarah Woodruff, von Humboldt Fleischer and Sophie Bieganski provide the nucleus of experience and the catalyst to action, but as the narrative progresses the flow of experience eventually passes them by. At the most crucial moments they leave the limelight, no longer confronting us face to face. Who or what atones for the rupture of that displacement? Who fills the

void which is now vacated? It is the first-person and largely autobiographical narrator, whose substance has long been one of the
daunting conventions in the history of the novel. He alone endures
and remains at the centre of the stage surrendered to him by the
tragic subject. It is he who, through his composed mastery in the
telling of the tale and his genuine sense of bereavement, emerges
triumphant as the sort of person with whom the reader can
identify. It is the orchestrating *alter ego* of John Fowles giving us
the shrewd benefit of historical hindsight and the choice of two
different endings. It is the guilty but successful Charlie Citrine,
who inherits Humboldt's dubious gift. It is the green and innocent
Stingo, deflowered in the deeper realms of hedonistic fantasy by
the camp-survivor who is soon to die. All three triumphantly
survive to give the reader solidity and strength in the act of
reading, to create the fictional illusion of an assured mastery placed
side by side with the genuine tragedy without which their fabulating would be the empty vessel of a worthless cause.

Of the three, Fowles has the clearest link to Durrell, through
The Magus, whose playful use of fabulation takes the Anglo-Saxon
fetish of the exotic to a new literary low. The novel fabulates
Greece and the eastern Mediterranean as the source of the erotic
and the irrational which the rational English hero must encounter
and survive. But the irrational itself turns out to be nothing more
than the testing-ground of a *rite de passage*, which in turn is an
elaborately contrived hoax. The tricks which Conchis plays on
Nicholas Urfe mirror the elaborate charade by which Fowles lures
the reader into his story. The continuity with Durrell is clear, but
the effect even thinner. Fabulation cannot prevent *The Magus* from
being bogus, because its masques and rituals, like those of
Durrell's, are predicated on the exploitation of a primal human
emptiness.

The French Lieutenant's Woman is altogether more substantial. In
writing it, Fowles was the beneficiary of a decade which saw the
release of *Lady Chatterley's Lover* from the tentacles of censorship
and thus enabled him to write about the damaging sexual
constraints of Victorian society with explicit irony and passionate
conviction. The novel reflexively contains the assumption that the
hedonistic push of the 1960s had made the distance between us
and the Victorians absolute. Fowles's informed and probing
contemporary narrator has the devastating advantages of anar-
chronistic hindsight, and the author appeals to the contemporary

reader by erecting his historical narrative on the grave of the historical romance. For not only does it deal explicitly with the hypocrisies of sexual constraint: it also demonstrates that sexual and social constraint were virtually inextricable. His knowing and playful narrator can express with ease what the greatest Victorian novelists were forbidden by convention to attempt. The narrator is thus the continuous lifeline between a closed Victorian society and a contemporary world of desublimated desire.

The knowing distance of the contemporary narrator, who cannot himself be a character in the novel, is similar to the dramaturgy of Brecht's 'complex seeing'. The narrator constructs the privileges and pitfalls of Charles Smithson's circumstances, charts his conventional stuffiness and gentlemanly pursuit of fossils. But when Sarah Woodruff appears he elides the distance between himself and the male hero, seeing her through Smithson's eyes, experiencing the same exasperation and compulsion, the same sense of enigma and mystery. At times Smithson's distant interpreter, he is also at times Smithson himself. Thus Fowles the fabulator manages to have his cake and eat it. In the first instance the reader can revel in the comparison between the 'destructive neurosis' of wealth in our own age and the 'tranquil boredom' which Victorian life produced in a gentleman such as Charles. He or she can be witness to the scandal of prostitution and the treatment of women in a way that poor Charles is not. There is no modern sensibility lurking in a Victorian skull, no fatal error comparable to that in Styron's *The Confessions of Nat Turner*, where the black slave-leader is cast as both epic hero *and* exclusive narrator, ending up in tone and sensibility like a prosaic and crudely anachronised James Baldwin. In the second instance the double focus still allows us the immediacy of witnessing the black hooded figure on the Cobb, of hearing her voice in the wood or on the Undercliff. We can thus experience Charles's sense of mystery directly, and at spaced intervals are drawn back from that rapt witnessing.

The portrait of Sarah Woodruff reproduces and parodies that of the Victorian heroine, but deliberately goes beyond the means of portraying transgression which were available to the Victorian novelist. Yet Sarah must also remain a figure of mystery. Her enigma is deeply rooted, and, if it did not have a deepening ambiguity, then she would merely ossify into a stereotype of the Hooded Temptress. Charles and Grogan can discuss her through the latest works on melancholia, and the narrator, *après* Freud, can add his own aphorisms, but she cannot ultimately be *known* in the manner in which the narrator treats her orthodox contemporaries. Sarah's infatuation is the nodal point of mystery, for, if Charles cannot fathom it, neither can his narrator. 'I cannot explain it', she tells Smithson. 'It is not to be explained'.[3]

Yet there is also a sleight of hand in Fowles's parodic passion for the Victorian heroine. Sarah Woodruff is closer to Emma Bovary than to the heroines of George Eliot or Charlotte Brontë. Her passion for the French Lieutenant is after all pure *Bovaryism*, an imaginative fancy of transgression and ostracism whose public performance is real in its consequences. The innovation of Fowles's part is to make Charles infatuated with her infatuation. Since the brief affair with the French Lieutenant was never actually consummated, he is infatuated with the infatuation of her inventive imagination when he wrongly believes himself to be infatuated with the tragedy of her aborted passion. The fancy is all the more powerful since the illusion of the passion that has already been is the catalyst for the consummation of desire which has yet to come. In a world of provincial constraint, whose consequences for someone like Sarah can be so severe, the fancy becomes the core of identity, the resource which enables her to endure the ostracism it engenders:

> 'I did it so I should never be the same again. I did it so that people *should* point at me, *should* say, there walks the French Lieutenant's Whore . . . I think I have a freedom they cannot understand. No insult, no blame, can touch me. I am hardly human any more. I am the French Lieutenant's whore'.[4]

Since Smithson's infatuation with infatuation later leads to a real consummation – and Sarah's loss of virginity – Fowles inventively traverses the whole territory of modern fiction which has been the subject of this book. Out of Flaubert's love of love, which remains tenuously on the margin of classical passion, he conjures the infatuation with infatuation which leads, in its deflowering of the wish-dreaming innocent, to what the Victorians could never express – the incident of desire. Yet that discovery of desire digs its own grave. Brief, awkward and abortive though it is, an orgasmic consummation for Charles alone through immediate ejaculation, it is an act of extinction for the novel itself. In being the point of revelation, the flashpoint of desire which nineteenth-century fiction had elided, it takes the Victorian novel it parodies outside of its moral universe into a vacuum where the author himself is lost. At a stroke Fowles explodes the fabric of his secure narrative world. Formally Sarah disappears after revealing her deception to Charles, her confession to the fancy which inverts Tess's concealment from Angel Clare of actual seduction and constitutes the 'motive' for her departure. But at this point Sarah's mystery becomes a mystification, since her disappearance lacks narrative credibility. The real reason is that Fowles, having reached the moment of desire, which is the point of no return, does not know what to do with her, since no Victorian convention is going to tell him.

The two endings which Fowles fabulates as an illustration of the arbitrariness of all story-telling is, despite the conspicuous stamp of post-modernism, an illustration of the arbitrary nature of the story *he* has told. The ingenuity in the double ending lies precisely in the juxtaposition of alternatives. Taken singly they are melodramatic and unconvincing, the figure of Mrs Roughwood a mere shadow of Sarah Woodruff, her voice a mere echo. But the equally weak credibility of both endings testifies to their equal insignificance. The arbitrariness of Sarah's disappearance dictates the arbitrariness of her reappearance. In order to pick up the pieces of the narrative frame he has exploded, Fowles must move back from his post-Lawrentian climax to a pre-Lawrentian convention where the beloved remains as mysterious in the house of Rossetti as she had been previously in the straitjacket of provincial Dorset.

III

In its scope and ambition, *The French Lieutenant's Woman* is none the less one of the few outstanding English novels to be written since the war. For the most part, its fabulations fit with the author's strategy of historical distancing, which in turn give an impetus to the play and intrigue of narrative often difficult to accomplish in fictions of contemporary life. In the process of historical and narrative distancing the subjects of that distancing must continue to remain significant. The difficulty of E. L. Doctorow's gimmicky *Ragtime*, or even the far superior *Gravity's Rainbow*, is that the historical subjects are usually treated as a pretext for fabulation.

Thus Pynchon's sublime and gyroscopic fabulations, which can read so majestically, burn off the page and leave in their wake a forbidding blankness. By comparison *Humboldt's Gift* and *Sophie's Choice* strike a better balance between narrator and subject in their fictions of recent history. The reader is cued into the message that, while the fabulations are there to be savoured, their subjects are also to be taken seriously.

The novels of Bellow and Styron, along with the later work of Updike, are more central to the reconstruction of realism than Fowles's fictions of contemporary life, whose tone is sporadically uneasy and uncertain. Despite the common existential legacy which Bellow and Styron share with Fowles, the strength of their fabulation comes from the distancing of the intrinsically *tragic* subject – that is to say, from off-stage tragedy. Narrative distance is essential in forging the tragic stature of Bellow's Humboldt, a paranoid and self-destructive poet who finds it impossible to sustain the difficult art of poetry in the cold and hostile climate of daily life in fifties America. Accusing all his friends of perfidy, he drifts downward into the gutters of Manhattan, and dies insane after endless bouts of drinking, drugs and shock treatment. But the whole of his story is told through the eyes of one of those friends accused of betrayal, the egregious Charlie Citrine, who looks on helplessly, feeling guilt and pity as Humboldt's nemesis coincides with the start of his own glittering success.

Bellow's narrative strategy is to intersperse Citrine's current life in Chicago with his memories of Humboldt in New Jersey shortly before the poet's death. But, unlike Mann's *Doktor Faustus*, where one finds a similar narrative interweaving of past and present in the story of the tragic artist, Bellow's novel presents us with a new departure. Humboldt's life ends a third of the way through the book. The story then shifts to Citrine's nefarious dealings in Chicago with gangsters, lawyers, mistresses and wives. With a self-indulgent slickness, Citrine parades his viscid talents in surviving life's misfortunes. Tragedy is distanced not only by giving way to Bellow's familiar existential concerns but, much worse, by being lost in the narrator's narcissistic bravado. The strength of the story lies in what happens to Humboldt. The long and tedious climax, or anti-climax, consists in what happens to Citrine twenty years later.

The formal connecting link is Citrine's discovery of a lost Humboldt screenplay he had co-written with the poet and which he now delivers to posterity with considerable financial reward. But Humboldt's 'gift' is hardly an apt metaphor for the book, except perhaps at a cynical level where one might regard Bellow as using the poet as a mere device for luring the reader into his more confessional and autobiographical story of Citrine. *Doktor Faustus* and *The Great Gatsby* both use a lesser person to narrate the story of their tragic hero. But the climax of the story belongs to the hero. In Bellow it belongs to the narrator, not simply because the narrator is more identifiably human and less remote, but because he is more like the author himself. The temptation to self-dramatise is fatal. Bellow loses Humboldt in the same way that Fowles loses Sarah Woodruff, to the self-love of his narrating *alter ego*.

The reappearance of the author is a function of that false composure which is meant to reassure the anxious reader in an age of electronic media of fiction's distinctive identity, an identity which can then be set against the limitless world of information by incorporating it into the fabulated text. It is strengthened in *Sophie's Choice* by a narrator whose life and name, Stingo, clearly approximate to Styron's own, even to the point where he fabulates the writing of *Lie Down in Darkness* in the New York City of the late forties. The knowing reader will see in the figure of the suicidal Marsha Hunt the literary embryo of Peyton Loftis, Styron's most powerful heroine. For better or worse, the author of the late seventies displays his earlier self with the explicit vantage of hindsight in ways which are easily, perhaps too easily, decoded. But the same narrative device is also used to introduce the historical catastrophe from which Styron wishes to distance the reader at the same time as engaging his or her attention. Unable and rightly unwilling to compete with the harrowing memoirs of camp-survivors, Styron deliberately holds his reader at arm's length until more than halfway through the novel. The reader discovers Auschwitz as Stingo does, through the ambiguous and with-holding confessions of Sophie in Brooklyn, where the Old World and the New tragically meet. We are thus softened up in advance, so the strategy gambles, for the deeper horror of the Holocaust.

The difficulty with Styron's strategy is that his American sense of place and period is much better realised, much more riveting, than its Polish counterpart. Though Sophie's animated Slavic-American is indeed a very distinctive confessional voice with its own compelling idioms, the Poland which it describes and which the author externally embellishes has a documentary flavour, the artificial odour of imported facts which have not been fully assimilated into the fable. While Stingo is more compelling than Charlie Citrine, Sophie is finally less compelling than Humboldt, because Styron finds it hard to give her history a genuine sense of place. There are occasions when the excessive reliance on documentation and Hannah Arendt seems to betray a loss of nerve. At one level, the weakness is exonerated because Sophie's masochism in her destructive affair with Nathan Landau comes across as a convincing transposition of her trauma at Auschwitz. But at another level, where Styron is trying to reformulate the compassion destroyed by Nathan in the friendship between Sophie and Stingo, he fails fully to separate the deeper horror of mass suffering from the daily pleasures of desublimated desire for which the virgin Stingo craves.

That ungratified desire is part of the comic play of fabulation, the mature author of the pleasure-loving seventies toying very amusingly with the horny torments of his young forties persona. As the eventual source of Stingo's carnal knowledge, Sophie lapses too easily into the stereotype of Eve, tempting with a voice of wisdom which is culled largely from sex manuals and littered with post-forties obscenities which are also distinctly post-Chatterley. Desublimated desire is an anachronised myth which desublimates language itself. Styron's lyrical narrative constantly loses its cadences in flat, uncharged reiterations of sexuality without erotic resonance. It is finally difficult to believe that the one-time household slave of Rudolf Höss can transform herself so easily into the slave of the blue movie and, as a voluptuous anachronism, change from the gaunt, emaciated and toothless camp-survivor whom Nathan has fed back into life to a corrigible Playboy pet of the seventies. Carried away by the freedoms of his own decade, the author inadvertently traverses what should be an unbridgeable abyss, from the world of Auschwitz to the world of *Deep Throat*.

The obscene brevity into which Styron has collapsed that immense distance becomes clear towards the end of the novel. Escaping with Stingo to the South in the late autumn, Sophie reveals the impossible choice which is the metaphor for the whole book. She had been asked, on entering Auschwitz, to sacrifice one of her children in order that the other survive. The story of that impossible choice is moving and powerful. But it is instantly deflated by what follows. 'We drank', Stingo reveals, 'ate crab cakes and managed to forget Auschwitz'.[5] That night he is luridly deflowered in the manner and cliché of the hedonistic seventies. Auschwitz is indeed forgotten, and, in a way, the reader is instantly reassured. The Holocaust is shunted back into history while the seduction is written in the idiom of its own decade. It 'belongs' to the present. When Sophie flees back to Nathan and a predictable suicide pact, the tragic ending takes place off-stage, no more than a coda to Stingo's initiation into the bitter-sweet joy of love's pleasure and desertion. A new man, chastened yet triumphant, he winningly mourns the dear departed.

There is a rich vein of vitality in the new narrative of Fowles, Bellow and Styron, in all three novels, which should not be overlooked. Realising that the world they convey contains and absorbs its tragic losses, they construct a narrative distance from the tragic subjects which allows them to avoid the pitfalls of melodrama, or excessive sentimentality. The autobiographical narrative is a confessional lens which in distancing the reader from the hero brings him or her closer to the author. The lens also acts as a protective glass, allowing the reader to grow in confidence with evidence of the narrator's human foibles, foibles with which the reader too can identify. With disarming frankness but great assurance, the narrator exposes the darkness of evil but anchors the reader to a conceit of normality in an abnormal world. Thus the reader is the accomplice of the teller before he or she is witness to the tale, enjoying humour and sampling irony on the rim of that firm outer surface that is untroubled by the void of a deeper darkness. The reader is thus hauled out of range of the anxieties of absence. The void is seen but the darkness never penetrated. All around it on its solid circumference is the triumphant graffiti of the new authorial slogan '*Alter Ego* rules OK.'

The narrator cannot be displaced as Ishmael is displaced by Ahab and Moby Dick, as Nick Carraway is displaced by Jay Gatsby, or as the insufferable pedant Serenus Zeitblom is finally forgotten in Adrian Leverkühn's climactic madness. Instead the author gains a pyrrhic victory. His own persona faces the audience like a master of ceremonies with strange hypnotic powers, purveying deadly commentary on nearby action which is hidden by the flimsiest of curtains. The narrator, reading the text of which he is a part, directs the gaze of the audience to the tragedy off-stage which he has cleverly and playfully orchestrated. But it is the curtain through which the action is viewed transparently, not the action itself, which is the necessary illusion.

Notes

CHAPTER 1. PASSION AND COMPASSION; ABSENCE AND DESIRE

1. Elizabeth Deeds Ermath, *Realism and Consensus in the English Novel* (Princeton, NJ: Princeton University Press, 1983) pp. 41ff. See also George Levine, *The Realistic Imagination: English Fiction from Frankenstein to Lady Chatterley* (Chicago: University of Chicago Press, 1981) pp. 12ff.
2. See Raymond Williams, 'Dickens and Social Ideas', in *The Sociology of Literature and Drama*, ed. E. and T. Burns (Harmondsworth: Penguin, 1973); Gillian Beer, *Darwin's Plots: Evolutionary Narrative in Darwin, George Eliot and Nineteenth Century Fiction* (London: Routledge and Kegan Paul, 1983); Leo Marx, *The Machine in the Garden: Technology and the Pastoral Ideal in America* (New York: Oxford University Press, 1964). Marx suggests that the nineteenth-century American experience of rapid industrialisation, i.e. machine production, amidst farming country which had only just been created out of vast tracts of wilderness – the machine in the garden – accentuated the disrelations in American thought of technology and the pastoral ideal. For his discussion of the fictionalisation of the dilemma by Hawthorne and Melville, see pp. 265–319.
3. J. Hillis Miller, *The Forms of Victorian Fiction* (University of Notre Dame Press: Notre Dame, Ind., 1970); Baruch Hochman, *The Test of Character: From the Victorian Novel to the Modern* (London: Associated University Presses, 1983). Though the special conjuncture of realism and romance in Hawthorne and Melville distinguishes them from the Victorian novelists of the same period, in Hawthorne the compassionate structure of feeling is clearly evident in *The Scarlet Letter* and *The House of the Seven Gables*. The relationships of Hester Prynne and her daughter Pearl, in the former, and of Phoebe and Holgrave, in the latter, both display the redemptive powers of compassion in the midst of Puritan severity and righteousness. For the literary form of the American romance, see Richard H. Brodhead, *Hawthorne, Melville and the Novel* (Chicago: University of Chicago Press, 1976) pp. 9ff.; and Michael Davitt Bell, *The Development of the American Romance* (Chicago: University of Chicago Press, 1980) pp. 126ff.
4. Denis de Rougemont, *Passion and Society*, tr. Montgomery Belgion (London: Faber and Faber, 1956).

5. See John Orr, *Tragic Realism and Modern Society* (London: Macmillan, 1977) pp. 53ff.
6. See Lionel Trilling, 'Art and Neurosis', in *The Liberal Imagination: Essays in Literature and Society* (Oxford: Oxford University Press, 1981) pp. 160ff.; Philip Rieff, *Freud: The Mind of a Moralist* (London: Gollancz, 1959) pp. 34ff.; Jean Laplanche, *Life and Death in Psychoanalysis*, tr. Jeffrey Mehlmann (London: Johns Hopkins University Press, 1976) pp. 25ff.

The important texts in Freud can be grouped around the themes of sexuality and metapsychology on which he wrote largely during the second decade of the century. Those needing special mention are *Three Essays on Sexuality* (1905), *On the Universal Tendency to Debasement in Love* (1912) and *Female Sexuality* (1931), in *On Sexuality*, Pelican Freud, vol. 7 (Harmondsworth: Penguin, 1977); *On Narcissism* (1914), *The Unconscious* (1915), *Instincts and their Vicissitudes* (1915), *Repression* (1915), *Mourning and Melancholia* (1917) and *Beyond the Pleasure Principle* (1920), in *On Metapsychology: The Theory of Psychoanalysis*, Pelican Freud, vol. 11 (Harmondsworth: Penguin, 1984).

One of the most fertile uses of Freudian, or psychocritical, analysis in literary theory is Leo Bersani's *A Future for Astyanax: Character and Desire in Literature* (Boston, Mass.: Little, Brown, 1976). The classic critical text on desire in the novel remains René Girard's *Deceit, Desire, and the Novel*, tr. Yvonne Freccero (Baltimore: Johns Hopkins University Press, 1966). Girard's study of Cervantes, Stendhal, Flaubert, Dostoevsky and Proust highlights the importance of imitative models, or what he calls 'triangular desire' in the European novel. Here the hero or heroine imitates a mediator, past or present, real or imaginary, in the development of attraction towards the beloved. The idealised nature of triangular desire makes it, in the context of this study, a specific dimension of passion in De Rougemont's sense, but one where, significantly, deceit is more common than compassion. See ch. 1 of Girard's study. The best study of a single novelist using the psychocritical method is John T. Irwin's *Doubling and Incest/Repetition and Revenge: A Speculative Reading of Faulkner* (London: Johns Hopkins University Press, 1975). This has had a seminal influence on my own, rather different, discussion of Faulkner, Lowry, Wright and Ellison.
7. Gerald Genette, 'Flaubert's Silences', in *Figures of Literary Discourse*, tr. Alan Sheridan (Oxford: Basil Blackwell, 1982).
8. Raymond Williams, *The English Novel from Dickens to Lawrence* (St Albans: Paladin, 1974) pp. 140–1.

CHAPTER 2. LAWRENCE: PASSION AND ITS DISSOLUTION

1. See Kim A. Herzinger, *D. H. Lawrence in his Time: 1908–1915* (London: Association University Presses, 1982) pp. 27ff.
2. Bersani, *A Future for Astyanax*, p. 70.
3. Joseph Conrad, *Victory* (Harmondsworth: Penguin, 1965) p. 13.
4. Ibid., p. 33.

5. See Roger Ebbatson, *Lawrence and the Nature Tradition: A Theme in English Fiction* (Hassocks, Sussex: Harvester, 1980) pp. 40ff.
6. John Lester, *Journey through Despair: A Transformation in British Literary Culture* (Princeton, NJ: Princeton University Press, 1968) pp. 46ff.
7. Detailed discussions of Darwin's influence on Hardy can be found in Roger Robinson, 'Hardy and Darwin', in *Thomas Hardy*, ed. N. Page (London: Bell and Hyman, 1980) pp. 128ff.; and Roger Ebbatson, *The Evolutionary Self: Hardy, Forster, Lawrence* (Hassocks, Sussex: Harvester, 1982) ch. 1.
8. D. H. Lawrence, 'Study of Thomas Hardy', in *Selected Literary Criticism* (London: Mercury, 1961) pp. 180ff.
9. D. H. Lawrence, 'Nottinghamshire and the Mining Country', in *Selected Essays* (Harmondsworth: Penguin, 1981).
10. D. H. Lawrence, *The Rainbow* (London: Heinemann, 1971).
11. Ibid., p. 100.
12. Ibid., p. 101.
13. Anaïs Nin, *D. H. Lawrence: An Unprofessional Study* (London: Neville Spearman, 1961) p. 6.
14. Lawrence, *The Rainbow*, p. 200.
15. Ibid., p. 234.
16. Ibid., pp. 318, 319.
17. Ibid., pp. 478–9.
18. Ibid., p. 480.
19. D. H. Lawrence, *Women in Love* (London: Heinemann, 1971) p. 239.
20. Ibid., p. 139.
21. Ibid., p. 142.
22. Hubert Zapf, ' "Taylorism" in D. H. Lawrence's *Women in Love'*, *D. H. Lawrence Review*, vol. 15 (1982) pp. 129ff.
23. Charles L. Ross, 'Homoerotic Feeling in *Women in Love*; Lawrence's "struggle for verbal consciousness" in the Manuscripts', in *D. H. Lawrence: The Man who Lived*, ed. R. B. Partlow Jr and H. T. Moore (Carbondale: Southern Illinois University Press, 1979).

CHAPTER 3. JOYCE: THE LINEAMENTS OF DESIRE

1. For Lawrence's relationship to Vorticism, see Herzinger, pp. 121ff.
2. James Joyce, *A Portrait of the Artist as a Young Man* (London: Jonathan Cape, 1968) p. 217.
3. Augustine Martin, 'Sin and Secrecy in Joyce's Fiction', in *James Joyce: An International Perspective*, ed. S. B. Bushrui and B. Benstock (Gerrards Cross, Bucks: Colin Smythe, 1982) pp. 147ff.
4. Joyce, *Portrait*, p. 101.
5. Ibid., p. 108.
6. Letter to Nora Barnacle Joyce, 2 Dec 1909, in Richard Ellmann (ed.), *Selected Letters of James Joyce*, ed. Richard Ellmann (London: Faber and Faber, 1975) p. 181.
7. Letter to Nora Barnacle Joyce, 16 Dec 1909, ibid., p. 191.

8. Arthur Powers, *Conversations with James Joyce*, ed. Clive Hart (London: Millington, 1974) p. 92.
9. Letter to Stanislaus Joyce, 13 Nov 1906, in *Selected Letters*, p. 129.
10. James Joyce, *Ulysses* (London: The Bodley Head, 1962) p. 21.
11. Ibid., pp. 10–11.
12. Ibid., pp. 24, 321.
13. Ibid., p. 37.
14. Ibid., pp. 99–100.
15. Ibid., p. 73.
16. Richard Ellmann, *The Consciousness of Joyce* (London: Faber and Faber, 1977) pp. 56ff.
17. *Ulysses*, pp. 237, 238.
18. Ibid., p. 244.
19. Ibid., p. 251.
20. For the first kind of approach see the perceptive article by Mark Spilka, 'Leopold Bloom as Jewish Pickwick: A Neo-Dickensian Perspective', *Novel*, vol. 13, no. 1 (1979–80) pp. 121ff. For the second, see Colin McCabe, *James Joyce and the Revolution of the Word* (London: Macmillan, 1978). The definitive study of Joyce's masterpiece which coherently fuses both perspectives is Marilyn French's *The Book as World: James Joyce's Ulysses* (London: Harvard University Press, 1976).
21. Joyce, *Ulysses*, p. 380.
22. Ibid., p. 382.
23. Ibid., p. 430.
24. Ibid., p. 476.
25. French, *The Book as World*, p. 187f. For an assessment of Joyce's place within the historical spectrum of literary realism, see Terence Doody, '*Don Quixote*, *Ulysses* and the Idea of Realism', *Novel*, vol. 12, no. 3 (1979–80) pp. 197ff.
26. Joyce, *Ulysses*, p. 606.
27. Ibid., p. 647.
28. French, *The Book as World*, pp. 249ff.
29. Joyce, *Ulysses*, pp. 931, 933.

CHAPTER 4. BITTER-SWEET: BARNES AND HEMINGWAY

1. F. Scott Fitzgerald, 'May Day', in *The Diamond as Big as the Ritz* (Harmondsworth: Penguin, 1962) p. 31.
2. Michael S. Reynolds, *Hemingway's First War: The Making of 'A Farewell to Arms'* (Princeton, NJ: Princeton University Press, 1976) pp. 61ff.
3. Ernest Hemingway, *A Farewell to Arms* (London: Jonathan Cape, 1975) p. 42.
4. Ibid., pp. 161–2.
5. Ibid., p. 95.
6. In Paris, Barnes and Hemingway moved in similar but never identical circles, and Barnes, of course, never knew the fame which Hemingway achieved during this period. But it is possible that Hemingway used Barnes's surname for the male hero of *The Sun also*

Rises. For the background to Barnes's stay in Paris and the real-life models for *Nightwood*, see the rather patchily written biography by Andrew Field, *The Formidable Miss Barnes* (London: Secker and Warburg, 1983).
7. Djuna Barnes, *Nightwood* (London: Faber and Faber, 1958) p. 29.
8. Ibid., pp. 49–50.
9. Ibid., p. 55.
10. Ibid., p. 60.
11. Ibid., pp. 65–6.
12. Ibid., pp. 77–8.
13. Ibid., p. 80.
14. Ibid., pp. 85–6.
15. Ibid., p. 202.
16. Ibid., p. 207.
17. Ibid., p. 71.

CHAPTER 5. FAULKNER I: THE FAMILY VOID

1. See C. Vann Woodward, *The Burden of Southern History* (Baton Rouge: Louisiana State University Press, 1960) pp. 89ff. and 141ff.
2. Eugene Genovese, *The World the Slaveholders Made* (New York: Vintage Books, 1971) pp. 119ff. For a comparison between the plantation stereotypes of nineteenth-century Southern writing and plantation realities, see John W. Blassingame, *The Slave Community: Plantation Life in the Antebellum South*, rev. edn (London: Oxford University Press, 1979) pp. 223–84. For the social construction of the white family as an integral part of the code of honour in the Old South, see Bertram Wyatt-Brown, *Southern Honour: Ethics and Behaviour in the Old South* (New York: Oxford University Press, 1982).
3. Flannery O'Connor provides a compelling criticism of the critics of Southern fiction in 'Some Aspects of the Grotesque in Southern Fiction', *Mystery and Manners: Occasional Prose* (London: Faber and Faber, 1984) pp. 36ff.
4. Louis D. Rubin Jr, 'Southern Literature: The Historical Image', in *South: Modern Southern Literature in its Cultural Setting*, ed. Louis D. Rubin Jr and Robert D. Jacobs (Garden City, NY: Doubleday, 1961).
5. For the historical significance of the story, see Bertram Wyatt-Brown, 'Community, Class and Snopesian Crime: Local Justice in the Old South', in *Class, Conflict and Consensus*, ed. Orville Vernon Burton and Robert C. McMath (London: Greenwood, 1982).
6. Blassingame, *The Slave Community*, pp. 265ff.
7. William Faulkner, *The Sound and the Fury* (London: Chatto and Windus, 1974) pp. 150–1.
8. Ibid., p. 176. For a more detailed Freudian analysis of Quentin's relationship with Candace, see Irwin, *Doubling and Incest*, pp. 37–49.
9. Ibid., p. 74.
10. Ibid., p. 193.
11. Ibid., p. 179.

12. Ibid., p. 295.
13. Ibid., p. 297.
14. Ibid., p. 288.
15. Ibid., p. 316.
16. William Faulkner, *As I Lay Dying* (London: Chatto and Windus, 1970) pp. 71–2.
17. Ibid., p. 76.
18. Ibid., p. 68.
19. Ibid., p. 135.
20. Ibid., pp. 163–4.
21. Ibid., p. 164.
22. Ibid., p. 243.
23. Ibid., p. 244.

CHAPTER 6. FAULKNER II: COLOURS OF ABSENCE; UBIQUITY OF DESIRE

1. Ralph Ellison, 'Twentieth Century Fiction and the Black Mask of Humanity', in *Confluence*, Dec 1953, pp. 3–21; repr in *Faulkner: The Critical Heritage*, ed. John Bassett (London: Routledge and Kegan Paul, 1975).
2. William Faulkner, *Sanctuary: The Original Text*, ed. Noel Polk (London: Chatto and Windus, 1981) p. 14.
3. Ibid., p. 15.
4. William Faulkner, *Sanctuary* (London: Chatto and Windus, 1952) pp. 13–14.
5. Ibid., p. 17.
6. Ibid., p. 177.
7. For a detailed analysis of Faulkner's use of montage, see Bruce Kawin, 'The Montage Element in Faulkner's Fiction', in *Faulkner, Modernism and Film*, ed. E. Harrington and A. Abadie (Jackson, Miss.: University of Mississippi Press, 1979) pp. 103–26.
8. Eric J. Sundquist, *Faulkner: The House Divided* (London: Johns Hopkins University Press, 1983) pp. 45ff.
9. Faulkner, *Sanctuary*, p. 5.
10. Ibid., pp. 6, 226.
11. Ibid., pp. 8, 9.
12. Ibid., p. 18.
13. Ibid., p. 40.
14. Ibid., pp. 237–8.
15. William Faulkner, *Light in August* (London: Chatto and Windus, 1968) p. 27.
16. Ibid., p. 204.
17. Ibid., p. 244.
18. Ibid., p. 246.
19. Ibid., p. 254.
20. Sundquist, *Faulkner: The House Divided*, pp. 71ff.
21. Faulkner, *Light in August*, pp. 106–7.

22. Ibid., pp. 107–8.
23. Ibid., pp. 424–5.

CHAPTER 7. FAULKNER III: ABSTRACTION

1. A distinction should be made here between the period of Faulkner's childhood and the period during which he wrote his major novels. It was during the first twenty-five years of segregation that the intimidation of blacks through violence and lynchings reached its height. Christmas's murder of Joanna Burden was partly based on an incident which took place in Oxford during Faulkner's childhood. By the time he came to write his major work, the incidence of racial violence had declined as a consequence of the system's greater effectiveness. For a discussion of the background to *Light in August*, see Joseph Blotner, *Faulkner: A Biography* (London: Chatto and Windus, 1974) vol. 1, pp. 702–4, 760–8. A wider discussion of the decline of racial violence in the 1920s can be found in Joel Williamson, *The Crucible of Race: Black–White Relations in the American South since Emancipation* (Oxford: Oxford University Press, 1984).
2. William Faulkner, *Absalom, Absalom!* (London: Chatto and Windus, 1960) p. 358.
3. Ibid., p. 7.
4. Cleanth Brooks, 'Thomas Sutpen: A Representative Southern Planter?', in *William Faulkner: Towards Yoknapatawpha and Beyond* (London: Yale University Press, 1978) pp. 289ff.
5. Faulkner, *Absalom, Absalom!*, p. 286.
6. Ibid., p. 263.
7. Ibid., p. 274.
8. Ibid., p. 303. For a detailed analysis of the relationship of narrative doubling to incest, see Irwin, *Doubling and Incest*, pp. 76ff.
9. Faulkner, *Absalom, Absalom!*, p. 299.
10. Ibid., p. 361.
11. William Faulkner, *The Wild Palms* (London: Chatto and Windus, 1970) p. 76.
12. Ibid., p. 116.
13. Ibid., p. 188.
14. Ibid., p. 190.

CHAPTER 8. LOWRY: THE DAY OF THE DEAD

1. Octavio Paz, *The Labyrinth of Solitude: Life and Thought in Mexico* (London: Allen Lane, 1967) p. 49.
2. Malcolm Lowry, *Under the Volcano* (London: Jonathan Cape, 1967) pp. 35, 41.
3. Ibid., p. 54.
4. Ibid., p. 55.
5. Ibid., p. 65.
6. Ibid., pp. 68–9.

7. Ibid., pp. 196–7.
8. Douglas Day, *Malcolm Lowry: A Biography* (London: Oxford University Press, 1974), p. 349.
9. Malcolm Lowry, *Selected Letters*, ed. Harvey Breit and Margerie Bonner Lowry (London: Jonathan Cape, 1967). Lowry writes,

> We also hear that the Consul has been suspected of being an English spy, or 'espider', and though he suffers dreadfully from the mania of persecution, and you feel sometimes, quite objectively, that he is indeed being followed throughout the book, it is as if the Consul himself is not aware of this and is afraid of something quite different: for lack of an object therefore it was the writer's reasonable hope that this first sense of being followed, might settle on the reader and haunt him instead. (p. 70)

The connecting figure of surveillance-as-presence is the ominous figure of Weber, the American smuggler who has flown Hugh down to Mexico, is talking in the Bella Vista bar in counterpoint to the conversation of Yvonne and Geoffrey when they first meet at seven in the morning, and is present at the Farolito in Parián when the Sinarchistas murder Geoffrey at seven in the evening (p. 72). Hugh's unexplained relationship to Weber suggests he is Hugh's fascist double just as Sanabria, the 'Chief of Gardens' and instigator of Geoffrey's murder, is Geoffrey's. See *Under the Volcano*, pp. 97, 359.

10. Dale H. Edmonds, '*Under the Volcano*: A Reading of the "Immediate Level" ', *Tulane Studies in English*, vol. 16 (1968) pp. 82ff.
11. Rather controversially, Freud located the origin of paranoia in suppressed homosexual desire. His more immediate contention was that delusions of persecution originate in the feeling of being watched during the sexual act by a disapproving persecutor. He interpreted this as a neurotic transformation of a normal process of watching by which our conscience measures the ego against the narcissistic satisfaction derived from the ego ideal. See the discussion in *On Narcissism* and *A Case of Paranoia* in *Standard Edition of the Complete Psychological Works of Sigmund Freud* (London: Hogarth Press, 1961) vol. 14, pp. 95–7 and 267ff.
12. Lowry, *Under the Volcano*, p. 372.
13. Ibid., pp. 370ff.
14. Ibid., p. 371.
15. Ibid., p. 55.
16. Ibid., p. 56.
17. Ibid., p. 144.
18. Ibid., p. 228.
19. Ibid., p. 256.
20. Ibid., p. 352.
21. Brian O'Kill, 'Aspects of Language in *Under the Volcano*', in *The Art of Malcolm Lowry*, ed. Anne Smith (London: Vision Press, 1978), pp. 73–9.
22. For Aiken's relationship with Lowry, see Day, *Malcolm Lowry*, pp. 170–80, 219–30. For Aiken's assessment of *Absalom, Absalom!*, see

'William Faulkner: The Novel as Form', in *William Faulkner: The Critical Heritage*, pp. 243ff.

23. Lowry, *Under the Volcano*, p. 291.
24. For a discussion of the relationship between the unconscious, time and memory, see Anthony Giddens, *The Constitution of Society* (Cambridge: Polity Press, 1984), pp. 45ff.
25. Sigmund Freud, *An Outline of Psychoanalysis*, in *On Metapsychology: The Theory of Psychoanalysis*, Pelican Freud, vol. 11, pp. 56–7; Giddens, *The Constitution of Society*, pp. 5–14, 41–5.
26. Bersani, *A Future of Astyanax*, pp. 55ff.
27. Ermath, *Realism and Consensus in the English Novel*, p. 65.
28. Giddens, *The Constitution of Society*, p. 132.
29. For a detailed account of Lowry's return see Ronald G. Walker, *Infernal Paradise: Mexico and the Modern English Novel* (London: University of California Press, 1978) pp. 299ff.

CHAPTER 9. COMPLETION: WRIGHT AND ELLISON

1. Robert B. Stepto, ' "I thought I knew these people": Richard Wright and the Afro-American Literary Tradition', in *Chart of Saints: A Gathering of Afro-American Literature, Art and Scholarship*, ed. Michael S. Harper and Robert B. Stepto (London: University of Illinois Press, 1979), pp. 200ff.
2. Mary Walker Alexander, 'Richard Wright', in *Richard Wright: A Collection of Critical Essays*, ed. Richard Macksey and Frank E. Moorer (Englewood Cliffs, NJ: Prentice-Hall, 1984) p. 25.
3. Richard Wright, *Native Son* (Harmondsworth: Penguin, 1984), p. 131.
4. Ibid., p. 223.
5. Ibid., pp. 152, 154, 233.
6. Ralph Ellison, 'The World and the Jug', in *Shadow and Act* (New York: Random House, 1964) p. 116.
7. Albert Murray, *The Omni-Americans* (New York: Outerbridge, 1970) p. 167. For a definitive account of the blending of blues narrative and doubling in the novel, see Leon Forrest, 'Luminosity from the Lower Frequencies', *Carleton Miscellany*, vol. 18, no. 3 (1980) pp. 82ff.
8. Ralph Ellison, *Invisible Man* (Harmondsworth: Penguin, 1983), p. 52.
9. Houston A. Baker Jr, 'To Move without Moving: Creativity and Commerce in Ralph Ellison's Trueblood Episode', in *Black Literature and Literary Theory*, ed. Henry Louis Gates Jr (London: Methuen, 1984) pp. 226ff.
10. Ellison, *Invisible Man*, p. 56.
11. Ibid., p. 39.
12. Ibid., p. 41.
13. Ibid., p. 68.
14. For Ellison's more personal account of the historical and phenomenological ironies of naming, see 'Hidden Name and Complex Fate', in *Shadow and Act*, pp. 144ff.
15. Ellison, *Invisible Man*, p. 354.

16. Kimberley W. Benston, 'I Yam what I Am: The Topos of (Un)naming in Afro-American Literature', in *Black Literature and Literary Theory*, pp. 162ff.
17. Ellison, *Invisible Man*, p. 380.
18. Ibid., p. 381.
19. Ibid., p. 469.
20. See John Orr, 'Confessions of Sophie: An Interview with William Styron', *New Edinburgh Review*, no. 51 (Autumn 1980), pp. 15ff.
21. William Styron, *Lie Down in Darkness* (London: Corgi, 1980) p. 317.
22. Ibid., pp. 321-2.
23. Ibid., p. 427.
24. Sylvia Plath, 'Daddy', in *Ariel* (London: Faber and Faber, 1965) pp. 54-5.
25. Plath, 'Lady Lazarus', ibid., p. 17.

CHAPTER 10: FALSE COMPOSURE: FOWLES AND STYRON

1. David Lodge, 'The Novelist at the Crossroads', *Critical Quarterly*, vol. 11 (1969), pp. 110ff.; see also Robert Scholes, *The Fabulators* (New York: Oxford University Press, 1967), pp. 3–31.
2. Robert Scholes, *Fabulation and Metafiction* (London: University of Illinois Press, 1980) pp. 7–9, 21–47.
3. John Fowles, *The French Lieutenant's Woman* (London: Jonathan Cape, 1969), p. 342.
4. Ibid., p. 171.
5. William Styron, *Sophie's Choice* (London: Jonathan Cape, 1979), p. 495.

Select Critical Bibliography

Aiken, Conrad, 'William Faulkner: The Novel as Form' in *William Faulkner: The Critical Heritage*, ed. John Bassett (London: Routledge and Kegan Paul, 1975) pp. 243ff.

Alexander, Mary Wright, 'Richard Wright', in *Richard Wright: A Collection of Critical Essays*, ed. Richard Macksey and Frank E. Moorer (Englewood Cliffs, NJ: Prentice-Hall, 1984).

Auerbach, Erich, *Mimesis*, tr. Willard Trask (Princeton, NJ: Princeton University Press, 1968).

Baker, Houston A., Jr, *The Journey Back: Issues in Black Literature and Criticism* (Urbana, Ill: University of Chicago Press, 1980).

——'To Move without Moving: Creativity and Commerce in Ralph Ellison's Trueblood Episode' in *Black Literature and Literary Theory*, ed. Henry Louis Gates Jr (London: Methuen, 1984).

Beer, Gillian, *Darwin's Plots: Evolutionary Narrative in Darwin, George Eliot and Nineteenth Century Fiction* (London: Routledge and Kegan Paul, 1983).

Benston, Kimberley W., 'I Yam what I Am: The Topos of (Un)naming in Afro-American Literature', in *Black Literature and Literary Theory*, ed. Henry Louis Gates Jr (London: Methuen, 1984).

Bersani, Leo, *A Future for Astyanax: Character and Desire in Literature* (Boston, Mass.: Little, Brown, 1976).

Binns, Ronald, *Malcolm Lowry* (London: Methuen, 1984).

Blassingame, John W., *The Slave Community: Plantation Life in the Antebellum South* (London: Oxford University Press, 1979).

Blotner, Joseph, *Faulkner: A Biography*, 2 vols (London: Chatto and Windus, 1974).

Brooks, Cleanth, *William Faulkner: The Yoknapatawpha Country* (London: Yale University Press, London 1963).

——, *William Faulkner: Towards Yoknapatawpha and Beyond* (London: Yale University Press, 1978).

Day, Douglas, *Malcolm Lowry: A Biography* (London: Oxford University Press, 1974).

De Rougemont, Denis, *Passion and Society*, tr. Montgomery Belgion (London: Faber and Faber, 1956).

Doody, Terence, 'Don Quixote, Ulysses and the Idea of Realism', *Novel*, vol. 12, no. 3 (1979–80) pp. 197ff.

Ebbatson, Roger, *Lawrence and the Nature Tradition: A Theme in English Fiction 1859–1914* (Hassocks, Sussex: Harvester, 1980).

——, *The Evolutionary Self: Hardy, Forster, Lawrence* (Hassocks, Sussex: Harvester, 1982).

Edmonds, Dale H., '*Under the Volcano*: A Reading of the "Immediate Level" ', *Tulane Studies in English*, vol. 16 (1968) pp. 63–105.

Ellison, Ralph, *Shadow and Act* (New York: Random House, 1964).

——, 'Twentieth Century Fiction and the Black Mask of Humanity', in *Confluence*, Dec 1953, pp. 3–21; repr. in *Faulkner: The Critical Heritage*, ed. John Bassett (London: Routledge and Kegan Paul, 1975).

Ellman, Richard, *James Joyce* (London: Oxford University Press, 1966).

——, *The Consciousness of Joyce* (London: Faber and Faber, 1977).

Ermath, Elizabeth Deeds, *Realism and Consensus in the English Novel* (Princeton, NJ: Princeton University Press, 1983).

Fabre, Michel, *The Unfinished Quest of Richard Wright*, tr. Isabel Barzun (New York: William Morrow, 1973).

Field, Andrew, *The Formidable Miss Barnes* (London: Secker and Warburg, 1983).

French, Marilyn, *The Book as World: James Joyce's Ulysses* (Cambridge Mass.: Harvard University Press, 1976).

Freud, Sigmund, *Standard Edition of the Complete Psychological Works of Sigmund Freud* (London: Hogarth Press, 1961).

——, *On Sexuality*, Pelican Freud, vol. 7 (Harmondsworth, Penguin, 1977).

——, *On Metapsychology: The Theory of Psychoanalysis*, Pelican Freud, vol. 11 (Harmondsworth: Penguin: 1984).

Genette, Gerald, *Figures of Literary Discourse*, tr. Alan Sheridan (Oxford: Basil Blackwell, 1982).

Genovese, Eugene, *Roll Jordan Roll: The World the Slaveholders Made* (New York: Vintage Books, 1971).

Giddens, Anthony, *The Constitution of Society* (Cambridge: Polity Press, 1984).

Girard, René, *Deceit, Desire and the Novel*, tr. Yvonne Freccero (Baltimore: Johns Hopkins University Press, 1966).

Herzinger, Kim A., *D.H. Lawrence in his Time: 1908–1915* (London: Associated University Presses, 1982).

Hochman, Baruch, *The Test of Character: From the Victorian Novel to the Modern* (Toronto: Associated University Presses, 1983).

Hollowell, John, *Fact and Fiction: The New Journalism and the Nonfiction Novel* (Chapel Hill: University of North Carolina Press, 1977).

Irwin, John T., *Doubling and Incest/Repetition and Revenge: A Speculative Reading of Faulkner* (Baltimore, Md: Johns Hopkins University Press, 1975).

Jenkins, Lee, *Faulkner and Black–White Relations: A Psychoanalytical Approach* (New York: Columbia University Press, 1981).

Joyce, James, *Selected Letters*, ed. Richard Ellmann (London: Faber and Faber, 1975).

Kawin, Bruce, 'The Montage Element in Faulkner's Fiction', in *Faulkner, Modernism and Film*, ed. E. Harrington and A. Abadie (Jackson, Miss.: University of Mississippi Press, 1979).

Laplanche, Jean, *Life and Death in Psychoanalysis*, tr. Jeffrey Mehlmann (London: Johns Hopkins University Press, London 1976).

Lawrence, David Herbert, *'Psychoanalysis and the Unconscious' and 'Fantasia of the Unconscious'* (New York: Viking Press, 1962).
——, *Selected Literary Criticism* (London: Mercury, 1961).
——, *Selected Essays* (Harmondsworth: Penguin, 1981).
Leavis, F. R., *D. H. Lawrence, Novelist* (London: Chatto and Windus, 1955).
——, *The Great Tradition* (London: Chatto and Windus, 1948).
Lerner, Laurence, *Love and Marriage: Literature and its Social Context* (London: Edward Arnold, 1979).
Lester, John, *Journey through Despair 1890–1914: A Transformation in British Literary Culture* (Princeton, NJ: Princeton University Press, 1968).
Levine, George, *The Realistic Imagination: English Fiction from Frankenstein to Lady Chatterley* (London: University of Chicago Press, 1981).
Lewis, C. S., *The Allegory of Love* (London: Oxford University Press, 1938).
Lowry, Malcolm, *Selected Letters*, ed. Harvey Breit and Margerie Bonner Lowry (London: Jonathan Cape, 1967).
Martin, Augustine, 'Sin and Secrecy in Joyce's Fiction', in *James Joyce: An International Perspective*, ed. S. B. Bushrui and B. Benstock (Colin Smythe, Gerrards Cross, Bucks., 1982).
McCabe, Colin, *James Joyce and the Revolution of the Word* (London: Macmillan, 1978).
Marx, Leo, *The Machine in the Garden: Technology and the Pastoral Ideal in America* (New York: Oxford University Press, 1964).
Miller, J. Hillis, *The Form of Victorian Fiction* (Notre Dame, Ind.: University of Notre Dame Press, 1970).
Millgate, Michael, *The Achievement of William Faulkner* (London: Oliver and Boyd, 1966).
Murray, Albert, *The Omni-Americans* (New York: Outerbridge, 1970).
O'Connor, Flannery, *Mystery and Manners: Occasional Prose* (London: Faber and Faber, 1984).
O'Kill, Brian, 'Aspects of Language in *Under the Volcano*', in *The Art of Malcolm Lowry*, ed. Anne Smith (London: Vision Press, 1978).
Orr, John, *Tragic Realism and Modern Society* (London: Macmillan, 1977).
——, 'Confessions of Sophie: An Interview with William Styron', *New Edinburgh Review*, no. 51 (Autumn 1980).
——, '*Sanctuary* and After', *New Edinburgh Review*, no. 55 (Autumn 1981).
——, 'Offstage Tragedy', *New Edinburgh Review*, no. 59 (Autumn 1982).
Paz, Octavio, *The Labyrinth of Solitude: Life and Thought in Mexico* (London: Allen Lane, 1967).
Powers, Arthur, *Conversations with James Joyce*, ed. Clive Hart (London: Millington, 1974).
Reynolds, Michael S., *Hemingway's First War: The Making of 'A Farewell to Arms'* (Princeton, NJ: Princeton University Press, 1976).
Rieff, Philip, *Freud: The Mind of a Moralist* (London: Gollancz, 1959).
Robinson, Roger, 'Hardy and Darwin', in *Thomas Hardy*, ed. N. Page (London: Bell and Hyman, 1980).
Ross, Charles L., 'Homoerotic Feeling in *Women in Love*: Lawrence's "struggle for verbal consciousness" in the Manuscripts', *D. H. Lawrence: The Man Who Lived*, ed. R. B. Partlow and H. T. Moore (Carbondale: Southern Illinois University Press, 1979).

Rubin, Louis D., Jr, *Thomas Wolfe* (Baton Rouge: Louisiana State University Press, 1955).
——, 'Southern Literature: The Historical Image', in *South: Modern Southern Literature in its Cultural Setting*, ed. Louis D. Rubin Jr and Robert D. Jacobs (Garden City, NY: Doubleday, 1961).
——, 'Regionalism and the Southern Literary Renaissance', in *The South and the Sectional Image*, ed. D. W. Grantham (London: Harper and Row, 1967).
Scholes, Robert, *The Fabulators* (New York: Oxford University Press, 1967).
——, *Fabulation and Metafiction* (London: University of Illinois Press, 1980).
Smith, Anne (ed.), *Lawrence and Women* (London: Vision Press, 1978).
Spilka, Mark, 'Leopold Bloom as Jewish Pickwick: A Neo-Dickensian Perspective', *Novel*, vol. 13, no. 1 (1979–80), pp. 121ff.
Stepto, Robert B., 'I thought I knew these people': Richard Wright and the Afro-American Literary Tradition', in *Chant of Saints: A Gathering of Afro-American Literature, Art and Scholarship*, ed. Michael S. Harper and Robert B. Stepto (Chicago: University of Illinois Press, 1979).
Sundquist, Eric J., *Faulkner: The House Divided* (Baltimore, Md: Johns Hopkins University Press, 1983).
Trilling, Lionel, *The Liberal Imagination* (London, 1961).
Walker, Ronald G., *Infernal Paradise: Mexico and the Modern English Novel* (London: University of California Press, 1978).
Walsh, Jeffrey, *American War Literature: 1914 to Vietnam* (London: Macmillan, 1982).
Werner, Craig Hanson, *Paradoxical Resolutions: American Fiction since Joyce* (London: University of Illinois Press, 1982).
Williams, Raymond, *The Country and the City* (St Albans: Paladin, 1975).
——, *The English Novel from Dickens to Lawrence* (St Albans: Paladin, 1974).
Williamson, Joel, *The Crucible of Race: Black–White Relations in the American South since Emancipation* (Oxford: Oxford University Press, 1984).
Wyatt-Brown, Bertram, 'Community, Class and Snopesian Crime: Local Justice in the Old South', in *Class, Conflict and Consensus*, ed. O. V. Burton and R. C. McMath (London: Greenwood, 1982).
Zapf, Hubert, ' "Taylorism" in D. H. Lawrence's *Women in Love*', *D. H. Lawrence Review*, vol. 15 (1982).

Index